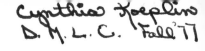

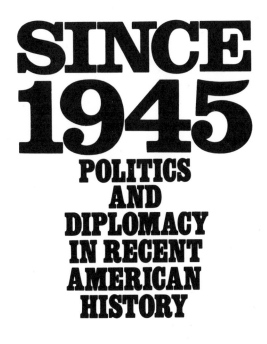

SINCE 1945

POLITICS AND DIPLOMACY IN RECENT AMERICAN HISTORY

ROBERT A. DIVINE

SINCE 1945

POLITICS AND DIPLOMACY IN RECENT AMERICAN HISTORY

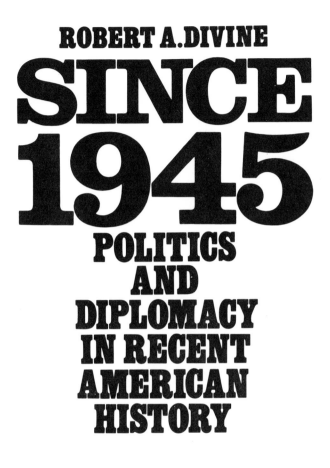

JOHN WILEY & SONS, INC.

New York   London   Sydney   Toronto

Library of Congress Cataloging in Publication Data:

Divine, Robert A
  Since 1945 : politics and diplomacy in recent American history.

  Bibliography: p.
  1. United States–Politics and government–1945–
  2. United States–Foreign relations–1945–
  I. Title.

E743.D54   320.9'73'092   74-30493
ISBN 0-471-21620-8
ISBN 0-471-21622-4 pbk.

Printed in the United States of America

10 9 8 7 6 5 4 3

To Barb

Preface

The Second World War had a profound effect on the United States, causing transformations of lasting impact in both foreign and domestic affairs. The change from an isolated nation that sought refuge in neutrality legislation into a superpower was the most dramatic shift. American bases overseas, American monopoly of the atomic bomb, American influence prevailing in Western Europe — all marked a radical change from previous national experience. The onset of the Cold War with the Soviet Union helped to institutionalize this new, active world role and prevented a return to isolation. For the next two decades, Americans found themselves caught up in a series of crises in strange-sounding places — Berlin, Suez, and Vietnam, to name only the most memorable. Despite an occasional yearning for the simpler days of the past, most Americans accepted the burdens of global leadership and some people even gloried in the futile quest for a Pax Americana.

The domestic changes were equally important, although they were often obscured by events overseas. The depressed economy of the 1930s gave way to a new affluence as the heavy military spending of World War II continued in the Cold War era and consumers displayed an insatiable appetite for automobiles, television sets, and the myriad of other products from the booming assembly lines. Not all Americans shared in the new abundance, however, and the quest for equality in social, political, and economic opportunities for the nation's black minority became a major theme in postwar politics. The reform impulse broadened beyond its New Deal limits to include not only civil rights

but aid to education, medical care for the aged, and protection of the environment. Under Democrats and Republicans alike, Americans sought to achieve a
just and equitable society and to fulfill the nation's most cherished aspirations.

The story was not always one of progress. The changing industrial society
brought new problems to replace the old. The alienation of youth by crass
materialism bewildered a depression-haunted generation that sought salvation
through economic advance; the fierce struggle for racial identity by northern
as well as southern blacks troubled the liberal white advocates of integration;
the exciting visions of American world leadership turned into a nightmare in
the devastated landscape of Indo-China.

In recounting the national experience since 1945, I have narrowed the focus
to the prism of politics. The vantage point is the White House; I have dealt
with the major foreign and domestic issues as they were perceived and grap-
pled with by successive presidents, from Truman through Nixon. There is no
attempt to deal with the many significant cultural, intellectual, and social
developments of the postwar years. Instead, I concentrated on the twin
themes of the Cold War abroad and the reform impulse at home. Too often,
historians separate these two broad aspects of postwar American life and treat
them in isolation. American presidents had to deal with them simultaneously,
and by integrating my account of policies pursued at home and abroad, I have
tried to demonstrate the interplay between them.

I originally intended to conclude the book in early 1973, since Nixon's reelection and the ending of the Vietnam War seemed to mark a natural stopping point. However, the rush of events that led to President Nixon's resignation—the galloping inflation, Vice President Agnew's resignation, the Watergate
revelations, and the movement toward impeachment — impelled me to add an
epilogue. These events are too recent to permit a fully balanced analysis; I
have tried simply to bring the story as close to the present as possible.

I express my gratitude to two close friends, Clarence Lasby and Lewis
Gould, for reading portions of the manuscript. I am also grateful to Gary W.
Reichard, Charles M. Dollar, and Walter LaFeber for their comments and criti-
cisms. Carl Beers and Wayne Anderson of Wiley contributed valuable support
at various stages of this project. Above all, I thank my wife, Barbara Renick
Divine, who read the entire manuscript with a keen eye toward style and content, and corrected errors in grammar, spelling, and meaning. She, more than
anyone else, had the interests of the reader at heart and constantly reminded
me of the need for clear, precise prose.

AUSTIN, TEXAS, 1974   ROBERT A. DIVINE

Contents

1
The Legacy of War

The bright flash that lit up the sky over Hiroshima on the morning of August 6, 1945 signaled both the end of World War II and the dawn of the nuclear age. A week later, Japan surrendered and the world was at peace after six years of fighting in Europe and eight in Asia. Yet Americans were never able to enjoy the peace they had looked forward to so fervently; the rapid onset of the Cold War with the Soviet Union kept international tensions at a dangerously high level and prevented any return to normalcy. Soon both superpowers possessed nuclear weapons and became locked in an escalating arms race that cast a long shadow over every aspect of postwar American life.

The man who made the decision to drop the atomic bomb had been in office only three months. Harry S. Truman became President on April 12, 1945 with the sudden death of Franklin D. Roosevelt, and he took up his duties with a staggering number of handicaps. Despite his declining health, FDR had failed to prepare his successor, keeping Truman in ignorance about vital military and diplomatic policies and refusing even to inform him of the atomic bomb project. In contrast to Roosevelt, Truman was a relatively obscure senator from Missouri who had built a modest reputation through his Congressional investigations of defense and war industries; he had won the respect of his fellow senators, but had made only a slight impact on the public at large. Powerful groups within the Democratic party, particularly southern leaders and big city bosses, had forced Roosevelt to dump Henry Wallace, his wartime Vice-President who leaned to the left, and Truman had emerged with the nom-

1

ination as an acceptable, middle-of-the road candidate from a border state. Already sixty years of age, the new President would have to master a broad range of information on policies new to him, display effective administrative ability in the difficult process of adjusting the nation to a peacetime status, and keep harmony in a political party already badly rent by internal dissension. It is not suprising that when Harry Truman tried to console Eleanor Roosevelt on her husband's death by asking, "Is there anything I can do for you?" she quickly replied, "Is there anything we can do for you? For you are the one in trouble now."

Harry Truman seemed to thrive on adversity. Born of hardy pioneer stock in Missouri, he had farmed for nearly ten years as a young man, risen to the rank of Major in the field artillery in World War I, and then suffered a humiliating bankruptcy in the clothing business, a victim of the economic slump of the early 1920s. He went into politics in Independence, a Kansas City suburb, serving as a county judge, an administrative position in which he distinguished himself with an honest and efficient road-building program. Though associated with Tom Prendergast, the corrupt boss of Kansas City, Truman developed a reputation for integrity and fair dealing that helped him win the election to the United States Senate in 1934, the year of the great New Deal landslide. A diligent but colorless legislator, he seemed doomed to defeat in 1940, but he never lost confidence in the voters of Missouri and, in a hard-fought campaign, he was reelected by a narrow margin. When the war in Europe led to heavy expenditures for defense preparedness in America, Truman won Congressional approval for his investigating committee, which uncovered inefficiency and corruption in industry as Truman displayed an impressive grasp of modern corporate practices.

Candor and forthrightness seemed to be Truman's most attractive traits. In contrast to FDR's fondness for political slight of hand, Truman liked everything out in the open. Sure of his own ability to handle problems, often to the point of cockiness, Truman tended to reduce complicated matters of national policy to simple questions of right and wrong and ignored the ambiguities. He prided himself on his blunt, frequently salty language, and on his ability to reach decisions without hesitation. He often acted too hastily, failing to give vital national issues the careful deliberation they demanded. Though fond of history and widely read, he was not an intellectual, and he had little use for those who played with ideas. He preferred to act, and once he had made up his mind, to act quickly and without regret. Above all, he prized loyalty as the supreme political virtue. A fierce partisan, he saw the Democratic party as the vehicle of national progress and he viewed Republicans with suspicion, and often contempt. He relied heavily on his friends, sometimes to his regret, in the case of cronies like Harry Vaughn, and he could be unforgiving to anyone he felt had slighted him or his family (like the music critic he called an s.o.b. for patronizing his daughter's singing). He seemed in many ways to be the epitome of the average American, and millions could easily identify with him, but he also felt keenly the prestige and dignity of the Presidency, and he was determined to do all he could to live up to the awesome responsibilities he had inherited.

The deteriorating relations with the Soviet Union posed the gravest problem for the new President. The wartime alliance, based on the common enemy in Hitler, began to disintegrate with the coming of victory. The Red armies flowed over Poland, Rumania, Hungary, and the other countries of Eastern Europe and Stalin was determined to impose regimes subservient to Moscow, as much for security as for ideological reasons. Churchill, trying desperately to save what he could, worked out a temporary division of influence with Stalin in 1944 to give Britain control of Greece, but Roosevelt refused to enter into these arrangements. The United States hoped to rely instead on a new effort at collective security in the form of the United Nations and on the principle of national self-determination in Eastern Europe. At Yalta, Roosevelt obtained Russian lip service to a Declaration of Liberated Europe promising free elections in these countries after the war, but there were no enforcement provisions, and in Poland, FDR had accepted an ambiguous formula that virtually insured a Communist-dominated regime. Roosevelt was probably prepared to write off both Poland and Eastern Europe, but he failed to inform either Truman or the American people of his intentions.

Truman had been a lifelong believer in the principles of Wilsonian internationalism and, as President, he moved quickly to implement his beliefs. He announced that the San Francisco conference would be held as scheduled to launch the United Nations, and he impressed his advisers, notably Ambassador to Russia Averell Harriman and Secretary of the Navy James Forrestal, who were already suspicious of the Soviets, with his determination to prevent postwar Russian domination of Eastern Europe. When Soviet Foreign Minister Molotov stopped off in Washington on his way to the San Francisco conference to confer with Truman, the President berated the Russians for their failure to allow the Poles self-determination. "I have never been talked to like that in my life," Molotov complained. "Carry out your agreements and you won't get talked to like that," Truman shot back.

Truman apparently believed that the Russians respected candor and toughness, and though he told his associates that he did not expect to receive 100 percent of what he asked for, he did feel that "we should be able to get eighty-five percent." Not only did he take a harder line on Eastern Europe than Roosevelt, but he dropped FDR's efforts to forge closer economic ties to Russia by abruptly terminating lend-lease, temporarily when Germany was defeated and permanently when Japan surrendered, and by ending discussion of a proposed billion-dollar loan to the Soviets to finance postwar reconstruction. Informed of the atomic bomb program and the imminent first test of the new weapon by Secretary of War Henry L. Stimson, he agreed to postpone the forthcoming summit meeting for several weeks. News of the successful detonation at Alamogordo reached Truman at Potsdam, where he was conferring with Churchill and Stalin, and led to a noticeable stiffening of his negotiating stance toward the Soviets. He informed Stalin of the new weapon in very sketchy terms; the Russian leader remained impassive as he remarked "make good use of it against the Japanese." Truman found the whole Potsdam experience to be a very heady one; "Churchill talks all the time," he wrote his mother, "and Stalin just grunts but you know what he means." Despite strenuous debate, Truman was unable to secure any Russian concessions on Eastern Europe, and on Germany the two sides finally accepted a compromise reparations settlement that provided for limited Russian acquisition of industrial goods from the Western zones in return for agricultural produce from East Germany.

The President's "get tough" policy did not achieve any noticeable gains as the Soviets gradually consolidated their grip on Eastern Europe during the remainder of 1945. James Byrnes, the man Truman appointed Secretary of State, met with complete frustration in September at the London Foreign Ministers meeting. Three months later, Byrnes traveled to Moscow and made some progress by acceding to Soviet control in Bulgaria and Rumania in return for Russian acquiescence to the exclusive American occupation of Japan. Byrnes angered the President by refusing to keep the White House informed of his negotiations and, when he returned to Washington, Truman read him "the real riot act" during a cruise aboard the Presidential yacht. "I told him our policy was not appeasement," Truman claimed, "and not a one-way street." Byrnes denied any breach with the President but, during his remaining year in office, he pursued a more vigorous line in his negotiations with the Russians.

By early 1946, the Cold War had clearly begun. The bright hopes for world peace embodied in the drive for the United Nations had disappeared in the confrontation over Eastern Europe. Russia remained firmly in control of this area, its planned satellite empire already well under way. The United States, on the other hand, remained the dominant force in Western Europe, loaning large sums to England and France while withholding such aid from the Soviets, and retaining its monopoly over the atomic bomb. There was as yet no open breach between the two superpowers, but Stalin was already talking about the incompatability between communism and capitalism as he called for the Russian people to prepare for "any eventuality." Winston Churchill answered for the West in March 1946. Speaking at Westminster College in Fulton, Missouri, with Truman sitting on the platform, the British leader declared that "an iron curtain" had dropped across Europe in calling for an Anglo-American alliance to preserve world order. The President had known in advance what Churchill planned to say; his presence indicated that he was prepared to lead the United States in a crusade against Soviet expansion.

I

The political situation facing Truman at home was nearly as difficult as the international crisis. Deep divisions had developed within the Democratic Party that had governed the nation since the depths of the depression. Urban bosses vied with liberal intellectuals; powerful labor leaders clashed with conservative southern representatives and senators. The Republicans had been gaining in congressional strength since FDR's great landslide of 1936. They had come very close to winning control of Congress in 1942, and only Roosevelt's fourth term victory in 1944 had restored a comfortable Democratic edge in the House and Senate. Southern conservatives resented the role labor, in the form of the C.I.O.'s Political Action Committee headed by Sidney Hillman, had played in the 1944 election, and many loyal New Dealers nursed a deep grievance over the dumping of Henry Wallace. Moreover, de facto control of Congress remained in the hands of a conservative coalition of southern Democrats and midwestern Republicans who had effectively blocked reform proposals since 1938.

In his first few months in office, Truman enjoyed a honeymoon period in his relations with Congress. Senators and representatives sympathized with a former colleague suddenly thrust into a challenging new position, and they concentrated on cooperating with him in the task of ending the war. The executive branch itself posed the most serious problems for Truman; it was filled with men loyal to FDR who viewed the new President with suspicion and often contempt. Truman wanted to establish a new team as soon as possible but, in the shock of Roosevelt's death, he had wisely asked the entire cabinet to stay on at their posts. In the next few months, however, he moved quickly to put his own men into key positions. In June, James Byrnes replaced Edward Stettinius in the vital office of Secretary of State and, though there was always a coolness between the two men, based on Byrnes feeling that he should have been Roosevelt's successor, the President felt that the South Carolinian had the ability and experience to build up public confidence in the Administration's foreign policy. In another significant move, Truman asked Fred Vinson, a former Kentucky congressman and federal judge who had replaced Byrnes as Director of Economic Mobilization under Roosevelt, to become Secretary of the Treasury. Vinson, a big rumpled man with sound judgment and middle-of-the-road views, had the expert knowledge of fiscal and economic affairs that Truman lacked, and he soon proved to be the strongest member of the new cabinet. In other shifts, the President appointed

Robert Hannegan, St. Louis politician and Democratic National Committee Chairman, as his Postmaster-General, former Washington Senator Lewis B. Schwellenback as the new Secretary of Labor replacing Frances Perkins, Clinton Anderson to the post of Secretary of Agriculture, and Tom Clark of Texas as Attorney General. Secretary of War Henry Stimson retired late in 1945 in favor of Robert Patterson and, in early 1946, Harold Ickes, the old curmudgeon, resigned in protest over a proposed Truman appointment and was succeeded as Secretary of the Interior by Julius Krug, one of his former subordinates. Henry Wallace stayed on as Secretary of Commerce until the fall of 1946, and only Navy Secretary James Forrestal lasted throughout Truman's entire first term in office, becoming the first Secretary of Defense when Congress finally unified the armed forces in 1947.

With the exception of Byrnes and Vinson, the new cabinet members lacked distinction and gave an air of mediocrity to the Administration. Yet Truman felt at home with these men, many of whom he had known well in Congress. He made equally significant changes in his White House staff. Harry Hopkins, after one last mission to Moscow, retired because of ill health and, of the men close to Roosevelt, only William Hassett, the correspondence secretary, and Judge Samuel Roseman, the gifted speechwriter and shrewd adviser, stayed on. Truman prevailed on his old school chum and veteran Washington journalist, Charlie Ross, to become his press secretary, and he brought Matt Connelly, who had worked on his wartime investigating committee, into the White House as appointments secretary. His selection of Harry Vaughn as military aide and John Snyder as economic mobilizer, and later Secretary of the Treasury when he made Vinson Chief Justice of the Supreme Court, reflected a tendency to favor old Missouri cronies whose friendship dated back to World War I days. But he also brought in bright, new faces in Clark Clifford, a young Navy lawyer who quickly became his most astute political adviser and all-around troubleshooter, and in John Steelman, a professional labor-management negotiator who handled economic issues. All in all, it was a reasonably competent group of men who could give an inexperienced President the advice and counsel he needed.

There were many other changes in the White House under Truman. Unlike FDR, who liked to keep late hours and spend the mornings in bed reading the day's newspapers, Truman arose promptly each morning at six and began his day with a brisk 45-minute walk, often with out-of-breath newsmen at his heels. His morning hours were filled with appointments, usually kept to 10-minute intervals and, in the afternoons, he conferred with government officials and conducted the business of the nation, ending the day with a heavy reading schedule of papers, memoranda and reports. Appalled by Roosevelt's messy administrative system, in which overlapping duties forced subordinates always to come to the President for ultimate approval, Truman tried to delegate as much of his authority as he could to cabinet members, reserving only the difficult decisions for himself. He won fame for asserting that "the buck stops here" but, in fact, he tried to pass it as far down the bureaucratic line as possible. He also differed from Roosevelt in his handling of the press, avoiding his predecessor's playful attitude and speaking his mind candidly, often too frankly, in his two weekly news conferences.

In the vital area of domestic policy, however, Truman sought continuity, not change. A staunch supporter of the New Deal as a senator, he intended to carry on and broaden the economic and social reforms that FDR had originated. Any doubt on that score ended on September 6, 1945, when Truman sent a twenty-one point message to Congress outlining his postwar domestic program. Picking up where Roosevelt had left off in proposing an economic bill of rights in his 1944 State-of-the-Union message, the new President called for legislation to ensure full employment, expand unemployment compensation, increase the minimum wage, create a permanent Fair Employment Practices Commission, and broaden the federal housing effort. The sweeping commitment to New Deal goals ended growing speculation that Truman would abandon the cause of reform. The program was sent to Congress, the President told one of his aides with a grin, "to let the Hearsts and the McCormicks know that they were not going to take me into camp." Four months later, in his 1946 State-of-the-Union message, Truman broadened the reform agenda by asking Congress to consider comprehensive health insurance, federal aid to education, and an increase in social security coverage and benefits. The President was not only perserving the New Deal; he hoped to move beyond it in such areas as health care and education, the nucleus of the future Fair Deal.

Despite his commitment to reform, Truman was never at ease with the New Deal liberals like Harold Ickes and Henry Wallace. He distrusted intellectuals with their heavy emphasis on principles; instead, he sought to achieve a better way of life for the common man out of the give and take of political compromise. He had a strong tinge of populism in his dislike of corporation executives and Wall Street bankers; he always viewed himself as fighting for the people against the special interests, He wanted to see the fruits of American prosperity distributed fairly to all groups in society — laboring men, farmers, small businessmen, white collar workers — yet he did not advocate any sweeping changes in the existing social and economic structures. In short, he was a pragmatic liberal who simply wanted to perfect the American way of life.

II

Truman's efforts to continue and broaden FDR's New Deal became lost in the nation's headlong rush to enjoy the fruits of peace. Neither the Congress nor the public cared about reform measures — they focused their attention instead on the liquidation of government controls and the return·to a free economy. The bitter memory of the great depression did lead to the passage of one significant piece of legislation, the Employment Act of 1946. It institutionalized the New Deal emphasis on government responsibility for the economy by setting forth full employment as a national policy goal and by creating a three-man Council of Economic Advisers to assist the President in achieving it. But the major concern in Congress and in the nation remained the end of wartime controls and the immediate return to normalcy in domestic life.

The President tried to meet this insistent demand without engulfing the nation in a disastrous inflationary spiral. On August 18, 1945, he issued an executive order easing up on many industrial controls, but at the same time he announced the continuation of the Office of Price Administration (OPA), which had succeeded in keeping the cost of living at reasonable levels throughout the war year. Truman's policy of "holding the line" on prices while industry reconverted to peacetime production quickly ran into difficulty. During the war, higher wages and a longer workweek, coupled with a lack of available consumer goods, had built up a huge nest egg of personal savings. Men and women who had survived the depression on a shoestring and who had gone without luxuries during the grim war years now wanted to spend their savings on new cars, appliances, furniture, and clothing so that they could enjoy the good life they had been denied for so long. They were willing to pay high prices, and even the under-the-counter payoffs many dealers insisted on for scarce goods, but they were unwilling to wait for industry to change its assembly lines over from the production of tanks and planes to the building of cars and refrigerators. Unable to get the goods they wanted, the people tended to blame the Administration and its cautious "hold-the-line" policy.

The OPA soon became the focus of the political struggle. In the fall of 1945, Congress reluctantly extended the wartime agency for six more months but, in the spring of 1946, the legislators greatly weakened its powers in a measure to give it another year's life. OPA had few friends. Consumers viewed it with distaste, angry over the way it had restricted their lives by rationing meat, shoes, and gasoline during the war; industrialists saw it as a "socialistic" device designed to interrupt the free enterprise system that alone could solve the problems of supply and demand. Paul Porter, head of the OPA, urged Truman to veto the Congressional extension, saying that its reduced powers would make it helpless to halt inflation. All but two cabinet members, however, urged the President to sign it, and Democratic Senate Majority Leader Alben Barkley told Truman that he had no choice since "it's the best bill we can get out of this Congress." With characteristic dispatch, Truman vetoed the bill on June 29, labeling it "a sure formula for inflation" and demanding that Congress enact a stronger measure.

For the next month, prices soared as consumers, freed from government restraints for the first time in three years, scrambled to acquire scarce commodities. Beef prices doubled to a $1 a pound and milk rose by 4 cents a quart. In late July, Congress finally enacted a slightly stronger measure and, though Truman realized that the legislation failed to give the OPA the power an effective price control program needed, he signed it, confident that he had proved his point. For the next few months, prices increased at an annual rate of 38 percent as alarming shortages developed in food supplies as well as in manufactured goods. Despite his efforts to hold the line on prices, Truman received most of the public criticism for the inflationary spiral and, finally, in an effort to satisfy his critics, he abandoned virtually all controls on wages and prices on November 9. The OPA lingered on for a few more months before its demise in 1947 becoming, in the mind of Paul Porter, the "office for Cessation of Rationing and Priorities," or more simply, OCRAP.

This rapidly rising cost of living intensified the postwar demands of organized labor and created even more serious problems for the beleaguered Truman Administration. During the war, labor had reluctantly agreed to a no-strike pledge to ensure full production and in 1942 had accepted the "Little Steel" formula, which tied wage increases to the cost of living. In his "hold-the-line" executive order on August 18, 1945 Truman approved increased wages for workers, provided that the new contracts did not lead to higher prices on manufactured goods. Management insisted it could not grant increased wages out of its profit margins; the workers countered with demands for heavy hourly pay increases so that take-home pay would remain constant as the work week fell from an average of over 48 hours during the war to the peacetime norm of 40 hours. Caught in the middle, Truman tended to side with labor at first, announcing on October 30 that wage increases were vital "to sustain adequate purchasing power and to raise the national income" and claiming that "there is room in the existing price structure for business as a whole to grant increases in wage rates."

A wave of strikes swept over the nation as business leaders refused to dip into profits to pay the requested wage hikes. On September 17, the oil workers walked out, paralyzing refineries and threatening a nationwide shortage of fuel oil and gasoline. The President seized the refineries and negotiated an 18 percent wage increase, setting a pattern for other industries. In the course of the next year, there were nearly 5000 strikes affecting over 4½ million industrial workers. The biggest involved General Motors, struck by Walter Reuther's United Auto Workers (UAW) in December 1945, and the entire steel industry, hit by the walkout of 750,000 workers in January 1946. Truman resorted to Presidential fact-finding boards in these strikes and, after lengthy negotiations, management finally granted raises averaging 18½ cents an hour. Angered by the greediness of both sides in the disputes, Truman began to take a more neutral position. "...labor has gone crazy, and management isn't far from insane in selfishness," he wrote to his mother in November 1945; six months later he prepared a message to Congress in which he planned to declare, "Let's give the country back to the people. Let's put transportation and production back to work, hang a few traitors and make our own country safe for democracy." Charlie Ross and Clark Clifford persuaded the President to delete these angry words, but they indicate how frustrated he had become with both labor and management.

Truman emerged as the champion of the public interest in contests with three of the nation's most powerful labor leaders. In the spring of 1946, Alvanley Johnston and A. F. Whitney, heads of the locomotive and trainmen unions respectively, refused to accept the recommendations of a presidential fact-finding board and began a nationwide rail strike, the first in American history. Outraged by this arrogant act, Truman seized the nation's railroads and went before Congress to ask for the power to draft the trainmen and locomotive firemen in order to restore rail service. While he was reading this drastic message to Congress, word arrived that Johnson and Whitney had given in, and Truman was able to announce to a cheering joint session that he had ended the rail strike. His critics denounced him for proposing to conscript workers and Johnson and Whitney vowed they would get their revenge at the polls, but Truman emerged in the popular mind as a man of courage who put the national interest first.

He won an even greater victory over John L. Lewis, the powerful and dramatic leader of the United Mine Workers. In the spring of 1946, the government took control of the mines and negotiated a wage settlement that favored the miners. In the fall, however, Lewis denounced the settlement and declared that his men would walk off the job on November 20. Truman called his aides together and told them, "This time I mean to slap that so-and-so down for good." The government, which was still formally operating the mines, sought an injunction from a federal judge to compel the miners to continue working. Judge T. Allan Goldsborough issued the order in Washington on November 18, but Lewis ignored it and the mines closed on November 20. The Truman Administration demanded that Lewis obey the court, and Judge Goldsborough finally cited the mine leader for contempt, fining the union $3,500,000 and Lewis himself an additional $10,000. Lewis stormed out of the court breathing defiance, but later that day he capitulated and ordered his men to return to work immediately, thus giving Truman his greatest victory on the home front. Two days later, the President boasted to his mother, "Well, John L. had to fold up. He couldn't take the gaff. No bully can."

Sweet as the triumph was over Lewis, it came too late to redeem Truman's sinking political fortunes. The inflationary spiral that began in the summer of 1946 built up dangerous discontent with the Administration's attempt to hold the line on prices. Though Truman tried to protect the public interest in the strike settlements, the steady series of wage hikes, together with Truman's veto of the Case bill designed to restrict union activities, tended to focus growing antilabor sentiments against the President. The Republicans, eager to gain power after their repeated defeats by FDR, capitalized on the mood of public dissatisfaction with the simple slogan, "Had enough?" The result was a Democratic rout in the Congressional elections; for the first time since 1928, the GOP won control of both houses of Congress. Overcome by the problems of reconversion, Truman had been unable to extend the New Deal reform program, and now he faced the possibility of a Congressional effort to dismantle it entirely.

III

The tension between the United States and the Soviet Union continued to build throughout 1946. In March, Secretary of State Byrnes delivered a sharply worded note to the Russians insisting that they remove their troops from northern Iran. The Red Army left this oil-rich Middle Eastern country by May, and later that year Russian forces also pulled out of Manchuria after stripping it clean of the industrial plant the Japanese had built up there. In Eastern Europe the Soviets continued to play a dominant role in internal politics and gradually consolidated their control of a satellite empire that stretched from Poland to Bulgaria. The temporary division of Germany into occupation zones began to harden into a permanent political split. In the East the Soviets transformed their sector in to another satellite, while General Lucius Clay, in charge of the American zone, halted the shipment of industrial reparations to the Soviet Union in May. During a speech in Stuttgart in September, Secretary Byrnes revealed that the United States would give the West Germans a measure of self-government and help them achieve a self-sustaining economy. The gravest showdown occurred at the United Nations, where Bernard M. Baruch presented the American proposal for the control of international energy. The Baruch plan called for the creation of an international atomic energy agency under the UN but exempt from the veto; international ownership and inspection of all atomic facilities; and a threestage transition period during which the United States would maintain its nuclear monopoly. Replying for the Soviet Union, Molotov rejected any form of inspection and called instead for the immediate destruction of all atomic weapons and a multilateral treaty to outlaw nuclear war. By October the arms talks had reached a stalemate over the veto and inspection issues, and it was clear that the Soviets intended to press forward with the development of their own atomic weapons.

Henry A. Wallace, the former Vice-President now serving as Truman's Secretary of Commerce, emerged as the chief critic of the Administration's "get tough" policy. In July he sent the President a 12-page, single-spaced letter in which he criticized Administration policy toward Russia as an attempt "to build up a preponderance of force to intimidate the rest of mankind." In particular, he attacked the Baruch Plan, charging that it constituted an effort to keep the Russians from developing their own nuclear weapons. Such an approach, he warned, would backfire, since the Soviets would "redouble their efforts to manufacture bombs, and they may also decide to expand their 'security zone' in a serious way." The President politely thanked the secretary for his unsolicited advice but made no changes in American foreign policy. The issue came to a head in September, when Wallace spoke to a left-wing political rally in New York City. Claiming that Truman had read and approved his speech in advance (in fact, the President had only glanced at it), the secretary expressed more moderate views than his pro-Soviet audience wanted to hear, but he nevertheless defended Soviet dominance of Eastern Europe and denounced the "get tough" policy by charging, "The tougher we get, the tougher the Russians will get."

"Then Wallace spoke and hell broke loose next morning," recalled Clark Clifford. "Oh, boy, it really did." Reporters wanted to know if the President had abandoned his earlier policy toward Russia; a flustered Truman bent the truth by denying that he had approved the speech in advance. From Paris, Secretary of State James Byrnes cabled to ask Truman to forbid Wallace from speaking out on foreign policy, threatening to resign if the President refused. Truman shot off an angry letter to Wallace demanding his resignation, a letter so personal and indignant that the Secretary of Commerce quietly returned it to the White House so it could be destroyed and, on September 20, the President formally announced Wallace's resignation. His departure marked the breaking of the last link with FDR's New Deal and the tactic of accommodation with Russia.

Brynes followed Wallace from the cabinet in early 1947, retiring from exhaustion after nearly two years of fruitless attempts to work out a European settlement with Molotov at the Council of Foreign Ministers meetings. General George C. Marshall, the organizer of victory as Army Chief of Staff in World War II, took his place and proceeded to revitalize a lethargic State Department. Marshall had little expertise in foreign affairs, but he brought in orderly administrative techniques, a powerful sense of dignity and purpose, and a highly developed ability to select and rely on gifted subordinates. In the first few months of 1947, the new Secretary of State combined with Dean Acheson, Will Clayton, and George F. Kennan to lay the foundations of America's cold war policy of containment.

The first step began in February, when the British informed the State Department that they could no longer support either the Greek government, then waging an intense campaign against Communist guerrillas, or Turkey, holding a key strategic spot between Russia and the Mediterranean. In fact, American officials had been planning for some time to extend aid to the Greek government, but the British action created a sense of extreme urgency. Marshall and Acheson convinced Truman that the United States must act quickly to bolster Greece and Turkey or lose the area by default to the Soviet Union, but the President worried about support from the Republican-controlled 80th Congress. On February 26, Marshall, Acheson, and Truman met with the Congressional leaders to outline the crisis and inform them of their plans. Marshall began the briefing, but then he turned to Acheson, who presented the case with a crusader's zeal. Comparing the situation to "apples in a barrel infected by one rotten one," Acheson warned that the fall of Greece and Turkey "might open three continents to Soviet penetration." "The Soviet Union," he recalled in his memoirs, "was playing one of the greatest gambles in history at minimal cost....We and we alone were in a position to break up the play." When he finished, to his intense relief Republican Senator Arthur Vandenberg told Truman that if he would present this crisis to the Congress "I will support you and I believe that most of its members will do the same."

For the next two weeks, the State Department experts worked on the President's speech. The basic request was simple enough—authorization to send military advisers and $400 million in economic aid to Greece and Turkey. The drafters struggled with the broader question of how to convince the Congress and the nation of the seriousness of the problem. Aware that few Americans were concerned with the fate of the Eastern Mediterranean, they couched the address in sweeping, global terms designed to follow Vandenberg's advice to "scare hell out of the American people." Thus, on March 12, President Truman informed the House and Senate that henceforth it would be American policy "to support free peoples who are resisting attempted subjugation by armed minorities or by outside pressures." The Truman Doctrine was thus a global pledge to resist Communist expansion, whether it took the form of internal subversion or external aggression. Senator Vandenberg summed up its meaning most fully when he told the Foreign Relations Committee that what Truman had in effect said was that "the fall of Greece, followed by the fall of Turkey, would establish a chain reaction around the world which could very easily leave us isolated in a Communist-dominated earth."

Commentators both in and outside the government were disturbed by the implications of the Truman Doctrine. George Kennan, then serving as chairman of the new Policy Planning Staff, had been one of the first to warn the Truman Administration of the dangers of Communist expansion and advocate a policy of containment, a phrase he himself coined. But Kennan viewed the Truman Doctrine as a dangerous overreaction to the Soviet threat, calling it "more grandiose and more sweeping than anything that I, at least, have ever envisaged." Walter Lippmann, the distinguished columnist, agreed. He warned that such unilateral action would greatly weaken the United Nations and he made an amazingly accurate prophecy of what the Truman Doctrine would mean in the future; "unending intervention in all the countries that are supposed to 'contain' the Soviet Union." The result could only be to strain the resources and will of the American people and give Russia the initiative in the ongoing Cold War.

Neither Kennan's reservations nor Lippmann's objections prevented Congress from approving the Truman Doctrine and voting the aid for Greece and Turkey in early May. By then, the State Department was far more worried about the basic economic health of Western Europe. Despite large American loans, neither England nor France had been able to regain its prewar level of production. Large Communist parties in Italy and France were making steady gains, and the people of Western Europe seemed apathetic and insecure. Aware that this area held the economic balance of power between the United States and Russia, the State Department officials decided that only a massive infusion of American capital could bring about European economic recovery and revitalization. Studies by Kennan's Policy Planning Staff and Clayton's economic experts reached the same conclusion and, on June 5, General Marshall presented the proposal to the world in the course of a commencement address at Harvard University. Citing the importance of Western Europe both for American security and prosperity, Marshall proposed that the United States provide the money for the Europeans, acting cooperatively to carry out a broad program of economic rehabilitation. Avoiding the narrowly anti-Communist tone of the Truman Doctrine, Marshall declared, "Our policy is directed not against any country or doctrine but against hunger, poverty, desperation, and chaos."

At Kennan's insistence, the original plan encompassed all the European nations including Russia and her satellites. The foreign ministers of the affected nations met in Paris in late June to discuss the American initiative; Molotov demanded that the American funds be given to each country to spend as it pleased and, when the others insisted on a cooperative plan for European recovery, Molotov walked out, thereby greatly improving the chances for Congressional approval. The Europeans presented a request for $28 billion over a four-year period. American negotiators quickly reduced the sum to $22 billion and, when Truman finally submitted the request to Congress in December, 1947, he had scaled it down to $17 billion over a three-year period. Despite the cuts, many economy-minded Republicans opposed the Marshall Plan as a giveaway program. Senator Robert A. Taft of Ohio, a prewar isolationist, dubbed the proposal a "European T.V.A." and other GOP senators viewed it as an "international W.P.A." and as a "bold Socialist blueprint." In a series of Congressional hearings, however, advocates of the plan offered compelling reasons for adopting it. Massive aid to Western Europe would restore America's best customers, and thus stimulate the domestic economy; it would provide a way to integrate a restored West Germany into a large European system; it would create a powerful barrier to the expansionist designs of the Soviet Union.

The last argument carried the most weight. With the outcome still in doubt, the Soviets cooperated with the Communists in Czechoslovakia to oust the coalition government and install a Stalinist regime that ended any pretense of democracy in that country. The American people, remembering the tragic role the Czechs had played in the coming of World War II, saw this coup as final proof of Communist designs for world conquest, a conclusion that was bolstered by the murder of former Foreign Minister Jan Masaryk, who mysteriously fell to his death from a window. A war scare quickly built up as General Clay informed Washington of his feeling that hostilities "may come with dramatic suddenness" and Secretary of State Marshall described the world situation as "very, very serious." In a special address to Congress on March 17, 1948, Truman claimed that Russia alone was blocking all efforts to achieve a peaceful world and called for the adoption of Universal Military Training and the resumption of the draft. The Senate, concerned over the Soviet threat, passed the Marshall Plan by a whopping 69 to 17 margin in mid-March, and two weeks later the House concurred by a vote of 318 to 75. A Democratic President and a Republican Congress had joined hands to save Western Europe from the menace of Communism. The Cold War, more than two years in the making, was now in full swing.

IV

Truman proved far less successful in handling domestic issues. The 80th Congress, which approved the Truman Doctrine and the Marshall Plan, rebuffed all his efforts to extend the New Deal. Proposals for health insurance, social security extension, and a comprehensive housing program all floundered in the face of Republican and southern Democratic opposition. The President fought hard to beat back conservative attempts to reduce taxes when a slight budget surplus developed, and the Senate barely sustained his veto of such a measure. The stormiest battle, however, came over labor legislation.

The Republican leaders made revision of the New Deal's Wagner Act their highest priority in the new Congress. In the House Representative Fred Hartley sponsored a very restrictive measure that would have prevented industry-wide bargaining; Robert Taft introduced a slightly milder bill in the Senate that tried to redress the balance between management and labor by defining unfair union practices. The resulting Taft-Hartley bill reflected a tough but not unreasonable approach. It outlawed the closed shop, prohibited secondary boycotts, forbade direct union participation in politics, and provided for 80-day cooling-off periods in strikes that caused national emergencies. Passed by overwhelming margins that included a majority of Democrats as well as Republicans in Congress, the Taft-Hartley Act posed a serious dilemma for the President. The legislation reflected such a growing national insistence for curbing the power of labor that Congress was certain to override a veto. But a group of Truman's advisers, led by Clark Clifford, urged him to deliver a strong veto message out of broader political considerations – primarily, the Administration's need to retain and intensify the support of labor. Truman's partisan distaste for the bill's authors ("Taft is no good and Hartley is worse," he wrote his mother) helped persuade him to accept Clifford's shrewd advice. On June 20, 1947, he delivered a ringing veto in which he called Taft-Hartley "a shocking piece of legislation" that was "bad for labor, bad for management, and bad for the country." Only three days later, Congress overrode the veto by even larger margins than on the original passage, but the President had succeeded in mending his fences with the union leaders, who stubbornly persisted in referring to the Taft-Hartley Act as "a slave labor law."

Truman needed political allies desperately as the New Deal coalition began to fracture under the strains of the Cold War. By mid-1947, the once united supporters of FDR had divided into two fractions. Henry A. Wallace led a powerful left-wing movement known as the Progressive Citizens of America (PCA), which advocated accommodation with the Soviet Union abroad and renewed reform at home, including an end to racial segregation. A competing group of liberal Democrats, including Eleanor Roosevelt, Reinhold Niebuhr, and Leon Henderson, agreed with the domestic goals of the PCA but clashed sharply with the Wallace faction's tolerance of Communists within their ranks and the willingness to compromise with the Soviet Union. In early 1947, they formed the Americans for Democratic Action (ADA) and adopted a six-point program calling for expansion of the New Deal "to insure decent levels of health, nutrition, shelter and education" in the United States coupled with "political and economic support to democratic and freedom-loving peoples the world over." In a key clause, the ADA rejected "any association with Communists or sympathizers with communism in the United States...."

The containment policy served to widen the split within liberal ranks. Wallace attacked the Truman Doctrine as "a military lend-lease program" and conducted a highly emotional and very popular nationwide speaking tour in which he raised more than $300,000 for the PCA. In criticizing the program of aid to Greece and Turkey, Wallace proposed instead "a major effort to restore the world economy by the use of American resources." When the

Secretary of State first presented the European Recovery Plan (ERP), Wallace hailed it as an embodiment of his own ideas but, by fall, when Russia had vetoed Eastern European participation, he was attacking the Marshall Plan as part of Truman's deliberate effort to "divide Europe into two warring camps." ADA spokesmen, on the other hand, though uneasy over the Truman Doctrine, backed the Marshall Plan wholeheartedly. In a *New Republic* advertisement, the ADA called the economic recovery program "the key to the fate of Europe" and, when Truman presented the final request to Congress in December 1947, the organization praised the Marshall Plan as "the highest point United States foreign policy has achieved since the death of Roosevelt."

The breakup of the liberal coalition had ominous political implications for the President. Despite the support the ADA gave to Truman's foreign policy, its leaders, notably James Roosevelt, the former President's son, who was active in California politics, felt that Truman lacked the stature to lead the nation at a time of crisis and began to sound out General Dwight D. Eisenhower on the possibility of accepting the Democratic nomination in 1948. The General continually discouraged these approaches but, when big city bosses such as Chicago's Jacob Arvey joined the Draft Ike movement, Truman's political stock began to fall rapidly. At the same time, the President faced a direct challenge from Henry Wallace, who announced, in December 1947, that he would run for the Presidency on a third-party ticket. In the early months of 1948, political experts predicted that while Wallace had no chance of winning, he might well drain off from 5 to 10 million Democratic votes in the large industrial states and thus insure a Republican victory in November.

While the pollsters and columnists casually wrote off Truman's chances of reelection in 1948 (indeed, many thought he could not even win the Democratic nomination), the President kept quiet while he and his aides mapped out their political strategy. Clark Clifford was the main architect. In a long memorandum to the President on November 19, 1947, Clifford advocated a hard-hitting presidential campaign designed to appeal to the various elements forming the New Deal coalition — farmers, labor, Negroes, Jews, and other ethnic groups — not in the expectation of achieving legislative results but to gain vital political advantage. He urged Truman to move to the left on domestic issues, even at the risk of alienating the South (which Clifford thought would grow mutinous but not rebel), in order to weaken Wallace's appeal to liberals, while at the same time doing everything possible "to identify him and isolate him in the public mind with the Communists." Clifford saw the Cold War as a great asset for Truman, and he advised him to play up his role as the man responsible for a get tough policy with the Kremlin. "The nation is already united behind the President on this issue," Clifford pointed out. "The worse matters get, up to a fairly certain point — real danger of imminent war — the more is there a sense of crisis. In times of crisis the American citizen tends to back up his President."

The President accepted Clifford's adroit but hypocritical plan and began to implement it in the early months of 1948, when his prestige had sunk to its lowest level. His veto of the Taft-Hartley Act had won him the support of labor, and Wallace's soft line toward Russia alienated many union leaders, who had been waging a hectic internal struggle to purge their ranks, especially in the C.I.O., of Communist organizers. Truman's strong advocacy of continuing the high price supports that stemmed from the war years made it unnecessary for him to do anything more to woo farmers, who were still enjoying a period of record prosperity. The Jewish vote presented a more difficult problem. Truman sympathized with the desire of those who survived Hitler's holocaust to creat a Jewish state in Palestine, and he had pressured Britain to admit 100,000 immigrants from Europe, but he also faced opposition from within his Administration, as State and Defense Department officials, notably James Forrestal, warned against alienating the Arab nations who controlled so much of the world's oil reserves. In March 1948, the State Department reversed Truman's stand in favor of a UN plan for the partition of Palestine into separate Jewish and Arab nations, and Zionist leaders condemned the Administration unmercifully. "It took the British 25 years to sell us out," commented Chaim Weizmann sardonically, "the Americans have done it in 2½ months." In May, with Jewish leaders preparing to proclaim the independence of Israel when British troops withdrew, Clark Clifford helped persuade the President to recognize the new nation despite the objections of the State Department. Eleven minutes after Israel came into existence on May 15, Truman extended *de facto* recognition, making the United States the first nation in the world to do so and thereby preventing any massive defection of Jewish voters from the Democratic ranks.

Truman also sought the support of the growing number of black voters in the country. Though his own racial attitudes were colored by his mother's southern sympathies and his border state's lack of tolerance for Negroes, as President, Truman had become a cautious advocate of civil rights. He had called on Congress to continue the wartime Fair Employment Practices Commission that a reluctant FDR had established in 1941 under the threat of a Negro march on Washington, but he had acquiesced in its demise, refusing to become engaged in a legislative showdown with powerful southern Democrats in Congress. A growing militancy among Negroes who had fought for their nation only to return home to be denied basic human rights led to a series of ugly incidents in the South, where a revived Ku Klux Klan used violence to maintain a segregated way of life. When a group of distinguished Negro leaders presented the President with shocking evidence of repression in September 1946, Truman responded by issuing an executive order three months later creating a presidential civil rights commission with the authority to inquire into ways to "safeguard the civil rights of the people," and to make recommendations "for the protection of civil rights." For the next eleven months the fifteen-member body, which included two liberal southerners and two Negro women but was controlled by northern whites, held extensive hearings and then submitted a report entitled *To Secure These Rights.* With the two southern members dissenting, the Committee on Civil Rights recommended the establishment of a permanent FEPC as well as a continuing civil rights commission, stepped-up Justice Department protection for blacks in the southern states, and most important, Congressional legislation to deny federal aid to any state that practiced segregation in schools, transportation, and public services.

The President received the civil rights report in October 1947 and kept silent while a storm of protest swirled up from outraged southerners. Then on February 2, clearly following Clifford's suggested strategy, he sent Congress his recommendations on civil rights. In calm, dignified prose, he discussed the "serious gap between our ideals and some of our practices," and then made ten specific proposals, including the creation of both a permanent Commission on Civil Rights and a new FEPC, federal efforts to end lynching and protect the right to vote, and a prohibition on discrimination in interstate transportation facilities. Liberal critics immediately noted the lack of any threat to withhold federal funds to force southern states to end segregation in schools and public accommodations, though they applauded Truman's announcement of plans to desegregate the armed forces and to guarantee the end of discrimination in all federal employment. Southern congressmen reacted angrily. Representative Eugene Cox of Georgia burst out, "The whole thing sickens me," while Mississippi Senator James O. Eastland responded with a call for his state to deny its electoral vote to the Democratic candidate and instead to promote the election of a "distinguished Southerner."

The threat of a southern bolt raised by Eastland, coming at a time when Wallace had defected and the ADA was wooing Eisenhower, forced Truman to back away from his bold rhetoric. When Strom Thurmond formed a movement of southern governors and congressmen to pressure the Democratic leadership, the Administration refused to repudiate the President's message but, at the same time, carefully refrained from having the party's Congressional leaders introduce any legislation designed to implement the civil rights program. Truman, pleased to learn from aides that the Negro press was referring to his February 2 message as "the greatest freedom document since the Emancipation Proclamation," felt that he had achieved his political goal and that any further steps would only drive the South into open opposition. Southerners continued to talk about bolting the party, however, despite Clifford's belief that they would remain loyal. Thurmond and his followers, according to historian William Berman, "failed to understand that Truman was engaged in symbolic action, that his rhetoric was a substitute for a genuine legislative commitment."

The President took advantage of events abroad to put the last part of Clifford's plan into effect. The Czech coup in February and the resulting fear of war with Russia led to massive liberal defections from Wallace's ranks. The third-party candidate accelerated the process when he accused the United States of provoking the events in Czechoslovakia by plotting a right-wing takeover. Truman capitalized on the change in the public mood in the course of a St. Patrick's Day address in New York City on March 17, the same day he had called on Congress to take stern measures to repel Soviet aggression. "We must not fall victim to the insidious propaganda that peace can be obtained solely by wanting peace," he told the audience. "I do not want and I will not accept the political support of Henry Wallace and his Communists." Pleased by the applause this line provoked, he wrote in his diary that he had spent the evening "reading Henry Wallace out of the Democratic Party."

The Russians provided an even more dramatic way for the President to profit from the Cold War. In late March the Soviets began harassing western rail and auto traffic to Berlin, which lay more than 100 miles within the Russian zone of Germany. Unhappy over American plans to give West Germany its sovereignty in the future, and perhaps hoping to force a solution to the whole German problem, Stalin ordered an absolute blockade of all ground routes to the city on June 24. Caught by surprise, the Truman Administration hastily canvassed the alternatives and rejected both the possibility of provoking a major war by sending an armed convoy into Berlin and the other extreme of simply withdrawing from an indefensible position. Instead Truman told his advisers that there would be no discussion of surrender ("We are going to stay period," Forrestal recalled him saying), and then gradually worked out a twofold policy: an airlift to feed and supply the 2 million civilians in Berlin and the ostentatious transfer of three squadrons of American B-29's, the plane that carried the atomic bomb, to bases in England as a somber warning to the Soviet Union. The crisis would continue for the remainder of 1948 as the airlift solved the immediate problem despite continued Soviet refusal to work out a settlement. It meant that day after day Truman received public acclaim for his refusal to back down in the face of stern Russian pressure. As Clifford had predicted, the American people rallied behind their President at a time of grave crisis, thus giving him a vital, if unnoticed, asset for the coming election.

Republicans paid little attention to Truman's efforts to strengthen his political position. Sure of winning in November, they concentrated on the all-important question of who would lead the party to victory. Governor Thomas Dewey of New York, the GOP's unsuccessful candidate in 1944, led the field, but his cocky refusal to take a stand on major issues and his smug, almost secretive personality made many leery of supporting him again. Midwest Republicans preferred Bob Taft of Ohio, "Mr. Republican," who stood for isolationism abroad and reduced federal activity at home, but he seemed to lack the personal charm needed for a successful presidential race and his foreign policy views alienated eastern internationalists. Harold Stassen, the former "boy" governor of Minnesota, offered a liberal alternative, while Arthur Vandenberg, the architect of a bipartisan foreign policy and General Douglas MacArthur, hero of the war in the Pacific, remained willing dark horses. Some Republicans turned to Dwight Eisenhower but, in January 1948, he definitely ruled himself out of the Republican primaries.

Forced to fight for the nomination, Dewey recovered from an upset at the hands of Stassen in the Wisconsin primary to post an impressive win in Oregon and enter the GOP convention in Philadelphia in a powerful position. Though Vandenberg became a declared candidate, Dewey led on the first ballot and, when Stassen and Taft failed to reach an agreement to merge their forces, the New York governor swept to victory on the third ballot. The party adopted a platform promising to preserve the gains of the New Deal while at the same time lowering taxes and bringing efficiency to the swollen federal bureaucracy. On foreign policy, Vandenberg's bipartisan approach prevailed. The Republicans pledged to support the United Nations and continue the policy of containment with surprisingly few recriminations for Democratic concessions at Yalta and Potsdam. The selection of liberal California Governor Earl Warren as the vice-presidential candidate confirmed the impression that the Republicans planned a campaign based on new leadership instead of on new programs; Dewey and Warren offered themselves to the voters as men who could preserve the existing prosperity and wage the Cold War more effectively than a discredited Harry Truman and a Democratic party that had grown listless and unresponsive after sixteen years in office.

The Democrats, in contrast, met in a pessimistic frame of mind after a last-ditch effort by Senator Claude Pepper to draft Eisenhower had failed. Making the best of what seemed a bad situation, the party nominated Truman and Senator Alben Barkley of Kentucky on a platform stressing Clifford's strategy of appealing to the various groups aided by the New Deal. The highlight came when Mayor Hubert Humphrey of Minneapolis led a successful fight to substitute an advanced civil rights plank for the moderate one Truman favored and thus provoked a walkout by several southern delegations. This defection from the right, coupled by Wallace's threat from the left, deepened the delegates' somber mood when they assembled to hear Truman deliver his acceptance speech. Displaying an amazing jauntiness, the President lambasted the 80th Congress and announced that he was calling a special summer session to enable the Republicans to enact the various progressive measures they had given lip service to in their platform. "In the space of 3,000 words," commented *Newsweek*, "Mr. Truman had given the Democratic Party its first real chance for hope in months."

The challenges from the right and left developed as planned during the summer. Three days after the Democratic convention closed, dissident southerners met at Birmingham, Alabama to form the States Rights Party and nominate two southern governors, J. Strom Thurmond of South Carolina and Fielding Wright of Mississippi, to run against the major party tickets. The Dixiecrats, as the new group became known, ran exclusively on a platform of preserving segregation in the South. In late July, Henry Wallace's followers assembled in Philadelphia and founded the Progressive Party, nominating Wallace and Idaho Senator Glen Taylor, best known as the singing cowboy, as their candidates. Communist leaders played a key role in the new party's deliberations by rigging a platform that followed the Soviet line in foreign policy and manipulating both the candidates and the rank and file, who simply sought alternatives to the Cold War policies of the Democrats and Republicans.

The special session of Congress met in late July and adjourned after twelve days of futile discussion without passing any significant legislation. Truman was pleased, because he now could make the 80th Congress the main target of his fall campaign. Using a whistle-stop technique novel for an incumbent, he traveled across the nation speaking eight to ten times a day from the rear platform of his train at small communities and then giving a major address every evening in a big city. Stiff and ill at ease reading formal speeches, Truman had developed an off-the-cuff style that suited his down-to-earth, folksy manner. Aides prepared cards with essential information and a few catch phrases, and Truman spoke from these few notes, expanding on topics that drew an enthusiastic audience response and skipping over matters that failed to excite interest. He condemned the Republican Congress everywhere he went — for passing Taft-Hartley in labor strongholds like Detroit, for favoring lower price supports in farm areas, for opposing conservation programs in western communities. The GOP was the party of special interests, he kept charging, while the Democrats stood for the people, as he reminded Jews of his recognition of Palestine and black voters of his civil rights stand. Sophisticated journalists ridiculed his methods, but reporters began to note that despite the polls, Truman was drawing large, enthusiastic crowds who responded to his peppery oratory with cries of "Give'em hell, Harry."

Dewey ignored the hubbub, dismissing it as the undignified last gasp of a losing candidate. Confident of victory, the GOP candidate adopted the traditional stance of a man already in power, refusing to discuss the issues or take specific stands for fear of limiting his freedom to act in the future. He used his melodious baritone voice to preach the doctrine of unity, and he directed his personal efforts toward local Republican leaders, not the mass of the people, as his meticulously precise campaign moved across the nation. Influenced by Senator Vandenberg and John Foster Dulles, his personal adviser on international affairs, Dewey hewed closely to the bipartisan foreign policy line.

He refused to attack the Democrats on Berlin, despite the fact that Roosevelt's failure in 1945 to secure definite access rights to the city offered a tempting target. Instead, as the Soviet blockade continued to dominate newspaper headlines throughtout the campaign, with the airlift Truman had ordered the focus of attention, Dewey called on the American people to stand loyally behind the Administration's policy.

Only Henry Wallace tried to engage in a meaningful debate on national issues. In a dramatic trip to the South in September, he broke precedent by speaking before integrated audiences and displayed great personal courage in braving ugly egg-throwing incidents while pleading the cause of racial equality. He continued to speak out bluntly on foreign policy. He condemned "the Truman-Dewey" policy of containment, calling for a withdrawal of American troops from bases overseas, including Berlin, and he argued that only direct negotiations with Moscow could resolve the Cold War and restore peace to the world. Truman became so concerned with Wallace's appeal to the peace vote that in early October he decided to send Chief Justice Fred Vinson to Russia for a face-to-face meeting with Stalin to ease world tension. After Secretary of State George Marshall flew home from a special UN meeting in Paris to persuade the President to abandon this proposed move, news of the mission leaked out, causing the Administration considerable embarrassment but also enabling Truman to let the people know of his strong desire to moderate the Cold War.

By late October, despite a growing shift to Truman, the pollsters and political commentators were unanimous in predicting a Republican victory. Elmo Roper stopped his surveys of public opinion in September, saying the outcome was certain. The New York *Times* concluded a canvass of political experts by saying that Dewey and Warren "appear certain to defeat" Truman and Barkley, while *Life* magazine captioned a picture of Dewey campaigning in California, "THE NEXT PRESIDENT TRAVELS BY FERRY BOAT OVER THE BROAD WATERS OF SAN FRANCISCO BAY." At times it seemed that only Truman himself refused to concede that defeat was inevitable. When Dewey took a week off from the stump in late October, the President stepped up his hectic pace. On October 30, he gave his last campaign speech in St. Louis, one long blast at "that Republican 'do-nothing' 80th Congress," and then returned to Independence to vote on November 2. Late in the day he slipped off to a resort hotel at Excelsior Springs some 22 miles north of Kansas City to await the returns. After listening to the early reports from the East, which showed him building a narrow lead, he nonchalantly went to bed, though nervous aides woke him several times in the night to inform him of the steadily growing margin over Dewey. Late results from the West confirmed the amazing upset victory the next morning and, shortly before noon, a stunned Dewey conceded. The final figures showed that Truman had outpolled Dewey by over 2 million votes to capture 303 electoral votes to 189 for the Republican. Wallace received only slightly more than 1 million popular votes (nearly half in New York alone) and failed to carry a single state; Thurmond won 38 electoral votes in the deep South.

Political commentators are fond of portraying Truman's triumph in 1948 as a lonely victory, the achievement of one man fighting an uphill battle by himself. The image is attractive to a nation that admires the underdog, but it is very misleading. Truman won because he appealed successfully to the enduring New Deal coalition, following closely the script Clifford had prepared a year before. Union workers unhappy over the Taft-Hartley Act, farmers suffering from a sudden decline in crop prices, Negroes whose hopes were suddenly raised by the civil rights promises, Jews gratified by the recognition of Israel – these were the traditional Democratic groups who rejected Wallace and Thurmond and stayed loyal to the political party that had enabled them to survive and prosper during the grim years of war and depression. 1948 was a Democratic triumph; the party regained control of Congress as Truman ran consistently behind the ticket across the nation. Above all, it was a final victory for the New Deal. "Harry Truman won this election," the *New Republic* concluded, "because Franklin Roosevelt had worked so well."

While the pundits sought an explanation, Harry Truman began a triumphal return to Washington aboard his campaign train, now dubbed "the Victory Special." Huge crowds greeted him at every stop ("Wednesday Democrats," he wryly remarked to aides), holding up copies of the Chicago *Tribune* headline, "DEWEY DEFEATS TRUMAN" and cheering mightily. When the party arrived in Washington, there was a mammoth crowd on hand at Union Station – a veritable sea of humanity to give the President "the greatest reception that I have seen in Washington," according to military aide William Leahy. Truman took it all in stride, enjoying the accolades from the only political experts he ever trusted, the American people. He now was President on his own; he had earned the right to return to what he called "the great white jail" on Pennsylvania Avenue.

2

The Price of Containment

Harry Truman was eager to greet the new 81st Congress, with its Democratic majorities in both Houses. He appeared in person on January 5 to outline his legislative program, basically the same measures that he had advocated in his first term and that the Republican-dominated Congress had rejected. He called for the extension of New Deal welfare reforms, especially the broadening of social security and a sharp increase in the minimum wage, for the adoption of new social advances in the form of aid to education, health care, and civil rights legislation, and for the repeal of the Taft-Hartley Act. The only real innovation came near the end of his address when, in summing up his program, Truman declared, "Every segment of our population and every individual has a right to expect from our Government a fair deal."

In proposing the Fair Deal, the President apparently ignored the fact that despite his victory in November, a conservative coalition of southern Democrats and midwestern Republicans still controlled the Congress. At best, skillful parliamentary handling might win passage for compromise proposals that would make modest advances toward the President's goals. But neither the White House nor the liberal interest group who felt it was time to collect on their campaign efforts displayed the caution and restraint the situation demanded. Instead, under pressure from his supporters, Truman tried to enact the entire Fair Deal at one time.

The fate of Taft-Hartley was typical. Pressed by union leaders who had played such a crucial role in his reelection, Truman demanded the total repeal of the law, spurning all attempts at compromise. Backed by strong public support for the existing act, especially for the 80-day cooling-off procedure in strikes affecting national welfare, both Houses of Congress rebuffed the Administration. In the civil rights area, the most Truman could hope to achieve would be a voluntary Fair Employment Practices Commission yet, pushed on by the NAACP and liberal advisers, he insisted on a compulsory FEPC and a federal antilynching act only to have all civil rights action cut off by a lengthy Senate filibuster. His proposal for a system of compulsory health insurance stirred up the bitter opposition of the American Medical Association, while the Roman Catholic Church came out against federal aid to education because it did not include subsidies for parochial schools. The greatest storm of controversy centered about the farm policy proposed by Secretary of Agriculture Charles E. Brannan, which sought to avoid the huge stockpiles of crops stored by the government under the price-support program by letting farm products be sold on the open market and then reimbursing farmers for any losses through direct federal payments. Conservatives branded the Brannan Plan dictatorial, and the American Farm Bureau Federation objected to its stringent controls; Congress finally rejected it completely in passing legislation to continue a variation of the existing price-support system.

By the end of 1949, Truman had succeeded only in enacting a comprehensive housing act, backed by Republican Senator Taft, which authorized construction of 810,000 new living units for low-income families, and in extending two key New Deal reforms by raising the minimum wage from 40 to 75 cents an hour and expanding the Social Security system to include nearly 10 million more Americans and doubling the level of benefits. The Fair Deal lay in shambles, victim of the excessive expectations raised by Truman's dramatic victory and the inability of liberal pressure groups to mold their programs to fit Congressional realities.

In foreign policy, the new Congress continued the bipartisan approach by approving American participation in the North Atlantic Treaty Organization (NATO), which became the capstone of containment. Dean Acheson, the new Secretary of State, worked closely with Republican Arthur Vandenberg in building up Senate support. Designed to encourage the nations of Western Europe, who were beginning to recover economically under the Marshall Plan, NATO committed the United States to defend ten nations stretching from Norway to Italy in case of military aggression, presumably from the Soviet Union or its satellites. A number of Republican senators, including Robert Taft of Ohio and Kenneth Wherry of Nebraska, objected to NATO as a military alliance that violated America's historic freedom of action, but the treaty's sponsors, notably Senator Vandenberg, tried to disarm the isolationist argument by asserting that NATO marked the extension of the Monroe Doctrine to Europe. In order to quiet Senate doubts, Acheson finally promised that the

United States would neither reinforce the two American divisions stationed in Europe nor work for the rearmament of West Germany. Just thirteen senators voted against NATO, but when Truman asked Congress for $1.5 billion for military equipment for our new European allies, he met with heavy opposition and only won grudging approval after months of debate.

The North Atlantic treaty marked the last achievement for bipartisanship. Many Republicans attributed their party's defeat in 1948 to the failure to challenge the Democrats on foreign policy. They were looking for an issue, and they found it in Asia. At the end of World War II, there were two groups vying for power in China: the Nationalists led by Chiang Kai-shek and the Communists under Mao Tze-tung. The Nationalists were recognized by most nations, including the Soviet Union, as the legitimate government of China, but Chiang's regime had grown corrupt and had lost the confidence of the Chinese people, who wanted to see their nation free of foreign domination. The United States unwisely backed a coalition policy, one that the Communists accepted for tactical reasons and the Nationalists entered into as a condition for American aid. General George Marshall, serving as Truman's personal representative, tried hard to make this shotgun marriage work, but by 1947 civil war had broken out between the two factions. Inflation weakened the Nationalists, whose strength lay in South China, and Chiang, ignoring the advice of American military men, stretched his numerically superior forces too thin in an attempt to occupy Manchuria. By the time Truman had won reelection in November 1948, the Nationalists had suffered a disastrous defeat in North China and their morale had cracked. The Communists, aided by American weapons captured from the fleeing Nationalists, drove quickly southward, finally forcing Chiang to flee with the remnants of his army to the island of Formosa, where he vowed he would someday return to rule all China.

Mao's victory, known in the United States as "the fall of China," shocked the American people. Nourished on a romantic myth of friendship with China based on the benevolent activities of American traders, missionaries, and philanthropists, the people blamed the Truman Administration for the outcome. Republican conservatives, long troubled by the Democrats' preoccupation with Europe, blamed the Foreign Service officers who had criticized Chiang's regime and advocated the coalition policy. "The greatest Kremlin asset in our history," declared Robert Taft, "has been the pro-Communist group in the State Department who promoted at every opportunity the Communist cause in China." Such Asia-first spokesmen as Congressman Walter Judd and Senator William Knowland called for all-out assistance for Chiang's forces, despite the fact that the United States had sent $2 billion in aid since 1945, but they stopped short of advocating actual American military intervention in the Chinese civil war. Even Democrats, like young Massachusetts

Representative John F. Kennedy, condemned the Administration for losing China. Finally, in August 1949, Acheson released a long White Paper that argued that nothing the United States did or did not do could have changed the outcome in China. The testimony of the commander of the American military mission to the Nationalists stated the case most effectively: "Their military debacles, in my opinion, can all be attributed to the world's worst leadership and many other morale-destroying factors that led to a complete loss of will to fight."

The belief that America had "lost" China persisted, however, and became a major factor in the demise of bipartisanship. Arthur Vandenberg tried hard to heal the breach but, with his death in early 1951, party leadership in foreign affairs passed to men like Taft and Knowland who had long wanted to challenge containment. Politically, they felt it had been poor tactics to defer to the Administration's conduct of foreign policy; emotionally, they chafed at the idea of engaging in a long, slow, and very expensive contest with the Soviet Union that gave no promise of early victory. Thus, from 1950 on, Truman faced a growing Republican opposition on foreign as well as domestic issues that made the 81th Congress an even more stubborn and persistent antagonist than its Republican predecessor.

I

"We have evidence that within recent weeks an atomic explosion occurred in the U.S.S.R.," President Truman announced on September 23, 1949. American planes taking air samples in the North Pacific detected the telltale radioactivity in early September; exhaustive scientific analysis indicated a Soviet atomic test had taken place in late August. Informed of this ominous development on September 21, Truman consulted with Congressional leaders and then broke the news as casually as possible to the American people, who seemed to take it in stride. After all, the Russians had only carried out a test; the United States still enjoyed a four-year lead in technology and a large stockpile of atomic bombs.

The men responsible for American security reacted very differently. They realized that the Soviet advance undermined the entire Cold War strategy of the United States, and they sought ways to offset the Russian achievement. Ever since the failure of the Baruch Plan, the Truman Administration had placed more and more emphasis on the atomic bomb as the key to American defense policy. Faced with Congressional demands for economy in government, the President had cut back sharply on spending for the armed forces, reducing the defense budget from $45 billion in 1946 to $13 billion by 1949. The result was a drastic drop in the Army and Navy and near total reliance

on the Air Force to protect the nation. In the Berlin blockade, Truman had
used the threat of atomic retaliation as his chief weapon against the Soviets
and, in 1948, a civilian commission headed by Thomas Finletter had concluded, "Our military security must be based on air power." Suddenly the
Soviets, who already possessed superior conventional forces, had broken the
atomic monopoly.

For the next six months, a secret debate took place within the highest
councils of government. A group of scientists led by Edward Teller, an
Hungarian physicist who had worked on the atomic bomb at Los Alamos,
and Ernest O. Lawrence, Nobel laureate and builder of the great cyclotron at
Berkeley, descended on Washington to urge the Atomic Energy Commission
(AEC) to embark on a crash program to build a hydrogen bomb. The Super,
as the new weapon was called, had been a theoretical possibility since 1942;
instead of splitting heavy elements like uranium and plutonium, it involved
the fusion of light forms of hydrogen to form helium, a process that released
fantastic amounts of explosive energy. Teller and Lawrence quickly persuaded
Senator Brien McMahon, chairman of the Joint Committee on Atomic Energy,
and Lewis Strauss, a member of the AEC, of the need to develop a fusion
bomb, which would be at least 1000 times more powerful than the atomic
bomb that destroyed Hiroshima. But a majority of the AEC, led by Chairman
David Lilienthal, hesitated, influenced by a negative report from the Commission's General Advisory Committee, a group of distinguished scientific advisers headed by Robert Oppenheimer, the man who had directed the wartime
effort at Los Alamos. Oppenheimer's group stressed the very great technical
problems involved in perfecting a fusion weapon, pointing out that it would
require the diversion of large quantities of scarce plutonium, the fissionable
material needed for atomic bombs. Moreover, they questioned the wisdom
and morality of developing a weapon of such great destructive power when
the world had not yet been able to adjust to the atomic bomb.

The AEC reported its inability to reach a unanimous decision to President
Truman in November, and he immediately appointed a special committee of
the National Security Council to study the problem and break the deadlock.
For the next two months, three men — Secretary of State Dean Acheson,
Secretary of Defense Louis Johnson, who replaced Forrestal in early 1949,
and AEC Chairman Lilienthal — went over the complex and sensitive issues
involved. Lilienthal kept pressing for a new attempt to reach an agreement
with the Soviets to limit the arms race, hopeful that the Russians would be
more reasonable now that they had broken the American atomic monopoly,
but neither Johnson nor Acheson would agree. The group finally reached a
compromise by which they would recommend that Truman authorize the AEC
to explore the feasibility of a hydrogen bomb (not quite a crash program)
while the National Security Council undertook a full-scale reexamination of

the country's entire military program in light of the Soviet breakthrough. On January 31, the three men reported in person to the President. Lilienthal voiced his reservations about continuing "our chief reliance upon atomic weapons in the defense of this country," but Truman brushed aside his objections as he signed a public statement announcing the decision to go ahead with the hydrogen bomb, telling Lilienthal he hoped he never had to use nuclear weapons. The AEC Chairman later recalled Truman adding, "but we had to go on and make them because of the way the Russians are behaving; we had no other course."

The National Security Council completed its review of America's strategic position in the world and handed the document, known as NSC-68, to the President in April 1950. The basic assumptions were exceedingly pessimistic. The planners believed that Russia was bent on world domination and that by 1954 the Soviets would have neutralized the American atomic advantage and upset the military balance in the world with their larger conventional forces. They forecast "an indefinite period of tension and danger" and said the United States had to choose among accepting an inferior military status, retreating back to a "fortress America" in the Western Hemisphere, launching a preventive war to redress the world balance of power in one stroke, or engaging in a "bold and massive program of rebuilding the West's defensive potential to surpass that of the Soviet world." The drafters of NSC-68 favored the last alternative as they recommended that Truman abandon the $15 billion ceiling and prepare the nation for defense spending of up to 20 percent of the gross national product, on the scale of $50 billion annually.

Without hesitation, Truman initialed this startling document, which he referred to as "my five-year plan for peace." In many ways NSC-68 was even more far reaching than the Truman Doctrine, since it meant that the United States would become a militarized nation, accepting the burdens of a large, permanent military establishment in peacetime. National security was now defined in global terms; containment was expanded into a military contest with the Russians for control of the world. Dean Acheson spelled out the diplomatic implications most fully in a speech in March 1950. "The only way to deal with the Soviet Union, we have found from hard experience," the Secretary of State proclaimed, "is to create situations of strength. Wherever the Soviet detects weakness or disunity — and it is quick to detect them, it exploits them to the full....when we have eliminated all the areas of weakness that we can — we will be able to evolve working agreements with the Russians." In other words, the Truman Administration would embark on a deliberate program of developing the full potential of America's economic and technological abundance, through the building of the hydrogen bomb and the expansion of conventional forces, so as to frustrate all Soviet efforts to expand their power and influence. The implication was that the Cold War could end only when the Russians acknowledged their inferiority and accepted a secondary place in the world.

II

While the Truman Administration forged a global response to the Soviet challenge, the American people suddenly discovered the Communist danger at home. The loyalty issue had been building slowly with the onset of the Cold War, but it developed startling momentum by 1950 as a result of the fall of China and the explosion of the Russian atomic bomb. Congressional investigations produced dramatic revelations of Soviet espionage rings working within the American government, culminating in the conviction of Alger Hiss in January 1950 and the sensational disclosure the next month that British scientist Klaus Fuchs had spied for the Russians at the Los Alamos project during the war. These events touched off a red scare that infected every aspect of American life with doubt and insecurity.

To some extent, the Truman Administration itself was to blame for the hysteria over subversives. The overblown rhetoric that Truman and Acheson used to describe the nature of the Communist threat abroad created the feeling that the United States was engaged in a crusade against evil. Tom Clark and J. Howard McGrath, the men who served as Attorney General under Truman, took a hard-line attitude toward Communism that fed the public concern. In a speech in 1949, McGrath declared that there were "many Communists in America." "They are everywhere — in factories, offices, butcher stores, on street corners, in private businesses," he continued. "And each carries in himself the germ of death for society." In reality, the American Communist party, though never large, had enjoyed some degree of success among intellectuals in the 1930s when a number of government employees, along with writers, artists, Hollywood personalities, union organizers, and college professors had joined party cells or, more often, had sympathized openly with Communist-backed causes and had thus become identified as fellow travelers, an elastic term used to describe nearly everyone on the left in American politics in the late 1940s. Many of those attracted to Communism tended to support the New Deal and, though most who were in government employ had ended any formal connection with the Communist party after the Nazi-Soviet pact of 1939, the Truman Administration realized it needed to protect itself against possible GOP charges of employing disloyal individuals as relations with Russia deteriorated. Accordingly, the President appointed a special commission in late 1946 and then issued an executive order on March 22, 1947 establishing a Federal Employee Loyalty Program. Each government agency and department was to create a loyalty board that would examine and decide on the trustworthiness of all its employees. At the top, a Loyalty Review Board headed by conservative Republican Seth Richardson would coordinate the program and serve as a final court of appeals.

The Administration's program failed to satisfy either the left or the right. Civil libertarians criticized it for the vague rule that permitted dismissal from · government service if "reasonable grounds exist for the belief that the person involved is disloyal to the Government of the United States." They also attacked the practice of using FBI reports for evidence of disloyalty and then refusing to let the employee in question confront his accuser. Conservatives were skeptical of the ability of the Administration to police itself, and the revelations of the House Un-American Activities Committee that Communist cells had existed within the Department of Agriculture, the Treasury Department, and the National Labor Relations Board lessened confidence in the loyalty program. Even the test of loyalty itself did not seem strict enough to many; self-annointed patriots wanted to change the standard for dismissal to the existence of "reasonable doubt as to the loyalty of the person involved," a radical change that Truman reluctantly approved in 1951 at the height of the red scare. In five years, the Truman Administration checked the loyalty of more than 4 million individuals and brought charges against only 9077. Some employees resigned under fire; of the 2961 who underwent formal hearings, the government dismissed 379, or 0.002 of all those whose loyalty was examined. The 379 were dismissed as security risks, not as spies; according to Chairman Richardson, "not one single case or evidence directing toward a case of espionage has been disclosed. . . ."

The strange case of Alger Hiss, more than any single event, discredited the loyalty program and confirmed the popular notion that spies had infiltrated the government. Hiss had been a State Department officer for fourteen years, serving in important roles at such crucial wartime meetings as Dumbarton Oaks, Yalta, and the San Francisco conference. After the war, he had resigned from government service to become the president of the prestigious Carnegie Endowment for International Peace. On August 3, 1948, Whittaker Chambers, a *Time* senior editor, testified before the House Un-American Activities Committee to having been a member of the Communist party from 1924 to 1937 and then named Hiss as one of several government employees in his cell. Two days later, Hiss appeared before the Committee to deny Chambers' testimony in an attempt to preserve his reputation and career. Hiss made an excellent impression on the Committee; he was so plausible and forthright that the majority wanted to drop the case. But Richard Nixon, then a young California Representative, and one other committee member insisted that the investigation continue. Nixon took personal charge of the quest, grilling Chambers at length to satisfy himself that he was telling the truth, and then arranging a private confrontation on August 17 between Chambers and Hiss in the Hotel Commodore in New York City. At that time, Hiss recognized Chambers as a man known to him in the 1930s as George Crosley, but he continued to deny any Communist activity. On August 25, the two men met again in a public confrontation before the full Committee that lasted nine hours. This time Chambers came off relatively well while Hiss seemed vague and evasive in his testimony. The matter might still have died had not Hiss, his reputation endangered, challenged Chambers to repeat his charges outside the committee hearings where he was immune to charges of slander. Chambers obliged by declaring on "Meet the Press" on August 30 that "Alger Hiss was a Communist and may still be one."

Two weeks later, Hiss filed suit in Baltimore for slander against Chambers, asking for damages of $75,000. In November, in a pretrial hearing, Chambers handed the court documents he had hidden in Brooklyn when he broke with the Communist party consisting of copies of 65 pages of confidential State Department communications he claimed Hiss had given him. Nixon immediately brought the House Committee back onto the Hiss case and, in early December, Committee investigators accompanied Chambers to his Maryland farm where he led them to a hollowed-out pumpkin that contained three rolls of microfilm, photographs of more than a hundred secret government documents. The statue of limitations prevented the Justice Department from trying Hiss on charges of espionage. Instead, a New York federal grand jury to which he had denied knowing Chambers indicted him on two counts of perjury. Hiss appealed to the liberal community for support, claiming that Nixon and the Committee were using him as the scapegoat to attack the New Deal and the United Nations, the causes for which he had worked as a government employee. Many liberals responded and, when Hiss was found guilty in his second trial (the first ended in a hung jury), those associated with him were discredited. The evidence indicates that Hiss probably was a Communist in the 1930s, though apparently he broke with the party before the war and made no attempt to influence American policy in a pro-Soviet direction. The tragedy lay in his guilt being extended to cover the people and movements identified with him and thus to confirm the popular belief that Communist subversion at home instead of Russian aggression abroad was the real threat to American security.

Senator Joseph McCarthy of Wisconsin immediately seized on the new public mood to rescue his declining political fortunes. A shrewdly opportunistic politician who combined a boyish friendliness with a surly contempt for conventions, McCarthy launched his anti-Communist crusade at an obscure GOP women's meeting in Wheeling, West Virginia on February 9, 1950. In the course of his rambling remarks, delivered extemporaneously from a bundle of notes, McCarthy startled his audience by charging that Communists inside the State Department were responsible for American setbacks in the world, waving a piece of paper as he claimed, "I have here in my hand a list of 205."

In speeches given the next few days in Reno and Salt Lake City, he cited new numbers, first 57, then 81 Communists in the State Department. Back in Washington, on February 20 McCarthy renewed his charges in a long and often incoherent speech that lasted until midnight. He referred to "81 known Communist agents in the State Department," but refused to give their names, apparently relying on discredited information dug up by another congressional committee in 1947. In an effort to rebuke McCarthy, Democratic Majority Leader Scott Lucas of Illinois secured passage of a motion to have the Foreign Relations Committee conduct a full investigation into the Wisconsin Senator's charges. Democrat Millard Tydings of Maryland chaired the hearings, which turned out to be a study in frustration. McCarthy proved impossible to pin down; he responded to attempts to force him to substantiate his charges by bringing forth a series of new accusations. He finally identified John Hopkins professor Owen Lattimore as "the top Soviet espionage agent" in the State Department, despite the fact that he was only an occasional consultant. Lattimore eventually cleared his name, but the Tydings committee failed to stop McCarthy's momentum. Republicans, eager to embarrass the Administration, rallied to his side, and the Senate divided along exact partisan lines in voting on the committee's report, thus taking the sting out of its condemnation of McCarthy's tactics as "a fraud and a hoax perpetrated on the Senate of the United States and the American people."

McCarthy gained revenge by helping Republican candidate John Marshall Butler defeat Tydings in the 1950 Congressional election in an unscrupulous campaign. The upset of a popular Senator threatened the political security of potential opponents and gave McCarthy virtual immunity from further attacks by his colleagues. He continued to campaign against the State Department, finding the elegant Dean Acheson, who had testified on behalf of Alger Hiss, a perfect target. He accused the Secretary of State of harboring the Communists who had sold out China, and he regularly referred to Acheson mockingly as "the Red Dean."

Historians and social scientists have offered a number of broad explanations for the phenomenon of McCarthyism. Some see it as the natural by-product of Truman's effort to whip up public enthusiasm for the Cold War against Russia — in the face of adversity, the people turned against those who had first roused them to a sense of danger. Others have attributed McCarthy's success to the "status anxieties" of such groups as the newly rich, rising middle-class ethnic groups, particularly the Irish and the Germans, and frustrated intellectuals. This new "radical right" applauded McCarthy's attack on the old, established groups in government and society. Still others see McCarthyism as a result of Truman's victory in 1948, which distorted the normal political rhythm and forced the Republicans to back an underhanded and distasteful attack on the Administration as the only way to insure victory in 1952.

All these external explanations offer some insight into the Wisconsin Senator's appeal, but they tend to minimize McCarthy's gifts as a supremely accomplished demagogue. In large measure, he succeeded because he exploited the basic insecurities of his time so skillfully. McCarthy manipulated the press, making some of his most severe critics his most useful allies. He knew the insatiable desire of reporters to write a fresh story for each new edition; his steady stream of charges met this need perfectly, and guaranteed him front-page coverage day after day. He knew that the American people are fond of documentation and so he always had papers in his hand to bolster his assertions and a briefcase bulging with official-looking folders to lend his statements an air of authenticity. In time he built a network of informers within the government itself, men and women who bore grudges against their superiors or their fellow employees and who provided McCarthy with a steady stream of leads to pursue. He failed to identify a single Communist spy or uncover a single genuine subversive within the government, but he succeeded in creating the impression that he was ferreting out the Reds who alone had denied the United States a victory in the Cold War by betraying Chiang Kai-shek and by giving the Russians the secret of the atomic bomb. In short, he catered to what Denis Brogan so aptly termed "the illusion of American omnipotence" to build up a personal following that made him the most dangerous man in public life since Aaron Burr.

III

On June 25, 1950 the Truman Administration received a far greater challenge than either the Soviet A-bomb or the McCarthy crusade when the North Korean army crossed the 38th parallel. The Communist assault in Korea could be viewed as a limited probing action designed to test the willingness of the United States to defend Syngman Rhee's autocratic regime in the south, or as a response to the recent American decision to negotiate a separate peace treaty with Japan, or even as the beginning of a full-scale Soviet effort to take over all Asia. Truman and Acheson instinctively reacted to the attack as a showdown for the principle of collective security. In the 1930s the democracies had allowed Hitler to take country after country by piecemeal aggression; the appeasement policy that reached a climax at Munich had ultimately led to the most devastating war in history. With this memory of the recent past uppermost in their minds, American leaders vowed they would take a resolute stand to halt aggression in Korea and thus prevent World War III.

When the first reports of the North Korean attack reached Washington, Truman was on a trip to Missouri. Dean Acheson immediately arranged for an emergency meeting of the UN Security Council and then informed the

President, who said he would return to the capital the next day to consult with his principal advisers. Events moved swiftly over the next seven days. The Security Council called on the North Koreans to withdraw behind the 38th parallel, a resolution made possible by the absence of the Russian representative, who was boycotting the UN over its refusal to seat Red China. When the Communists ignored the Security Council request and pressed deeper into South Korea, Truman issued new orders, authorizing General Douglas MacArthur, the American commander in the Far East, to begin air strikes against the invaders south of the 38th parallel and instructing the American Navy to patrol the Formosa Straits in order to prevent a Chinese attack against the Nationalists. On June 27, American delegate Warren Austin asked the Security Council to condemn North Korea as an aggressor and to call on all members of the United Nations to "render such assistance to the Republic of Korea as may be necessary to repel the armed attack and to restore international peace and security to the area." Seven nations voted for this affirmation of collective security, with Yugoslavia opposed and the Soviet Union again absent. On June 30 after a personal report from MacArthur describing the rout of the weak South Korean army, Truman ordered American ground troops into battle in Korea. He had consulted with Congressional leaders before taking this move, but he acted solely on his authority as Commander-in-Chief. His bold stand met with nearly unanimous approval; only Robert Taft criticized Truman for usurping the Congressional power to declare war.

The President never had any doubt about the decision he made in Korea. At the time, he compared the situation to that in Greece in 1947, saying, "If we are tough enough now, they won't take any next steps....There's no telling what they'll do, if we don't put up a fight now." In his memoirs, he contrasted his actions with the appeasement of the 1930s, asserting, "Communism was acting in Korea just as Hitler, Mussolini, and the Japanese had acted ten, fifteen, and twenty years earlier. If this was allowed to go unchallenged it would mean a third world war." He presented the conflict to the American people as a violation of the UN Charter, telling a press conference that the United States was not engaged in a war but, instead, was attempting "to suppress a bandit raid on the Republic of Korea." When a reporter asked if it would be accurate to call the fighting "a police action under the United Nations," the President replied, "Yes, that is exactly what it amounts to." For the next three years, the United States maintained the fiction that the war in Korea was simply a UN police action. Sixteen nations contributed troops, but the United States furnished the bulk of the ground forces and nearly all the air and naval units and, while the UN was consulted on major policy questions, the world body simply ratified decisions made by the American Joint Chiefs of Staff. In time, it became clear that the United States was engaged in a unilateral struggle to contain Communist expansion in Asia and prove to the world that aggression did not pay.

At first, it appeared that even full-scale American intervention might not stem the Communist advance. The postwar demobilization had left the United States Army woefully unprepared for battle. There were only 592,000 troops in service in 1950, less than half the army's strength at the time of Pearl Harbor; the 80,000 soldiers MacArthur had on hand consisted mainly of recent draftees who had no wartime experience and little combat training. Moved suddenly from their occupation duties in Japan, these green troops had difficulty in stopping the well-trained and highly motivated North Korean soldiers who continued their steady advance down the peninsula. MacArthur simply tried to slow the enemy while building up a defense perimeter around the crucial port of Pusan at the southern tip of Korea. The long supply line and the constant American aerial assaults finally halted the North Korean invasion some fifty miles north of Pusan. Instead of fighting his way back over the rugged Korean terrain to the 38th parallel, MacArthur decided to capitalize on superior American air and naval power with a daring amphibious strike deep behind the enemy lines at Inchon, located on the west coast of Korea near Seoul. This risky operation, on which MacArthur himself claimed the odds were 5000 to 1 against success, went off beautifully on September 15. Within two weeks the American forces had recaptured Seoul and had cut off and decimated most of the North Korean army.

MacArthur's startling victory induced the Truman Administration to broaden its goals in Korea. In June, consistent with the police action statement, Truman had announced that the United States was fighting simply to restore the 38th parallel as the dividing line between North and South Korea. On September 1, after the Communist offensive had been stopped, the President began to speak publicly about the need to unify Korea. On September 11, the Joint Chiefs, with Truman's approval, authorized MacArthur to advance beyond the 38th parallel and begin occupying North Korea, provided "there was no indication or threat of entry of Soviet or Chinese Communist elements in force." This proviso was crucial. The Chinese shared a common border with North Korea along the Yalu River and they might well regard the destruction of a neighboring Communist state as a threat to their security requiring a military response. Dean Acheson told the American people on September 10 that it would be "sheer madness" for the Chinese to intervene in Korea, and the Administration continued to discount this possibility. On October 1, MacArthur permitted South Korean troops to cross the 38th parallel, and six days later the UN adopted an American-drafted resolution recommending that "all appropriate steps" be taken "including the holding of elections" to establish "a unified, independent and democratic government in the sovereign State of Korea." The war, originally limited to the single goal of driving the invaders out of South Korea and thus uphold the principle of collective security, now became a crusade to destroy the Communist regime in the north and establish a democratic Korea on the very doorstep of China and Russia.

General MacArthur was delighted with the Truman Administration's decision to fight an expanded war in Korea. He had long felt that those in power in Washington had neglected the Communist menace in Asia in their pursuit of a Europe-first policy and he welcomed the chance to unify Korea by force. He chafed at the ambiguity of his orders, however, which advised him to restrict his military movements if he had any evidence of Chinese intervention.

Communist China quickly reacted to the escalation of the Korean conflict. On October 1, Chou En-lai, Peking's Foreign Minister, informed the Indian ambassador that "if the United Nations forces crossed the 38th parallel, China would send in troops to help the North Koreans." Washington ignored this warning when it was relayed through diplomatic channels, evidently in the belief that the Chinese were bluffing. American intelligence indicated that there were less than 150,000 Chinese troops stationed along the Yalu, and Far East experts argued that the Communist regime was too exhausted from the recent civil war to engage in any new adventures. Truman still worried about China, however, and he decided to hold a personal meeting with MacArthur on Wake Island in the Pacific to discuss the problem at first hand.

The two men approached each other with considerable uneasiness. In August the President had forced the General to retract a speech he had planned to have read to the Veterans of Foreign Wars that contradicted Administration policy in the Far East by placing excessive emphasis on defending Chiang on Formosa. MacArthur resented the way in which Truman allowed the Joint Chiefs to phrase his orders, giving him wide discretion but forcing him to bear the responsibility if anything went wrong. At Wake Island, after a tense scene in which the President refused to leave his plane until the General appeared at the airfield to greet him, the two men first held a private conversation and then met with their aides. Truman brought up the problem of China and MacArthur assured him, "We are no longer fearful of intervention." He went on to say that at most the Chinese could move only 50,000 to 60,000 men across the Yalu, and if they tried to do so without air cover, "there would be the greatest slaughter." Truman accepted these reassurances and returned to the United States in a more confident frame of mind. The President had undoubtedly benefited politically from this highly publicized meeting with one of the nation's great heroes, and he could look forward to a speedy end to the Korean conflict as MacArthur announced a new offensive designed to bring the boys "home by Christmas."

IV

The outbreak of the Korean War killed off the President's lingering hopes of enacting the Fair Deal. When Congress reconvened in early 1950, Truman had pushed once again for passage of the Brannan Plan, adoption of federal aid to education, creation of a compulsory health insurance plan, and repeal of the Taft-Hartley Act. He failed to secure any of these goals before the North Korean aggression turned Congressional attention exclusively to the Asian conflict.

Other issues combined in 1950 to weaken the Democrats' political position still further. Estes Kefauver, a crusading Tennessee senator who wore a coonskin cap to prove that he was no one's "pet coon," headed a Senate investigation of organized crime. Already nursing presidential ambitions, Kefauver focused on gambling in a series of hearings held in major cities, culminating in the nationally televised grilling of underworld chieftain Frank Costello in New York. The hearings failed to produce any solution to the crime problem, but they did serious political damage by revealing the close ties between the big city machines the Democrats controlled and the criminal syndicates. The continuing red scare also hurt the Administration. In September, Senator Patrick McCarran of Nevada sponsored an omnibus bill to deal with subversion. The McCarran Internal Security Act required all Communists and Communist-sponsored groups to register with the Attorney General, forbade the employment of Communists in defense plants, and gave the government the power to deny passports to them and to order the deportation of any alien who had been a member of the Communist party and, most frightening of all, to detain during a national emergency "any person as to whom there is reason to believe he might engage in acts of espionage or sabotage." Congressional Democratic leaders, worried about the upcoming November elections, urged the President to accept this measure despite its flagrant violations of individual liberties. Charles Murphy, Truman's special counsel, countered by recommending a veto, warning the President that the bill would "greatly enlarge the field of activity of self-appointed loyalty censors, vigilantes and super patriots." Truman responded with a stinging veto message on September 22; despite intense White House lobbying and a determined fight led by freshman Senator Hubert Humphrey, Congress overrode the veto by huge majorities, 286 to 48 in the House, 57 to 10 in the Senate.

By early November, Democratic prospects in the Congressional elections had become quite bleak. Even the success in the Korean War failed to build up support for the Administration as Chinese "volunteers" began to appear in North Korea, the first sign of a massive intervention that would reverse the course of that conflict. The Republicans had begun blaming the war on Dean Acheson, claiming that he had invited the Communist attack in a January 1950 speech in which he had declared that Korea lay beyond the American defensive perimeter in the Pacific. Amid a rising demand that Truman fire Acheson, the President stood loyalty behind his Secretary of State. Neither man could appreciate the irony in the fact that the GOP search for political advantage had transformed the hardest of the hard-liners into a symbol of softness toward Communism.

The Republicans succeeded in making impressive gains in the midterm election, picking up 28 seats in the House and 5 in the Senate. In addition to Millard Tydings in Maryland, whose defeat was attributed primarily to McCarthy's intervention, Scott Lucas, the Senate Majority Leader who was hurt both by his opposition to McCarthy and the exposures of the Kefauver committee, lost to Representative Everett McKinley Dirksen in Illinois. The Republican candidates exploited the Communist issue across the nation to unseat Democrats, none more effectively than Richard Nixon, who defeated Helen Gahagan Douglas by associating her with "pinks and fellow travelers." Although the Democrats retained a narrow majority in both Houses, thus avoiding the disaster of 1946, the Administration was in serious trouble. Unable to enact the Fair Deal after the 1948 victory, Truman now faced the opposition of an aroused Republican Party eager to capitalize on the red scare and the Korean War to regain possession of the White House after twenty years of frustration.

V

Foreign policy became the first battleground between the Republicans and the Truman Administration in the new Congress. A new disaster in Korea set the tone for the increasingly bitter partisan debate. General MacArthur had ignored the presence of Chinese troops in North Korea in early November and had proceeded with plans to advance to the Yalu River in order to complete his victory. His forces moved up the east and west coasts of Korea as it widened out toward Manchuria, cut off from each other by the mountains in the center. Unknown to MacArthur, 300,000 Chinese had crossed the Yalu; on November 26, they struck, achieving complete surprise and forcing the Americans into a headlong retreat. By the end of December the Chinese had regained all North Korea, and it seemed possible that the Communists would succeed in driving the UN forces off the peninsula. In a press conference on November 30, Truman ominously hinted at possible use of the atomic bomb to stem the Chinese advance and, in Tokyo, MacArthur warned the Administration that it faced the loss of all Korea unless he was allowed to expand the war against China. Specifically, the General wanted permission to bomb the supply lines in Manchuria, institute a blockade of the entire China coast, and use Chiang Kai-shek's troops both in Korea and in diversionary raids against mainland China. After a flying visit from British Prime Minister Clement Attlee, who expressed the European fear of full-scale American involvement in a war with China, Truman dropped any further mention of atomic attacks. Acting on the advice of the Joint Chiefs, he also rejected MacArthur's strategy, and by mid-January General Matthew Ridgway, who had taken command of the army in the field after the death of General

Walton Walker, had halted the Chinese advance south of Seoul and began a slow but steady counterattack that would reach the 38th parallel by April.

Truman reacted to the defeat in Korea by preparing for a long and costly conflict. Meeting with the National Security Council in early December, he decided to accelerate NSC-68, already being implemented during the Korean War, in order to achieve the projected expansion of American military strength by 1952, two years ahead of the original schedule. He asked Congress for an additional appropriation of $16.8 billion for national defense, which brought the total for fiscal year 1951 to a staggering $52 billion, four times the pre-Korean War level. Finally, after consulting with Congressional leaders, who gave him conflicting advice, Truman announced to the nation plans for wage and price controls and tax increases necessitated by the war and then declared a state of "national emergency."

The first sign of a Republican rebellion against this ambitious program came over European commitments. At a NATO council meeting in September, Acheson had agreed to United States participation in the formation of a NATO army under an American commander to defend Europe. Truman made this commitment public on December 19, naming Dwight D. Eisenhower as the Supreme Commander of the Allied Powers in Europe and announcing that several additional American divisions would join the two already in Europe. This bold step, taken at a time when the outcome in Korea was still uncertain, reflected the Administration's fear that the Russians were masterminding a "trap play" in which American overinvolvment in Asia would permit them to expand in Europe. Former President Herbert Hoover gave the Republican response in a widely publicized speech criticizing any attempt to fight a land war against the Communist hordes in either Europe or Asia. Instead, Hoover recommended writing off Western Europe in favor of relying on air and naval power to defend the Atlantic and Pacific approaches to the New World. In a statement reminiscent of pre-World War II isolationism, he declared, "The foundation of our national policies must be to preserve for the world this Western Hemisphere Gibraltar of Western Civilization." Senator Taft immediately endorsed Hoover's new version of Fortress America, and when Congress convened in January GOP Minority Leader Kenneth Wherry touched off what the press called "the great debate" with a Senate resolution to force the President to secure the consent of Congress before sending any more American troops to Europe.

The Administration fought hard against the Wherry resolution. Dean Acheson ridiculed its backers for advocating a policy of "sitting quivering in a storm cellar waiting for whatever fate others may wish to prepare for us." In the Congressional hearings that followed, internationalist Republicans, led by Governor Thomas Dewey of New York, warned against the United States becoming "an island of freedom in a Communist world." General Eisenhower returned to plead with the senators, telling them that Western Europe was too vital to American security to sacrifice, and despite Taft's complaint that both Eisenhower and the Joint Chiefs of Staff "are absolutely under the control of the Administration," his testimony had a significant impact. The result was finally a compromise weighted heavily in the Administration's favor; in early April the Senate voted to send four more divisions to Europe but warned Truman not to commit any additional troops without "further Congressional approval."

The "great debate" had barely ended when Truman set off a far greater controversy by removing General MacArthur from his command on April 11, 1951. The immediate cause was insubordination, but the real issue was the concept of limited war. MacArthur refused to accept the restraints that the Truman Administration insisted on in Korea after the Chinese intervention. Not only did Washington turn down MacArthur's plan to widen the war against China, but when Ridgway's forces began to approach the 38th parallel, the Administration decided to seek a negotiated peace with the Communists instead of striving again to unify Korea by force. MacArthur, already resentful of the ban on bombing north of the Yalu, which made Manchuria "a privileged sanctuary," decided to sabotage the forthcoming Presidential call for truce negotiations by issuing an ultimatum to the Chinese, telling them they faced certain destruction unless they sued for peace on UN terms. The Chinese naturally rejected this demand, forcing Truman to cancel his peace appeal. This incident convinced him that he had to dismiss MacArthur. The President waited for the right moment, which came in early April when GOP House Minority Leader Joseph Martin released a letter from the General objecting strenuously to the Administration's restraints on his conduct of the war and concluding, "There is no substitute for victory...." By appealing to the opposition party, MacArthur had sealed his fate. Truman carefully consulted once more with his military advisers. General Marshall, who had come out of retirement to serve as Secretary of Defense, read the file on MacArthur and then told Truman, "The S.O.B. should have been fired two years ago." Acheson warned the President that if he removed the General, "you will have the biggest fight of your administration." Undaunted, Truman issued the orders relieving MacArthur of his command.

The General returned to enjoy a hero's welcome home, as Americans poured out in record numbers to express their appreciation for his services in World War II and Korea. Republicans heaped scorn on Truman. Richard Nixon denounced the President for "appeasement" of Communism and demanded the reinstatement of MacArthur; Representative Martin spoke darkly of impeachment, while McCarthy called the President "a sonofabitch" who would let "red waters...lap at all of our shores." MacArthur drew tumultuous applause when he appeared before a joint session of Congress to plead for an all-out effort to defeat the Communists in Asia, and then closed dramatically by reciting the lines of an old West Point ballad, "Old soldiers never die, they just fade away."

To his astonishment, that is precisely what happened to the General. The Senate held public hearings conducted jointly by the Foreign Relations and Armed Services Committees under the scrupulously fair chairmanship of Senator Richard Russell of Georgia. The Administration relied heavily on General Marshall and members of the Joint Chiefs of Staff to defend the strategy of limited war. Any other course, they contended, would alienate the NATO allies and expose Western Europe to Soviet attack. General Omar Bradley offered the classic refutation of MacArthur's proposals when he claimed that they would "involve us in the wrong war, at the wrong place, at the wrong time and with the wrong enemy." MacArthur stubbornly insisted that any limitation on the use of force amounted to "appeasement," and he repeatedly asserted his belief that a theater commander should have the right to use all the power at his disposal. The hearings did not lead to any final conclusions, but the Administration succeeded in proving that MacArthur was challenging the considered judgment of the military establishment, not just the views of Harry Truman. Moreover, as the proceedings droned on, they drained the situation of emotion and thus robbed MacArthur of his most valuable asset. By the time the hearings ended, the American people had reluctantly accepted the wisdom of the Administration's decision to limit the war in Korea. Armistice negotiations, delayed by MacArthur in March, finally got under way in July as the fighting settled into a stalemate just north of the 38th parallel. The conflict would continue to sap the political vitality of the Truman Administration, but at least the President had succeeded in his effort to prevent any further escalation.

VI

Everything seemed to go wrong during Truman's last two years in office. Joe McCarthy, emboldened by his apparent success in making Communism a key political issue in the 1950 election, grew more reckless than ever with his charges. He renewed his attacks on the State Department as he hammered away on the thesis that foreign service officers had betrayed China to the Communists. He listed twenty-six security risks inside the State Department and he singled out one, John Carter Vincent, for "the Lattimore treatment." Vincent, serving in 1951 as minister to Switzerland, had been an influential State Department adviser on Far Eastern affairs. McCarthy claimed Vincent was a Communist who had sponsored the "Hiss-Acheson-Jessup-Lattimore-Vincent plan" to sell out Chiang Kai-shek. Though loyalty boards exonerated Vincent on all these charges, McCarthy ruined his career by forcing the State

Department to demand that he resign "in the best interests of the U.S." McCarthy scored a similar success against Philip C. Jessup, Truman's nominee for delegate to the United Nations General Assembly in 1951. A distinguished professor of international law, Jessup had served as Acheson's leading trouble-shooter and ambassador-at-large. McCarthy accused him of association with "six communist fronts" and with following "the Communist line," particularly in proposing recognition of Red China. After lengthy hearings, a Senate Foreign Relations subcommittee voted 3 to 2 against his nomination, effectively blocking confirmation by the full Senate.

McCarthy made his most sensational attack on the Senate floor on June 12, 1951. His target was General George C. Marshall, the man Truman admired above all others in his Administration. Reading a speech prepared by his staff, the Senator promised to reveal "a conspiracy so immense and an infamy so black as to dwarf any previous such venture in the history of man." What followed was a detailed attack on postwar American foreign policy, dull and tedious enough to cause so many listeners to leave the gallery and the Senate floor that McCarthy read only one third of the 60,000 words. The full text, which appeared in the *Congressional Record,* insinuated that Marshall had deliberately permitted the Communists to win victory after victory, but he offered no evidence of treason, and lamely concluded by claiming that he had laid bare "a conspiracy of infamy so black that, when it is finally exposed, its principles shall be forever deserving of the maledictions of all honest men."

"No comment," snapped Harry Truman when a reporter asked him about McCarthy's accusation against Marshall. Privately, he called it "one of the silliest things I ever heard." Earlier the President had tried to defuse McCarthy-ism by telling reporters, "I think the greatest asset that the Kremlin has is Senator McCarthy." The President appointed a special task force to provide cabinet members and Democrats in Congress with material to rebut the Senator's charges, but the denials rarely caught up with the original accusations. At one time, Truman denounced "scandal mongers and character assassins" in Congress; no names were mentioned, but McCarthy prevailed on the three networks to give him free radio time to reply. Sadly, Truman came to realize that he could not stem McCarthyism with words and so he remained silent, placing his confidence "in the good sense of the American people," as he said in his memoirs, and the knowledge that "this period of hysteria would eventually run its course."

In the midest of the red scare, charges of corruption in government further embarrassed the Truman Administration. In the hectic atmosphere of reconversion after the war, bewildered businessmen seeking government contracts or trying to find their way through the maze of federal regulatory agencies sought the help of influence peddlers, men who claimed to know the right people in the bureaucracy and who collected fees of 5 percent on the contracts

they secured for clients. As the dedicated men and women originally attracted to government service by a commitment to the New Deal or wartime patriotism left, their places were taken by loyal party workers with far lower ethical
standards. When Congressional committees began probing into the executive
branch, they found some disturbing practices. General Harry Vaughn, the
President's military aide and poker-playing pal, had naively used his position
to allow five percenters to gain government favors and, in return, he had
received a deep freeze, a gift that became a symbol of laxity in the Truman
Administration. Far more serious, a Senate committee revealed in 1951 that
White House aide Donald Dawson had used his considerable authority to persuade the Reconstruction Finance Corporation to make questionable government loans to fly-by-night entrepreneurs and speculators. Later in the year,
an alarming pattern of corruption in the Bureau of Internal Revenue came to
light as witnesses told of high tax officials shaking them down for sums ranging
up to $500,000 to cover up fraudulent returns. The tax scandal involved an
assistant attorney general and eventually reached into the White House with
the conviction of appointments secretary Matthew Connelly on bribery charges.

Truman himself remained above reproach, but his excessive feeling of loyalty prevented him from punishing men like Vaughn and Dawson for their in-
discretions. He failed to take the swift and effective action necessary to reassure the public about the basic honesty of the federal bureaucracy. Instead,
he asked Attorney General J. Howard McGrath, a professional politician with
an easy-going tolerance of shady practices, to take charge of the cleanup effort and then, after an outcry from his critics in Congress, appointed Newbold
Morris, a liberal Republican lawyer from New York, as a special investigator.
Morris, an utterly tactless individual, soon antagonized eneryone involved and
brought about a showdown when he insisted that all high government officials
fill out a questionnaire listing their sources of income. McGrath refused to
allow the questionnaire to be used, Morris resigned, and Truman finally replaced McGrath with a new attorney general who quietly removed some 66
Internal Revenue and Justice Department employees, with nine eventually
receiving jail sentences. The Truman scandals had never been very great, hardly on a par with those of Grant or Harding, but the President's inept handling
of the situation, together with the way Republicans exploited the juicy details
of deep freezes and mink coats, created the impression that there was "a mess
in Washington" on such a scale that only a thorough housecleaning could restore integrity to government.

The continuing stalemate in Korea added to the growing public disenchant-
ment. The truce talks had quickly bogged down on the prisoner-of-war issue.
The UN had captured 132,000 Chinese and North Koreans; nearly half did
not want to return to their homelands, and Truman refused to repatriate these
men against their will. The Communists, unwilling to admit that anyone would

refuse to return to their way of life, insisted that all prisoners be exchanged. And so the war went on, with heavy casualties as each side tried to seize the high ground and improve its position along the battleline just north of the 38th parallel. The American people, while sympathetic to the President's stand against forced repatriation, grew more and more weary of a conflict in which the United States had already given up any prospect of victory.

McCarthyism, corruption in government, and the Korean deadlock led to a massive loss of public confidence in the Truman Administration. By the spring of 1952, the President's standing in the Gallup poll had dropped to an all-time low of 26 percent. In only three years, Truman had gone from the pinnacle of victory to the depths of political failure, an object of ridicule to his opponents and of embarrassment to his own party. In early 1950, long before things had become so bleak, he had decided against another term, and he informed his aides of this decision in 1951. He kept his intentions from the public while he searched for a worthy successor, first trying to persuade his old friend Fred Vinson to run, and then when Vinson declined on grounds of age, he approached Adlai Stevenson, the Governor of Illinois. To Truman's surprise, Stevenson first hesitated, then turned down the opportunity. After an embarrassing defeat in the New Hampshire primary, where the President had let his name be entered simply to block the ambitious Estes Kefauver, Truman finally announced at a Jackson-day dinner in late March, "I shall not be a candidate for re-election." "I do not feel that it is my duty to spend another four years in the White House," he concluded. Cries of "oh no" came up from the party faithful, but most Democrats breathed a sigh of relief as they began the quest for a more attractive nominee.

VII

Time has dimmed the sense of disappointment and near disgrace that surrounded Truman as he ended his presidential career. His reputation has steadily improved, with historians polled in the early 1960s ranking him among the "near great" Presidents of all time. House Speaker Sam Rayburn gave an evaluation of the man from Missouri that many have come to share, "Right on all the big things, wrong on all the little ones." The prevailing view has been that Truman performed well on the issues that really mattered, particularly in foreign policy, with the Truman Doctrine, the Marshall Plan, and the decision to fight in Korea as examples of the firm way he halted postwar Soviet expansion. His failures, according to the conventional wisdom, came at home, in his inability to secure passage of legislation from Congress, his reliance on mediocre men to administer domestic programs, and his helplessness in the face of McCarthy and the red scare. Truman's fondess for petty political bickering and his penchant for engaging in personal squabbles cost him dearly in public esteem but, in the long run, these failures seem minor compared to his Cold War achievements.

As we gain perspective on the Truman years, a reevaluation that reverses the usual assessment becomes more plausible: Truman's actions were more notable and admirable in the domestic than in the foreign field. While it is true he did not enact his Fair Deal program, he did astonishingly well in protecting New Deal reforms and extending them substantially in such areas as social security and the minimum wage. Faced with a conservative coalition that dominated Congress even when the Democrats were in the majority, he blocked all efforts to roll back earlier advances, with the single exception of the Taft-Hartley Act, which modified but did not revoke the basic collective bargaining system created by the Wagner Act in 1935. More important, Truman broadened the reform agenda he had inherited from FDR by advocating federal responsibility for health care, education, and civil rights. Despite the cautious nature of his program and his refusal to launch a full-scale attack on segregation, he brought civil rights squarely into the political arena and did more to advance the interests of black Americans than any of his predecessors. Near the end of his Administration, the Justice Department filed briefs as a friend of the court to aid those seeking to overturn the prevailing pattern of segregation in the nation's public schools, thus abetting a process that would lead to the historic Supreme Court integration decision of 1954. He was less successful in the fields of federal aid to education and health care, but he did begin the long process, so necessary in a democracy, of building a case for these advanced social programs and thus bequeathed to future Democratic Presidents measures that would become their primary legislative goals.

At the same time, his foreign policy accomplishments, which seemed so constructive to a generation deeply involved in the Cold War, appear much more questionable in the post-Vietnam decade. One does not have to accept extreme revisionist charges that the United States provoked the Cold War to realize that Truman and his associates badly overreacted to the Soviet danger. In the vacuum of power that existed in 1945 after the defeat of Germany and Japan, the United States needed to take firm but restrained steps to check Russian expansionist tendencies. Instead, fearful of repeating the mistakes that led to Munich and urged on by hard-line advisers like Harriman, Forrestal, and Acheson, Truman encouraged the American people to engage in a crusade against the Soviet Union. With exaggerated rhetoric, the President and his associates compared Stalin to Hitler and spoke of a contest between the free world and slavery. The resulting containment policy did preserve Western Europe from Soviet penetration and eventually produced relative stability on that troubled continent. But inevitably the call to arms against the infidel ked to a global commitment to halt communist expansion that bred frustration when Mao seized power in China and when the Korean War ended in a stalemate. By the end of his second term, Truman had committed the United States to the defense of the status quo in a changing world, with German rearmament and Japanese economic resurgence the main pillars of policy in Europe and Asia. The United States ignored the rising force of nationalism in the Third World as it tied its destinies firmly to industrialized nations and thus identified itself with the imperialism of the past.

Such was Truman's legacy, an intensified Cold War abroad and a promising but unrealized reform program at home. He had shown amazing fortitude after stepping almost totally unprepared into the world's most difficult job, and he had done better than anyone had expected. He helped guide the nation's economy through the difficult reconversion process, preventing a return to depression conditions and keeping inflation within reasonable bounds. He proved to be a more adept politician than the experts realized as he gave the average American a feeling that the President cared about his welfare. He limited Russian expansion in Europe, avoided a potentially disastrous involvement in the Chinese civil war, and brought the nation safely through the unpopular Korean conflict. His greatest failure lay with the Congress, where his fierce partisanship and determination to uphold executive prerogatives cost him dearly. Amid the travails of his second term he lost the confidence of the American people, but he never lost the belief that he was doing all he could for his country. He summed up his attitude toward public service in April, 1952 when he told reporters, "I have tried my best to give the nation everything I have in me." "There are a great many people...who could have done the job better than I did it," he continued. "But I had the job and I had to do it." In time, the American people would come to agree with Truman's favorite epitaph, "He done his damnedest."

3

A Return to Normalcy

In 1952, Dwight D. Eisenhower seemed to millions of Americans the one man who could provide the leadership the times demanded. Ike had emerged from World War II as a popular hero, a genial man who had directed the war against Hitler, culminating in the successful D-day invasion and the rapid destruction of German resistance. He had also earned the respect of knowledgeable observers for his great skill in reconciling differences with temperamental Allied leaders, ranging from Charles de Gaulle to Field Marshal Bernard Montgomery, and for his organizational genius in equipping, arranging, and deploying more than 2 million men on the European continent. Anything but a "man on horseback," he delighted the American people with his infectious grin and forthright manner, accepting their accolades with becoming modesty, and quietly refusing to exploit his great popularity. Democrats as well as Republicans tried unsuccessfully to woo him into politics in 1948; he chose the presidency of Columbia University instead. A firm believer in collective security, he returned to active duty in late 1950 when Truman asked him to organize the new NATO armed forces. As Supreme Commander of the Allied Powers in Europe, he grew more and more concerned with Truman's clumsy handling of the Cold War and with McCarthy's challenge at home. Extremely confident of his own ability, he had resisted earlier presidential overtures out of distaste for domestic politics, but he now began to listen to the appeals of businessmen, politicians, and wartime comrades who came to Paris to persuade him to seek the Presidency.

The movement to draft Eisenhower reflected an attempt by eastern internationalist Republicans to prevent Ohio Senator Robert A. Taft from gaining the GOP nomination by default. A bitter critic of Truman, Taft represented the dominant element within the party. A prewar isolationist who only grudgingly backed the containment policy, the Senator felt that Democratic preoccupation with Europe had enabled the Communists to seize power in China and nearly win in Korea. Above all, he believed the Cold War threatened the nation with bankruptcy; as a foe of big government he wanted to reduce federal spending both at home and abroad. Like many Republicans, he resented the way the eastern wing had dominated the party's presidential efforts under Wendell Willkie and Thomas Dewey and had accepted the Democratic foreign and domestic policies in waging "me-too" campaigns. Taft held himself out as a man who would offer clear-cut alternatives; he promised to invigorate the free enterprise system and cut back on America's dangerous overcommitment abroad.

Eisenhower cared little about Taft's promise to roll back the New Deal; it was the Senator's threat to America's active world role that moved him. Prodded by General Lucius Clay, now chairman of the board of the Continental Can Company, and Senator Henry Cabot Lodge, the General finally agreed in April to seek the GOP nomination. At first he thought his entry alone would be enough, but he quickly learned he would have to fight a major battle to wrest the nomination away from a man the party's rank-and-file looked on as "Mr. Republican." Ike began the quest at Abilene, Kansas, his boyhood hometown, in a speech on June 4 that revealed that he stood even to the right of Taft on domestic issues. Despite the Senator's efforts to mute his isolationist leanings, the two men divided sharply on foreign policy, but the struggle ultimately turned on the ability of Eisenhower's advisers to transform Taft's attempts to control southern delegations into an emotional issue. At the Chicago convention in July, Ike won a decisive victory over Taft as the majority of delegates reluctantly accepted the argument that only the popular General could guarantee a Republican victory in November.

The Democrats responded by offering the American people a new and attractive spokesman in Adlai E. Stevenson, the Governor of Illinois. Unhappy with Truman's record and perhaps unsure of his own fitness for the Presidency, Stevenson resisted all attempts at a draft until the convention opened in Chicago with Estes Kefauver, the maverick Tennessee Senator who had antagonized the party leaders but won most of the primaries, in the lead. Stevenson finally agreed to serve, and after his nomination on the third ballot, he gave an eloquent acceptance speech in which he set a high moral tone for his campaign. He promised to "talk sense to the American people" and, though he won the undying loyalty of intellectuals with his keen wit and lofty rhetoric, he failed to excite the average American or to separate himself in the public mind from the discredited Truman Administration.

Eisenhower waged a long and intense campaign that began slowly but gradually grew in strength and appeal. His advisers persuaded him to avoid Dewey's tactic of appealing to independent voters with a "me-too" approach; instead, they had him attack the Democrats for "creeping socialism" and excessive spending at home and inept waging of the Cold War abroad. Their target was not only disaffected Democrats and independents, but the great numbers of Americans who never participated in presidential elections. Relying heavily on television, the Republicans planned to use Ike's prestige and popularity to win the "stay-at-home" vote.

The GOP campaign was a long series of compromises with the principles Eisenhower cherished. He detested the Republican witch-hunters, especially Indiana Senator William Jenner, who had called his idol General Marshall "a living lie," and Joe McCarthy, who had accused Marshall of being a traitor. Yet, in Indiana, Ike appeared on the same platform with Jenner (wincing visibly when the Senator embraced him) and in Wisconsin the General deleted a flattering reference to Marshall's patriotism from a Milwaukee speech at the request of McCarthy's supporters. In September, with the campaign hurt by the obvious coolness of Senator Taft and his supporters, Eisenhower held a breakfast meeting with the Ohio Senator, who emerged triumphantly to read a statement the two men had agreed on. Minimizing the very real differences between them in foreign policy, Taft's announcement stressed their common goal of limiting the growth of big government and sharply reducing the federal budget. Eisenhower's greatest embarrassment came later in the month when the press reported that his handpicked running mate, Richard M. Nixon, had used a secret fund to meet many of his political expenses as a Senator from California. The General had stressed the issue of corruption in attacking Truman for the "mess in Washington"; now as he commented privately to reporters, how could he carry on his crusade "if we ourselves aren't as clean as a hound's tooth?" The eastern Republicans, led by Governor Dewey of New York, urged him to dump Nixon from the ticket; Ike wisely waited, preferring to let his running mate work out his own fate. After Nixon won enormous public support with an emotional speech, highlighted by a reference to his dog Checkers, the General forced him to fly hurriedly to his campaign train in West Virginia, and only then gave him his blessing.

Even in the realm of foreign policy, Eisenhower found that politics had a distorting impact. Despite reservations, he had gone along with the slogan of liberation advocated by GOP foreign policy expert John Foster Dulles as a substitute for the Democratic policy of containment. Ike, however, insisted that any promises to free Eastern Europe must be limited to peaceful means (even chewing out Dulles by telephone when he omitted this vital qualification in one speech). In an address to the American Legion in late August, Eisenhower elaborated on the liberation concept, promising to help free the captive peoples in the Soviet satellites. When the Democrats hit back hard, pointing out that liberation, if taken seriously, meant risking nuclear war, Eisenhower dropped the phrase from his speeches, though other Republicans continued to use it.

Eisenhower reversed himself even more dramatically on the Korean War. In his homecoming remarks at Abilene in June, the General had endorsed the Truman Administration's conduct of the Asian conflict, saying he had no alternatives to offer. In the fall campaign, he first avoided the Korean War but, as the fighting resumed with heavy casualties, he found his audiences more and more receptive to references to the conflict. In Illinois, in early October, Eisenhower advocated the use of South Korean troops in the front lines, saying, "If there must be a war there, let it be Asians against Asians...." When Truman, who was barnstorming the country for Stevenson, began taunting Eisenhower, demanding that he offer a solution to the Korean stalemate, the Republicans were ready. Emmet John Hughes, a *Life* journalist turned speechwriter, had drafted an address that the GOP high command was saving for the campaign's climax. In Detroit on October 24, Ike delivered it. After reviewing the deadlock in Asia, he stressed his determination to end the fighting and then announced, "That job requires a personal trip to Korea. I shall make that trip....I shall go to Korea...."

"That does it — Ike is in," reporters exclaimed when they read the advance text of Ike's speech. The promise to go to Korea, coming from the man identified in the public mind with the victory in World War II, clinched the election. A record number of voters went to the polls two weeks later to give Eisenhower a sweeping triumph. Stevenson carried only nine states (all but two in the South) as Ike won 55 percent of the popular vote. The Republican party fared less well, gaining control of the House by a scant eight votes and splitting even in the Senate. Eisenhower's enormous personal popularity, so shrewdly exploited in the stress on the "stay-at-home" vote, had combined with the public's disillusionment with the Korean War and Truman's leadership to give the Republicans control of Washington for the first time in twenty years. The General had proved surprisingly flexible as a candidate, but his real test as a politician was yet to come as he faced the task of governing the nation with a divided and suspicious party.

I

Dwight Eisenhower held a very different view of the Presidency from his Democratic predecessors. Both by temperament and ideology, he preferred a less active role in guiding and shaping national policy; he planned to delegate authority more broadly in the Executive branch and to restore a greater degree of balance in relations with Congress and the Supreme Court. Hostile critics saw Ike's passive philosophy as an expression of disinterest, if not laziness.

Treating the Presidency as a reward for services already rendered to the nation, Ike was content to restore public confidence by symbolic acts while his subordinates actually ran the government. Friendlier commentators argue that Eisenhower acted out of a deeply held belief that the essence of presidential leadership was "the ability to decide what is to be done and then to get others to want to do it." According to this view, the President's task was one of patient conciliation, pacifying those with conflicting views, encouraging the emergence of a consensus, but never browbeating Congress or the public in an effort to achieve action. Above all, Ike believed in conserving his great public esteem. He refused to engage in lost causes, and he always preferred to work quietly, behind the scenes. Richard Nixon, who came to have an acute appreciation of Ike's political skills, summed up his technique best when he noted: "An Eisenhower characteristic was never to take direct action requiring his personal participation where indirect methods would accomplish the same result."

The staff system Eisenhower established in the White House reflected his belief in delegating authority and reserving himself for the truly significant issues. Sherman Adams, the taciturn former Governor of New Hampshire who had served as Ike's campaign director, stayed on as the President's chief assistant. Not only did he control access to the President, but he handled so many of the routine White House duties that he was in effect an Assistant President, at least in the domestic area. He made many enemies, especially in Congress, for his zealous determination to protect his boss, but he rarely tried to influence the making of policy. Adams shared with Eisenhower the belief that the real task was simply to keep the machinery of government moving efficiently; neither man had any sense of mission nor any desire to alter the prevailing patterns of American life. General Wilton Persons handled relations with Congress skillfully; James Hagerty did a professional job of keeping the press reasonably well informed on Administration policies; Gabriel Hauge and Arthur Burns offered the President the conservative economic and fiscal advice he wanted.

In keeping with his restrained view of the Presidency, Eisenhower gave members of his cabinet considerable responsibility. Three men stood out as the dominant members. John Foster Dulles finally fulfilled his lifelong ambition to become Secretary of State. Steeped in the traditions of diplomacy both by family ties and experience ranging from the Second Hague Peace Conference in 1907 to the negotiation of the Japanese Peace Treaty in 1951, Dulles combined a Presbyterian moralism reminiscent of Woodrow Wilson with a shrewd realization of the need to placate and reassure a suspicious Congress. He achieved both ends by publicly espousing a rigid Cold War ideology while pursuing a more flexible and realistic policy in private. Ponderous in speech and aloof in his personal relations, Dulles worked hard to win Ike's trust and, though the two men were never really close friends, the President gave him wide latitude in the conduct of foreign policy. Dulles guarded his mandate carefully, keeping Eisenhower fully informed of his activities and resisting any encroachment on his domain from others in the Administration.

George Humphrey, the Secretary of the Treasury, exerted an even greater influence on Administration policy. The head of the Mark Hanna Company in Cleveland, Humphrey reflected the Taftite concern with excessive government spending, even though Taft had not recommended his appointment. A genial, balding man of great personal charm, he got along easily with Ike, winning his friendship in a way Dulles never could. Humphrey discovered that Eisenhower shared his belief in fiscal restraint, and he waged an unending battle to achieve a balanced budget. The Treasury Secretary's concern for economy brought him into every aspect of Administration policy, and as a result he helped influence foreign as well as domestic decision making.

The new Secretary of Defense, Charles E. Wilson, appeared at first to be on a par with Humphrey and Dulles. The former president of General Motors, Wilson personified the hard-driving executive who came to Washington to run the government on a businesslike basis. A frank, outspoken man with opinions on every subject imaginable, Wilson quickly put Eisenhower off with his loose tongue and frequent complaining. At the first cabinet meeting, held before the inauguration, Wilson objected to the President's suggestion for more trade with Iron Curtain countries by commenting tartly, "Well, I'm a little old-fashioned — I don't like selling firearms to the Indians." His famous remark to a Congressional committee that he thought that "what was good for our country was good for General Motors, and *vice versa*," made him good copy for the Washington press but lowered his influence with Eisenhower, who constantly had to ride herd on him at the Pentagon.

The other cabinet members included men of wisdom and ability, notably Herbert Brownell, the Attorney General, and Sinclair Weeks, the conservative Secretary of Commerce; Republican regulars rewarded for their campaign efforts such as Douglas McKay, the Secretary of Interior, and Postmaster General Arthur Summerfield; an ardent advocate of reducing the government's role in farming, Secretary of Agriculture Ezra Taft Benson; a woman, Oveta Culp Hobby, the first Secretary of Health, Education, and Welfare (this new department was created in the spring of 1953), and Martin Durkin, an A.F. of L. plumbing union official who lasted only a few months as Secretary of Labor but whose presence enabled a liberal journal to describe Ike's cabinet as "eight millionaires and a plumber."

The President met regularly with this group, seeking its advice on all major domestic and foreign policy issues before he acted. He encouraged cabinet members to express their views freely, but he always reserved the right to make the final decision himself. Once the President had made up his mind,

Sherman Adams noted, "the minority views were well and carefully buried." At the suggestion of Ezra Benson, a devout Mormon, the cabinet members bowed their heads for a brief silent prayer before they began their deliberations. This pious practice was sometimes overlooked in the rush of business; on one occasion an aide informed Ike of the oversight and he burst out, "Oh, goddammit, we forgot the silent prayer."

Eisenhower placed equally strong emphasis on his weekly session with the National Security Council. Where Truman had used this group sparingly, Eisenhower made it the primary agency for providing information and developing policy positions on every aspect of the Cold War. He expanded its membership to include Treasury Secretary Humphrey and Budget Director Joseph Dodge and he appointed Robert Cutler, a Boston banker who had served as his personal aide during the campaign, to the post of Special Assistant for National Security Affairs. Cutler kept careful track of all decisions reached by the NSC and pursued them through the bureaucratic maze to be certain the President's wishes were translated into effective action. Eisenhower dominated these meetings, asking probing questions of his advisers and lecturing them sternly on the realities of world affairs. "The mythical Eisenhower, who left decision-making to subordinates, whose mind was 'lazy' and/or not very bright," commented one official who served on the NSC under both Ike and Truman, "cannot be found in these records of the most important business he conducted for the nation."

II

Eisenhower concentrated on problems arising from the Cold War in his early months in office. Two closely related issues stood at the head of his agenda — ending the Korean War and balancing the federal budget. Nearly all Republicans agreed on the second objective; indeed, the President's difficulty would be to cut spending rapidly enough to please the Taft wing of the party. Korea raised greater complications. Eisenhower hoped not only to end the fighting in Korea quickly but to reduce the American commitments in Asia in order to restore to Western Europe the primacy it had once enjoyed in United States foreign policy. Both his wartime experience on the continent and his recent tour with NATO had convinced Ike that a stable, prosperous Europe would lead eventually to peace in the Orient. Asia-first Republicans, however, wanted to end the Korean conflict with a great victory that would serve as a prelude to returning Chiang Kai-shek to power in China. In a formal dinner at the Chinese Embassy, GOP Senators William Knowland and Styles Bridges joined their Nationalist hosts in a shouted toast, "Back to the Mainland." It would take all of Eisenhower's skill at conciliation to persuade such men to accept the limited retreat from Asia he contemplated.

Less than a month after his election, Eisenhower fulfilled his dramatic campaign promise by flying to Korea. His brief inspection convinced him that an all-out ground offensive against the more than 1 million Chinese and North Korean troops would by prohibitively expensive. On his way home, he discussed his strategic options with John Foster Dulles and Admiral Arthur Radford, then commander of American naval forces in the Pacific. Dulles brought up the idea of relying primarily on America's nuclear superiority to halt Communist aggression, an idea eventually known as "massive retaliation." Eisenhower had objected to this concept in May, when Dulles had first raised it, but now he began to change his mind as Admiral Radford argued that Korea proved it was impossible for the United States to fight a ground war in Asia against the Communist hordes. The proper strategy, Radford argued, would be to rely on local forces to meet initial threats, with the United States maintaining a strategic reserve in the Western Hemisphere based primarily on nuclear striking power. The men apparently discussed the possibility of using atomic bombs to break the Korean stalemate and, though no final decision was reached, Ike gave a broad hint of his plans when he announced to the press that his Korean visit had convinced him that "we face an enemy whom we cannot hope to impress by words, however eloquent, but only by deeds — executed under circumstances of our own choosing."

After the inauguration in January, Eisenhower began to work out a solution to "the great equation" of balancing America's global commitments against the nation's finite fiscal resources. As a professional military man, he was not impressed with the Pentagon's demands for more and more funds for defense. The huge arms buildup begun under NSC-68 and accelerated by the Korean War meant that nearly 70 percent of the federal budget went to national defense items. Eisenhower moved quickly to regain control over these expenditures. He put economy-minded George Humphrey on the NSC and he insisted that every new security proposal include an estimate of its eventual cost. He forced Defense Secretary Wilson to make sharp cuts in the armed services' requests for new funds, bearing down with special force on the Army and Navy in keeping with the Dulles-Radford emphasis on nuclear retaliation as the nation's main line of defense. As a result, Eisenhower was able to pare new military appropriations by $7 billion and thus to cut back Truman's projected deficit from nearly $10 billion to less than $4 billion. Shocked military men learned what speechwriter Emmet Hughes had already discovered to his own surprise: "The internationally minded leader of the Western World was a frugal Kansan."

The President informed the nation of his "new look" in defense at a press conference on April 30. He explained the importance of keeping "our country free and our economy solvent" and listed as a primary goal, "maximum effectiveness at minimum cost." Earlier in the day he had reported on his budgetary cuts to a group of Congressional leaders, proudly pointing out that he had cut the projected Truman deficit in half. To his amazement, Robert Taft, now the Senate Majority Leader, exploded at Eisenhower's failure to achieve a completely balanced budget. "With a program like this," the Senator snapped, "we'll never elect a Republican Congress in 1954. You're taking us down the same road Truman traveled. It's a repudiation of everything we promised in the campaign," Taft shouted as his fist slammed down on the table. An omnious silence ensued as Ike's face flushed with anger, but he held his temper as others spoke to clear the air. Later the President expressed his wonder that anyone would challenge his grasp of defense issues. Taft eventually apologized for his outburst, but it undoubtedly helped Eisenhower realize how difficult it would be to satisfy his own party.

Korea remained the real test. Budgetary considerations alone seemed to dictate a negotiated settlement and Eisenhower decided to pursue Truman's policy of arranging a truce, an effort still blocked by the Communist insistence that all prisoners be returned, including those who opposed repatriation. Dulles went along reluctantly with the President, although he preferred a clear-cut military victory. "I don't think we can get much of a Korean settlement," he told Emmet Hughes, "until we have shown – before all Asia – our clear superiority by giving the Chinese one hell of a licking." The Secretary did persuade the President to issue a statement in January announcing that the American Seventh Fleet would no longer patrol the Formosa Straits, thereby "unleashing" Chiang Kai-shek from the restraints Truman had imposed at the outbreak of the Korean War (in reality, the original order had been designed to block a Communist invasion of Formosa rather than prevent a Nationalist return to the mainland). Eisenhower and Dulles also began dropping hints that a Communist failure to resume negotiations would lead to American use of atomic bombs against China, eventually using Indian diplomats as the go-betweens to make sure the message got to Peking.

The sudden death of Joseph Stalin on March 5, 1953 probably had a greater impact on the Chinese leaders, creating as it did uncertainty about the future leadership and foreign policy of the Soviet Union. In late March, the Chinese ended three months of diplomatic silence by responding favorably to an Indian suggestion for the exchange of wounded prisoners. Truce talks resumed at Panmunjon in April and, after several setbacks, most notably when South Korean President Syngman Rhee threatened to obstruct any settlement, the negotiators finally worked out armistice terms on July 27 that permitted 21, 809 Chinese and North Korean prisoners to avoid forced repatriation (along with 359 members of the United Nations forces, including 23 Americans) and ended the fighting without providing any long-term solution to the Korean political problem. The country remained divided at the truce line, just north of the 38th parallel. Most Americans felt a sense of relief at the end of a long, unpopular struggle that had taken over 33,000 lives. Eisenhower and Dulles defended the settlement as a vindication for collective security, pointing out that Communist aggression had been checked and the sovereignty of South Korea preserved. But right-wing Republicans expressed open contempt for the Administration's refusal to achieve a genuine victory in Korea. William Knowland, who succeeded Taft as Majority Leader when the Ohioan was stricken with cancer in late May, voiced the views of many within the party when he termed the truce, "peace without honor."

Eisenhower winced under such criticism, but he took solace in the fact that he had accomplished a major campaign objective within his first six months in office. The Korean settlement, moreover, ended an enormous drain on the Treasury and gave him assurance that he could solve the great equation between adequate defense and financial solvency that he believed in so passionately.

III

The Cold War dominated domestic politics as well as foreign policy during Eisenhower's first year in office. The Republican right pressed for vigorous action to reverse past Democratic mistakes and remove all those suspected of being soft on Communism from government service. The Administration, however, needed Democratic support for its legislative program and thus could not indulge in this partisan desire for revenge. The result was an increasingly bitter struggle within the GOP over the loyalty issue.

John Foster Dulles and the State Department stood at the heart of the storm. Aware that Dean Acheson had lost Congressional support by his stubborn defense of foreign service officers against McCarthy's charges, the Secretary set out to appease the Congressional witch-hunters. He appointed Scott McLeod, former aide to Senator Styles Bridges and close friend of McCarthy, to head up the State Department's security program; he concurred in dubious loyalty findings that removed such dedicated diplomats as John Paton Davies, John Carter Vincent, and John Stewart Service; and he outraged the Department's staff by telling them that he would demand their "positive loyalty," a phrase that suggested a new test of allegiance was to be imposed as a condition of continued employment. Dulles' most cowardly action came in his treatment of George Kennan, the nation's foremost expert on the Soviet Union who had recently served as ambassador to Russia. Despite the need for Kennan's expertise, particularly when Stalin's death raised new uncertainties about Russian policy, the Secretary quietly forced the author of containment to resign from the foreign service by failing to appoint him to a new ambassadorial post within the required 90 days.

In two other areas, Dulles, backed up strongly by the White House, took a bolder position. The first dealt with the wartime arrangements Roosevelt and Truman had made with the Soviets that the Republicans claimed had led to the enslavement of the peoples of Eastern Europe. Congressional leaders interpreted the GOP victory as a mandate to pass legislation to repudiate the agreements made at Yalta and Potsdam; the Administration, realizing that Democrats in Congress would never go along, countered with a draft resolution denouncing "any interpretations or applications" of secret deals that "have been perverted to bring about the subjugation of free peoples." In an angry exchange with Senator Taft, Dulles explained that Roosevelt and Truman had not signed away Eastern Europe; it was subsequent Russian violations that led to the satellite empire. GOP leaders refused to accept the Administration's wording but, after Stalin's death, both sides agreed to let the issue drop, though later in the decade Republican Congressmen finally did secure passage of a vague resolution decrying the fate of the "captive nations."

The question of Kennan's successor provoked a more heated debate. After careful consideration, Dulles suggested the appointment of Charles E. Bohlen as the new ambassador to Moscow, an idea that met with Eisenhower's approval. Bohlen had been a member of the first diplomatic mission to Russia following recognition in 1933, headed up the Russian desk of the State Department during World War II, and served as Counselor to Secretaries Marshall and Acheson during the formative years of the Cold War. Despite these impressive credentials, right-wing Republicans identified Bohlen with what Richard Nixon had referred to during the campaign as "Dean Acheson's Cowardly College of Communist Containment" and seized on the fact that Bohlen had been FDR's interpreter at Yalta to oppose his confirmation. The Senate Foreign Relations Committee voted unanimously for Bohlen, but then Joe McCarthy jumped in, claiming that Scott McLeod had refused to clear the appointment because the FBI files contained some damning evidence on Bohlen's loyalty. When Dulles denied this allegation, McCarthy called the Secretary's statement "completely untrue" and commented that calling Bohlen "a security risk" was "putting it too weak." Dulles called Bohlen in for a talk, hinting that he might consider withdrawing his name, but Eisenhower came out strongly for the appointment, calling Bohlen "the best qualified diplomat" he could find for this crucial post. Taft came to the Administration's rescue by proposing that he and Democratic Senator John J. Sparkman examine the FBI file and report their evaluation to the full Senate. After seeing the evidence, the two Senators gave Bohlen a clean bill of health and Taft then secured Senate confirmation by an impressive margin, 74 to 13. The Majority Leader, however, found the task unpleasant, telling Eisenhower and Dulles afterwards, "no more Bohlens!"

McCarthy's action on the Bohlen appointment underlined the delicate problem facing the Administration. Republicans had benefited politically from the Wisconsin Senator's probes and charges as long as the Democrats were in power; now he was an embarrassment to the party. Hoping to sidetrack his activities, the GOP agreed to let him chair the relatively insignificant Committee on Government Operations while Senator Jenner, who was much more responsive to party discipline, headed the heretofore crucial Internal Security Subcommittee. Though McCarthy assured the Administration, especially Vice-President Richard Nixon, who served as Eisenhower's liaison with the extreme right, that he would be cooperative, he quickly transformed his obscure committee into a major investigating body, hiring a staff headed by Roy Cohn, a young New York lawyer whose brash arrogance matched McCarthy's, and proceeding to go after the State Department with a vengeance. After a brief examination of the Department's security program, McCarthy held a series of hearings on the Voice of America program, which Republicans claimed was run by "Communists, left-wingers, New Dealers, radicals and pinkos." Failing to make any substantial disclosures, the Senator turned his attention to the Department's overseas information libraries. Claiming that they were filled with books by "communists, fellow-travelers, *et cetera*," he sent Cohn and G. David Schine, a wealthy volunteer investigator, on a whirlwind trip through Europe. Panicky State Department employees withdrew books by avowed Communists such as Howard Fast and Soviet sympathizers like Joseph E. Davies, and in one case even burned books offensive to McCarthy.

Inside the Administration, a small group of advisers led by C. D. Jackson, a former *Life* editor serving as a special White House assistant on psychological warfare, urged the President to speak out forcefully against McCarthy. The Senator's attacks, they claimed, hurt American foreign policy by undermining State Department morale and by making the United States appear ridiculous in the eyes of the world. Only the President, with his great esteem and personal popularity, could challenge McCarthy effectively, argued Jackson. Other advisers, notably Sherman Adams, expressed distaste for witch-hunting but feared an intraparty fight, while still others, particularly Vice-President Nixon, warned that such an attack would doom the Administration's program in Congress. Eisenhower himself expressed his instinctive reaction when he told Jackson, "I will not get into the gutter with that guy." He steadfastly resisted growing pressure to condemn McCarthy publicly, sticking to his belief that such an attack would only play into the Senator's hands. "Nothing would probably please him more," Ike wrote to a friend about McCarthy, "than to get the publicity that would be generated by public repudiation by the President." Yet Eisenhower did regret the effect of McCarthy's activities. "It is a sorry mess," he told the same friend in May 1953; "at times one feels almost like hanging his head in shame when he reads some of the unreasoned, vicious outbursts of demagoguery that appear in our public prints."

The attack on American overseas libraries finally compelled Eisenhower to speak out obliquely against McCarthy. In the course of a commencement address at Dartmouth College, the President departed from his prepared remarks to advise the graduates, "Don't join the book-burners....Don't be afraid to go in your library and read every book as long as that document does not offend your own ideas of decency." The press hailed his words as an effective rebuttal to the Wisconsin demagogue but, at a press conference three days later, Eisenhower refused to link book-burning with McCarthy (who had innocently told reporters that Ike could not have meant him, saying, "I have burned no books") and in muddled responses the President even indicated that he had no objections to destroying flagrantly Communist literature. An outrageous charge that Protestant clergymen composed "the largest single group supporting the Communist apparatus in the United States" made by J. B. Matthews, an employee of McCarthy's investigating committee, gave White House aides a chance to urge the President to make a rebuttal. After two days of intricate maneuvering, Eisenhower released a statement deploring "Generalized and irresponsible attacks that sweepingly condemn the whole of any group of citizens." An hour later, McCarthy fired Matthews, leaving the impression that the President had forced him to act when in fact he had planned to take this step earlier.

By mid-1953, Eisenhower's cautious and typically indirect tactics seemed to be working. Three liberal Democrats resigned from McCarthy's investigating committee over the Matthews affair, while several conservative southerners broke the long silence in the Senate by rebuking McCarthy in floor speeches. Yet, despite the apparent decline of McCarthy's influence, the red scare continued. State governments enacted their own security programs, firing those suspected of Communist sympathies in the schools and universities and imposing loyalty oaths as a condition for employment. Entertainers and writers accused of being fellow travelers encountered blacklists that deprived them of the opportunity to earn a living and denied them the chance to confront their accusers. In Washington, Eisenhower made a significant change in the federal loyalty process in an effort to weed out "security risks," defined broadly to include individuals whose personal habits, political views, or radical associations might make them betray the national interest. As a result, the President announced in early 1954 that during his first year in office he had removed 2200 security risks from the government, many more than Truman had fired in five years. Eisenhower expressed indifference over the outcries of civil libertarians, telling his cabinet, "We know we've been just in this matter." Ike revealed how insensitive he was to liberal pleas in June 1953, when the Supreme Court overruled the stay that Justice Douglas had granted for the execution of Ethel and Julius Rosenberg, convicted atomic spies. Despite the fact that no American citizen had ever been put to death under the Espionage

Act of 1917, Eisenhower ignored a worldwide protest in refusing to grant executive clemency. "The execution of two human beings is a grave matter," he declared in a public statement. "But even graver is the thought of the millions of dead whose deaths may be directly attributable to what these spies have done."

IV

The struggle with the Republican right affected nearly every aspect of Eisenhower's relations with Congress. Time and time again the President ran into stubborn opposition from members of his own party that forced him to appeal to more cooperative Democrats to secure his legislative goals. Eisenhower became especially angry when economy-minded Republicans cut over $1 billion from the mutual security program to show their disdain for foreign aid. The Administration was more successful in blocking the attempt of New York Representative Daniel Reed, Chairman of the House Ways and Means Committee, to cut taxes by moving up the scheduled end of an 11 percent personal income surtax by six months. Stressing the need to balance the budget before reducing taxes, Eisenhower finally persuaded Congress not only to table Reed's bill but to continue until January 1954 the excess profits tax enacted to help finance the Korean War.

Eisenhower proved no more successful than Truman in securing Congressional action on his more modest social and economic legislation. A growing shortage of classrooms induced by the post-World War II baby boom led the Administration to request federal funds for school construction, but Congress refused to go beyond limited aid to those local school districts whose resources were strained by the children of federal employees. Eisenhower did not advocate a sweeping health plan, but he did suggest a reinsurance scheme whereby the federal government could help protect private health insurance groups from unusual losses. Republican Congressmen, fearful of "socialized medicine," rejected the plan, voting only for federal funds for medical research and hospital construction. Thanks to Democratic support, the President was more successful in extending earlier welfare programs. In 1954, Congress voted to extend Social Security benefits to more than 7 million additional workers, including farmers, domestics, and government employees. At Eisenhower's request, both Houses made 4 million more Americans eligible for unemployment payments and raised the minimum wage from 75 to 90 cents an hour. Congress also enacted modest housing legislation and enabled Eisenhower to redeem a campaign promise by enacting the tidelands bill, twice vetoed by Truman, to give states control over the oil from submerged land within their historic boundaries.

In the controversial area of civil rights, Eisenhower made no attempt to carry on Truman's initiatives. He refused to support the bipartisan efforts of Senators Hubert Humphrey and Irving Ives to establish a Fair Employment Practices Commission, voicing his objection to "punitive or compulsory federal law" and expressing a naive faith that "states will move on this in an enlightened and forward-looking way." In the early months of his Administration, there was no action on civil rights until Negro Congressman Adam Clayton Powell, an outspoken advocate of black interests, released a telegram to the White House accusing Eisenhower's subordinates, particularly HEW Secretary Hobby, of condoning discrimination in federal programs and appealing to Ike "to decisively assert your integrity." Powell's shock tactics worked. The President's aides arranged for an exchange of letters with the Congressman in which Eisenhower declared, "There must be no second-class citizens in this country," and he issued directives to end all discriminatory practices in federally funded programs. As a result, Secretary of the Navy Anderson quietly integrated naval installations to complete the desegregation of the armed forces Truman had begun and in 1954 Eisenhower created a Committee on Government Contracts headed by Vice-President Nixon to insure equal opportunity for blacks and other minorities in industries supplying the federal government. In addition, Eisenhower appointed J. Ernest Wilkins, a Negro attorney, Assistant Secretary of Labor, and elevated E. Frederick Morrow to the position of Assistant to the President, making him the first black aide in the White House.

By far the most significant step toward racial equality, however, came from the Supreme Court. In *Brown* v. *Board of Education,* Chief Justice Earl Warren, an Eisenhower appointee, ruled for a unanimous Court that segregation in the nation's public schools violated the Constitution. Eisenhower's response to this epoch-making decision reveals his basic indifference to civil rights. Publicly, he refused to comment, saying only that, "I am sworn to uphold the constitutional process in this country; and I will obey." Privately, Ike told one of his aides two years later, "As a matter of fact, I personally think the decision was wrong." His subsequent actions indicate that while he believed the federal government should offer equal opportunities to all citizens, he felt under no obligation to urge the American people to change their traditional racial attitudes. He refused to consider taking any legislative steps to carry out integration in the schools and on several occasions he voiced his belief that race relations involved personal considerations that lay beyond the scope of governmental action. Eisenhower apparently shared a southern distaste for racial intermingling. In his relatively sheltered military career, he had not been exposed to the fundamental indignities of discrimination and he seemed unmoved by the plight of the Negro. Thus he was intellectually and emotionally unable to provide the Presidential leadership the nation so desperately needed as it entered a new era in American race relationships.

An economic decline that began in the summer of 1953 and lasted for the next year worried the President a good deal more than desegregation. The recession was a natural result of decreasing government expenditures stemming from the end of the Korean War and the Administration's own budget-trimming efforts. The sudden drop in federal spending removed a vital stimulus to the economy; by early 1954, unemployment had risen by more than 1 million as manufacturing production dropped 10 percent. When Arthur Burns, chairman of the Council of Economic Advisers, first warned the President about the state of the economy in September 1953, Eisenhower responded with a strong assertion that he would take whatever steps were necessary to prevent "another 1929." His greatest fear, however, was an unbalanced budget and, though he approved standby plans for increased federal spending, he steadily resisted demands from labor and liberal Democrats for a massive public works program. Instead he followed Burns' advice and relied on the Federal Reserve Board and the Treasury Department to increase the money supply and ease credit through lower interests rates. Though unemployment continued to rise through early 1954, consumer spending, stimulated by the end of Korean War price controls and the tax reductions that went into effect in January, remained relatively high. The recession gradually ended in mid-1954, giving way to a new period of prosperity. By using fiscal and monetary controls, Eisenhower had overcome the economic crisis without departing from his cherished goal of a balanced budget.

Eisenhower's rather uneven record in domestic affairs during his first two years in office reflects his conscious decision not to be an activist President. He saw no need for sweeping changes in American life; after a period of internal turmoil, he hoped to usher in a time of tranquility at home so that the American people could concentrate on fulfilling their world responsibilities. He occasionally lost his temper with right-wing obstructionists in Congress, denouncing in private "those damn *monkeys* on the Hill," but he left Congressional relations to his aides, refusing to engage in the kind of personal controversy that he felt had undercut Truman's legislative program. He came to appreciate the cooperation of the Democrats, especially the two Texans, Senate Minority Leader Lyndon B. Johnson and House Speaker Sam Rayburn, and he even contemplated the idea of founding a third party to escape the Republican right. He talked more seriously about reshaping the GOP along lines of "modern Republicanism" but, at heart, Eisenhower did not place much faith in the party system. He believed he could best serve as President of all the people and that men of good will would abandon partisanship to follow his lead. His failure to speak out strongly on such vital issues as civil rights and McCarthyism, however, disappointed the millions of Americans who looked to him for leadership and destroyed whatever opportunity existed in the 1950s for remedying the nation's ills.

V

On August 12, 1953, Washington officials learned that the Soviet Union had exploded a hydrogen bomb. The United States had detonated its first thermonuclear device in November 1952; now both nations possessed a weapon 1000 times more powerful than the original atomic bomb dropped on Hiroshima. Robert Oppenheimer, the distinguished physicist, compared the United States and the Soviet Union to "two scorpions in a bottle, each capable of killing the other, but only at the risk of his own life," and led a group of scientists who urged the President to inform the American people of these nuclear facts of life and death. Eisenhower appointed C. D. Jackson to head an interdepartmental committee dubbed Operation Candor, but Admiral Lewis Strauss, the conservative chairman of the Atomic Energy Commission, invoked security considerations to block all efforts at public disclosure. Strauss ultimately succeeded in removing Oppenheimer as a government consultant by convincing Eisenhower that the physicist was a security risk, but the AEC chairman failed to dissuade the President from taking the initiative on nuclear disarmament.

News of the Soviet H-bomb reached Eisenhower while he was vacationing in Colorado. Realizing its implications, he searched for a way to renew international efforts to control the atom, stymied since the impasse on the Baruch Plan in 1946. On his return to Washington in September, he called in Robert Cutler and outlined a new approach to the problem: "Suppose the United States and the Soviets were each to turn over to the United Nations for peaceful uses X kilograms of fissionable material...." Cutler passed on the President's idea to Strauss and Jackson. For the next four months, Jackson wrote thirty-three drafts of a presidential speech developing Eisenhower's formula as he sought to overcome the objections of the AEC, the Pentagon, and especially the State Department, where Dulles viewed any attempt at nuclear disarmament with great skepticism. The President, however, insisted on going ahead, and finally on December 8 he presented his concept in a dramatic speech before the United Nations in New York City. After citing the awesome destructive power of nuclear weapons, he proposed the creation of an International Atomic Energy Agency to which the United States and other nuclear powers would contribute fissionable material "to serve the peaceful pursuits of mankind." Such a step, he concluded, would help the world "find the way by which the miraculous inventiveness of man shall not be dedicated to his death, but consecrated to his life."

The audience of 3500 greeted the "atoms for peace" address with sustained applause and the American people, watching on television, joined in the enthusiastic acclaim. The Soviets, though alerted in advance by Ambassador Bohlen to the speech's significance, refused to cooperate, preferring instead to close the American technological lead before entering into meaningful steps toward disarmament. The United States probed the peaceful uses of the atom with its allies until 1957, when the Soviet Union finally participated in the founding of the International Atomic Energy Agency. In the meantime, the arms race continued as the world entered an era described so aptly by Winston Churchill as "a balance of terror."

Despite the Soviet success in neutralizing America's nuclear advantage, John Foster Dulles decided to make public the concept of massive retaliation that he and Admiral Radford had persuaded Eisenhower to adopt in 1953. In a speech to the Council on Foreign Relations, Dulles elaborated on a phrase Eisenhower had used five days earlier in his annual State-of-the-Union message, "a massive capability to strike back" against aggressors. Reliance on conventional forces to stem an attack was inadequate, Dulles explained. "Local defenses must be reinforced by the further deterrent of massive retaliatory power....The basic decision is to depend primarily upon a great capacity to retaliate, instantly, by means and at places of our choosing...." These awkward words sent a chill through the hearts of millions of Americans as they interpreted them to mean that the United States would launch a nuclear war to stop any Communist act of aggression. Critics saw the policy as one designed to deter Soviet expansion by threatening to use nuclear weapons; in view of Russian possession of the hydrogen bomb, they did not believe the American threat was credible. Disgruntled military men, particularly Army Chief of Staff Matthew Ridgway, feared that the excessive reliance on air power and the corresponding reduction of available ground forces would prevent the United States from responding effectively to limited Communist advances and probes.

The deteriorating situation in Indo-China quickly underlined the inadequacies of massive retaliation. The French had been fighting a war against Communist guerrillas led by Ho Chi Minh since late 1946. President Truman had authorized limited American economic aid to the French in May 1950, and after the outbreak of the Korean War, he had greatly stepped up this assistance. Despite the substantial American help (by 1954, the United States was paying 78 percent of the cost of the fighting), Ho's Viet Minh guerrillas, winning the support of many non-Communist Vietnamese nationalists, controlled much of the countryside. In late 1953, General Navarre, the French commander in Indo-China, sent 10,000 crack troops into the hamlet of Dien Bien Phu, presumably to cut off supplies coming to the Viet Minh from Communist China by way of Laos. The Viet Minh quickly surrounded the garrison and began a siege that became the focus of international attention. The loss of Dien Bien Phu would make little strategic difference, but the French had staked their prestige on holding this position. Thus the whole outcome of a nine-year guerrilla war turned on the fate on the besieged French troops in this remote jungle outpost.

The American stake in Indo-China seemed clear to most contemporaries. France was a vital European ally and, though the United States had repeatedly urged Paris to give the Vietnamese genuine independence, a humiliating French defeat in Asia was bound to weaken NATO. As early as 1950, moreover, the Joint Chiefs of Staff had warned that "the fall of Indochina would undoubtedly lead to the fall of the other mainland states of Southeast Asia" and thus create a "Soviet position of dominance over Asia" that would "constitute a major threat to United States security." In a famous press conference on April 7, 1954 Eisenhower indicated his acceptance of this strategic assessment by invoking the "falling domino" principle. "You have a row of dominoes set up, and you knock over the first one," Ike said in reference to Indo-China, "and what will happen to the last one is the certainty that it will go over very quickly."

The dilemma facing the Eisenhower Administration was how to prevent the loss of Southeast Asia within the limitations imposed by massive retaliation. "Involvement of U.S. forces in the Indochina War should be avoided at all practical costs," advised Admiral A. C. Davis, the officer in charge of Foreign Military Affairs in the Pentagon. General Ridgway backed him up, estimating that it would take at least seven American divisions to defeat the Viet Minh, and a total of twelve if the Chinese entered the conflict. Davis also warned against being "self-duped into believing the possibility of partial involvement — such as 'naval and air units only.' One cannot, " he observed drily, "go over Niagara Falls in a barrel only slightly." Eisenhower concurred in this judgment, writing in his memoirs that while the use of air power might lift sagging French morale, "I had no intention of using United States forces in any limited action when the force employed would probably not be decisively effective."

Unaware of these considerations, General Paul Ely, the French Chief of Staff, flew to Washington on March 20 to appeal for American military intervention in Indo-China. Meetings with the Joint Chiefs of Staff, Secretary of State Dulles and President Eisenhower produced only repeated expressions of sympathy and the offer of twenty-five B-26 bombers. Finally, Admiral Radford, now serving as Chairman of the Joint Chiefs, came forth with Operation Vulture, a desperate plan to have sixty B-29 bombers in the Philippines destroy the Viet Minh besiegers of Dien Bien Phu with a massive aerial strike that would include three tactical A-bombs. Although the other members of the Joint Chiefs advised against Operation Vulture, Eisenhower and Dulles did not rule it out immediately. Both men hoped to avoid unilateral American intervention, and in a speech on March 29 Dulles expressed the Administration's preference for "united action" — a statement that reflected Eisenhower's insistence that our allies join us in any attempt to rescue the French in Indo-China.

On Saturday morning, April 3, Dulles and Admiral Radford met with a small delegation of Congressional leaders to consider a request for a resolution authorizing the President to use American troops in Indo-China. The Senators and Representatives reacted critically when Radford outlined Operation Vulture; Senator Lyndon Johnson spoke for his colleagues when he pointed out that after Korea the American people would oppose involvement in another Asian war. The Congressional leaders reaffirmed Eisenhower's emphasis on collective efforts, reluctantly agreeing "that if such cooperation could be assured, it was probable that the U.S. Congress would authorize U.S. participation in such 'United Action.'" The next evening the President met again with Dulles and Radford and endorsed the Congressional position. Instead of a massive air strike to relieve Dien Bien Phu, the United States would seek the assistance of Great Britain, Thailand, the Philippines, and the people of Vietnam themselves in forming a new coalition to resist Communist expansion in Indo-China. In an appeal to Winston Churchill, Eisenhower urged the British to join this venture, reminding the English Prime Minister, "we failed to halt Hirohito, Mussolini, and Hitler by not acting in unity and in time."

England held the key and, though both Churchill and Foreign Minister Anthony Eden gave Dulles some encouragement about participating in "united action," Eden subsequently refused to sanction the use of force in Indo-China. Dulles made a final effort to get British approval on the eve of the Geneva Conference, originally called to negotiate a permanent Korean settlement but that ended up dealing primarily with Vietnam. Eden remained steadfast and, when the French, facing imminent defeat at Dien Bien Phu, tried to resurrect Operation Vulture, Dulles told them that while it "seemed to me out of the question under existing circumstances," he would refer the issue back to Eisenhower. The President refused to reconsider, writing in his memoirs, "There would be no intervention without allies."

Dien Bien Phu fell on May 7. Two months later, after the emergence of a new French government under Pierre Mendès-France, representatives of England, France, Russia, and Communist China signed two agreements providing for a truce between the Viet Minh and the French, temporary division of Vietnam at the 17th parallel, with all French forces moving south of that line, and the holding of elections within two years to provide a unified government for all Vietnam. In addition, the accords banned the introduction of additional foreign troops and forbade the Vietnam states from joining military alliances. The United States was not a signatory (Dulles refused to take part in negotiations with Red China) but, in a separate statement, the Administration announced its support for the idea of free elections and warned against any "aggression in violation" of the Geneva accords.

The Indo-China crisis revealed Eisenhower's skill as a leader. Relying on his wartime experience, he refused to be rushed into an unwise military adventure by Admiral Radford, but at the same time he took account of the domestic political risks in appearing to approve Communist gains abroad. Accordingly, he let Congressional insistence on cooperative action and the outright British refusal to condone a resort to force negate the French appeals for American intervention. Apparently Dulles was as opposed to the use of force as Eisenhower but, in playing an active role in seeking Congressional and British approval for a united policy, he emerged as an eager hawk held in check by a wiser and more mature President.

VI

While Eisenhower and Dulles worried over the spread of Communism in Southeast Asia, McCarthy's crusade against the Red menace at home created an even graver crisis. McCarthy made a series of attacks on the Administration in late 1953 that brought him new headlines and apparent public approval; by January 1954, the Gallup poll showed a record high of 50 percent of the American people responding favorably to the Wisconsin Senator, 29 percent unfavorably, and 21 percent expressing no opinion. Emboldened by this strong showing, McCarthy began an assault on the U.S. Army that led to his undoing. In February, he discovered that the Army had promoted and honorably discharged Dr. Irving Peress, an obscure dentist with leftist political views who had pleaded the Fifth Amendment in refusing to testify before McCarthy's investigating subcommittee. McCarthy called on General Ralph W. Zwicker, Peress' commanding officer and a much-decorated veteran of World War II, to explain the Army's action. Zwicker's answers failed to satisfy McCarthy, who began browbeating the General, claiming he was "not fit to wear that uniform" and did not have "the brains of a five-year old."

Eisenhower winced under these attacks on a fellow officer and on the Army itself. Yet he continued to resist the pressures of those within the Administration who wanted him to go after McCarthy personally. Instead he let Secretary of the Army Robert Stevens attend a famous fried chicken luncheon with McCarthy and conservative Republicans, arranged in part by Vice-President Nixon, at which Stevens capitulated to virtually all of the Wisconsin Senator's demands. A White House group led by Sherman Adams drafted a stronger statement for Stevens that Eisenhower approved, but the President refused to become involved in the resulting uproar. In mid-March, the Army counterattacked, releasing a chronological account of efforts by McCarthy and Roy Cohn to secure preferential treatment for Private G. David Schine, Cohn's wealthy assistant, who had been drafted in 1953. McCarthy immediately charged that the Army was trying to "blackmail" him into ending his investigation, an accusation that led directly to the Army-McCarthy hearings.

The televised proceedings began in April and lasted for 36 days. The original issues became lost in a welter of charges and countercharges as McCarthy fought for his political life. The remorseless eye of the television camera became his most deadly enemy as day after day he alienated more and more Americans with his sarcastic comments, his disdain for legal procedure, and his constant cry, "Mr. Chairman, point of order." He finally went too far when he suggested that one of the junior aides to Army counsel Joseph Welch was a fellow traveler. In a dramatic speech, Welch condemned the Senator's "reckless cruelty" and interrupted his reply to ask the question that millions of Americans were beginning to ask themselves, "Have you no sense of decency, sir, at long last? Have you left no sense of decency?" Welch left the room with tears streaming down his face, seemingly overcome with emotion but still alert enought to ask a colleague, "Well, how did it go?"

By the time the hearings ended in May, McCarthy's standing in the Gallup po l had dropped to 35 percent, while opposition to him had risen to an impr ssive 49 percent. More important, his attacks on the Administration and hi declining popularity made him a political liability for the Republican party. Sickened by the spectacle, Senator Ralph Flanders, a conservative Vermont Republican, introduced a censure resolution in July. Senate Minority Leader Lyndon Johnson carefully kept liberal Democrats silent; instead, he let the Republicans deal with their own problem free of partisan considerations. A special Senate committee headed by Arthur Watkins, another GOP conservative, conducted a deliberately low-key investigation and then recommended on September 27 that McCarthy be censured on two counts for contempt of the Senate.

The impending Congressional elections led to a decision to delay the vote until late November. Meanwhile Republicans tried to overcome the burden McCarthyism had placed on the party. Declining farm prices and the continuing high rate of unemployment stemming from the recent recession further weakened GOP candidates. Dwight Eisenhower campaigned vigorously, although sporadically, appealing to voters to return a Republican Congress that would continue the "great work" of his Administration. The President dodged the issue of McCarthyism, but Vice-President Nixon, who concentrated on traditionally Republican states, castigated the Democrats for "softness" toward Communism. Boasting of the Administration's success in "kicking the Communists and fellow travelers and security risks out of government," Nixon claimed that Democratic candidates represented the "party's left-wing clique which. . .has tolerated the Communist conspiracy in the United States." Despite these appeals, voters gave the Democrats a slim victory, enabling them to control the Senate by the margin of 1 seat and the House by 29. Although this outcome reflected little more than the usual off-year loss for the party in power, it meant that Eisenhower would have to work with Democratic leadership in Congress for the next two years.

When the Senate reconvened in late November, right-wing Republicans fought a losing battle against the report of the Watkins committee. Minority Leader Johnson wisely let conservative Democrats speak for his party; Mississippi's John Stennis condemned McCarthy for pouring "slush and slime" on the Senate while North Carolina's Sam Ervin wanted to go beyond censure and expel McCarthy permanently. On December 2, all forty-four Democrats voted to censure the Wisconsin Senator. The Republicans divided evenly, twenty-two for and twenty-two against. McCarthy snarled his anger at the Administration by expressing regret that he had voted for Eisenhower in 1952 and changing his charge of "twenty years of treason" to "twenty-one." But his colleagues' censure had broken his power. No longer able to intimidate other Senators, he gradually faded from the scene until his death in 1957.

The evil McCarthy did lived long after him, however. The unreasoning fear of Communism he had exploited continued to influence American attitudes toward the Cold War, stifling debate and preventing the growth of healthy dissent. The loyalty oaths, blacklists, and censorship McCarthy had encourged continued to be a familiar aspect of American life throughout the decade of the fifties. In a sense, Eisenhower's tactics of allowing the demagogue to destroy himself through his own excesses had worked, but the nation had to pay a heavy price. Ike's refusal to use his enormous popularity and great prestige not only to condemn McCarthy but to repudiate all that he stood for remains his greatest failure as President.

VII

The problem of containing Communist expansion in Asia continued to worry the Eisenhower Aministration. In August 1954, the National Security Council concluded that the Geneva accords on Indo-China had been a "disaster" that "completed a major forward stride of Communism which may lead to the loss of Southeast Asia." The French had simply sought to save face in agreeing to the elections scheduled for 1956, which they realized would probably result in a victory for Ho Chi Minh. Dulles, determined to save at least half of Indo-China, persuaded Eisenhower to accept NSC recommendations for extending military, economic, and political aid to the Vietnamese nationalists in the South led by Prime Minister Ngo Dinh Diem. In a letter to Diem in October, the President made a firm offer of assistance to help create "a strong, viable state, capable of resisting attempted subversion or aggression through military means." Direct aid to the South Vietnamese meant that the United States had now taken over the French role in Indo-China; by the end of the year, American military advisers had arrived in Saigon to begin the task of teaching the Vietnamese to defend themselves against the Communists in the North. In 1955, Diem became the outright ruler of South Vietnam and, with American backing, refused to hold the general elections called for in the Geneva accords.

Despite this unilateral policy in Vietnam, Dulles still sought to implement his "united action" proposal in Southeast Asia. He finally achieved a degree of success in September 1954, when representatives of Britain, France, Australia, New Zealand, Pakistan, Thailand, and the Philippines joined with the United States in forming the Southeast Asia Treaty Organization (SEATO). Though modeled after NATO, SEATO lacked the binding commitments for the use of force (the signatories agreed only to consult in case of aggression) as well as the homogeneous cultural and geographical makeup of the European alliance (the Philippines and Thailand were the sole Southeast Asian members). Nevertheless, Dulles felt that he had secured the necessary international support for his policy of extending containment to Asia.

Communist China remained the central issue. Upon taking office the Eisenhower Administration had ruled out the possibility of recognizing Mao's regime and had freed Chiang Kai-shek to attack the Communists by removing the Seventh Fleet from the Formosa Straits. Right-wing Republicans hoped for Chiang's speedy return to the mainland but, by 1954, a Communist invasion of Formosa seemed more likely. A crisis began to develop in the Formosa Straits in September as Red Chinese forces bombarded three groups of off-shore islands still in Nationalist hands: the Tachens, Quemoy, and Matsu. Eisenhower called an emergency meeting of the NSC at the summer White House in Denver to consider what Dulles called "a horrible dilemma." Admiral Radford and two other members of the Joint Chiefs advocated a commitment to defend the islands and to help the Nationalists bomb the mainland. General Ridgway disagreed and Eisenhower quickly backed him up. "We're not talking now about a limited, brush-fire war," he reminded the Chiefs. "We're talking about going to the threshold of World War III."

Eisenhower insisted on a diplomatic solution and, despite grumblings from right-wing Republicans in Congress, including Minority Leader Knowland who called for a total blockade of the China coast, Dulles worked out a compromise with Chiang Kai-shek. In return for a new security treaty by which the United States guaranteed Formosa and the nearby Pescadores Islands, the Nationalists agreed to stop their guerrilla raids on the mainland. Eisenhower, remembering GOP criticism of Truman's use of troops in Korea without prior Congressional approval, sent a message to Congress in late January 1955 requesting a resolution authorizing him to use force to defend Formosa, the Pescadores, and "related localities." The House complied quickly but, in the Senate, Democratic liberals tried to limit the President's authority by specifically ruling out the off-shore islands. This amendment received only thirteen votes in a debate characterized by Senator Wiley's declaration, "Either we can defend the United States in the Formosan Straits — now, or we can defend it later in San Francisco Bay." The Senate then voted 83 to 3 to give the President authority to "employ the armed forces of the United States as he deems necessary" to defend Formosa, the Pescadores, and "related positions" against armed attack.

Eisenhower used his broad powers wisely. When the Communists threatened to overrun the Tachens, he persuaded Chiang Kai-shek to evacuate these islands without a fight. As the Chinese Communists began shelling Quemoy and Matsu, the President refused to announce whether he would use American forces to defend these outposts, saying his decision would depend on whether he considered an attack a prelude to a full-scale invasion of Formosa. At the height of the crisis in March, Eisenhower answered a reporter who asked him if he contemplated using atomic weapons by saying, "I see no reason why they shouldn't be used just exactly as you would use a bullet or anything else." A few days later, Dulles publicly threatened the use of "new and powerful weapons of precision, which can utterly destroy military targets without endangering unrelated civilian centers," a clear reference to tactical atomic bombs. The Chinese never tested the willingness of Eisenhower and Dulles to carry out these nuclear threats. Instead, they gradually eased their bombardment of the islands and, by May, the danger of war in the Formosa Straits had passed.

Eisenhower's combination of firmness and restraint impressed the American people; his standing in the Gallup poll rose to a high of 68 percent in the spring of 1955. Dulles would later cite the Formosa Straits crisis in an indiscreet interview with a *Life* journalist as an example of preserving peace by going to the brink of war. In his account of Dulles' brinksmanship, the journalist neglected to point out that Eisenhower kept the crisis under control from the outset, overriding the military's desire for precipitate action and overseeing a deliberately ambiguous policy that kept the Chinese Communists off balance without committing the United States to the defense of a few barren islands off the China coast.

VIII

The fear of war, quickened by the crisis in the Formosa Straits, led in 1955 to the first summit conference since World War II. America's allies, especially British Prime Minister Winston Churchill, had been calling for such a meeting since Stalin's death. The hydrogen bomb had made the Cold War more perilous than ever before; a face-to-face encounter between the leaders of the East and the West would reassure an anxious world and might even lead to some tentative agreements to lessen tensions. Dulles regarded direct negotiations with the Soviets with great skepticism, but once the Russians demonstrated good faith by suddenly agreeing to the long-delayed Austrian peace treaty, he went along with Eisenhower's suggestion for a summit conference in Geneva in mid-July.

Two items headed the agenda. The first was Germany, divided since the blockade in 1948-1949, despite the official commitment of both sides to reunification. By 1955, the United States had succeeded in overcoming French resistance to German rearmament and had brought a sovereign West Germany into NATO; the Russians had thoroughly communized East Germany and, in 1955, made it a member of the newly formed Warsaw Pact, the Eastern European equivalent of NATO. The Soviets proposed a neutral, demilitarized Germany; the West countered with demands for unification under free elections. Nuclear disarmament, the second issue, raised even graver problems. The initial talks in the UN had bogged down in 1947 over the crucial issue of inspection. The United States refused to give up its nuclear advantage without an ironclad system of verification to prevent cheating; the Soviets refused to open up their closed society to foreign inspectors. Seeking to break this impasse, a group of American officials, led by Presidential assistants Nelson Rockefeller and Harold Stassen, formulated a proposal for mutual aerial inspection. Dulles showed little enthusiam for the idea, but Eisenhower liked it and decided to have Rockefeller and Stassen stand by in Paris, ready to come to Geneva if the President decided to make a new disarmament proposal to the Russians.

The leaders gathered in Geneva on July 18: Eisenhower, accompanied by Dulles, who warned him not to have a smiling picture taken with the Communists, representing the United States; Anthony Eden, who had recently succeeded Churchill, leading the British delegation; Edgar Faure, the Premier of France; and the two Russian leaders, Marshall Nikolai Bulganin, the handsome but powerless Soviet Chairman, and the rotund Nikita Khrushchev, Secretary of the Communist Party and the real ruler of the Soviet Union. Eisenhower opened the meeting with an earnest plea for "a new spirit that will make possible future solutions of problems which are within our responsibilities." During the next three days, however, the old differences manifested themselves in the discussions on Germany, nuclear disarmament, and methods of increasing cultural contacts between the East and West. When Bulganin offered the usual Soviet disarmament package, a reduction on conventional forces followed by a ban on the use of nuclear weapons, Ike decided it was time to propose something new. He called Stassen and Rockefeller to Geneva and asked them to prepare a speech embodying the concept of aerial inspection.

The next day, without any prior warning, Eisenhower unveiled the "open skies" proposal to Bulganin and Khrushchev. The United States and Russia, he suggested, should exchange "a complete blueprint of our military establishments" and open their countries to unlimited aerial reconnaissance. The open skies approach, Eisenhower argued, would reduce "the possibility of great surprise attack, thus lessening danger and relaxing tension." With the problem of inspection solved by this novel system, the two countries could then move toward more substantial disarmament. Eden and Faure immediately voiced their support for "open skies" and, to the surprise of many Western observers, Bulganin said it had real merit and would receive careful and sympathetic study by the Soviets. A few minutes later, however, Khrushchev told Eisenhower over cocktails, "I don't agree with the chairman," dismissing "open skies" as simply a way for the American Air Force to improve its targeting of Soviet military sites. At the end of the summit conference, the leaders formally referred "open skies," along with the deadlock on Germany, to subsequent meetings of the Council on Foreign Ministers, scheduled for the fall.

The Geneva meeting failed to bring about the long-hoped for detente in the Cold War. The foreign ministers proved unable to unravel the problems of either German reunification or nuclear disarmament, though they did implement the general agreement reached at Geneva for cultural exchanges that would help lower the Iron Curtain by permitting reciprocal visits of musicians, entertainers, and scientists. At the very least, the summit symbolized, as Emmet Hughes pointed out, "the acceptance by the major powers of the common necessity to shun recourse to nuclear war." The simple fact that the leaders of the East and West met in polite discourse bred a "spirit of Geneva" that eased the tensions that had been building steadily since the late 1940s. Eisenhower was the unquestioned beneficiary of this new feeling of optimism. His "open skies" plan won him worldwide applause and, at home, his popularity soared to a record 79 percent in the August Gallup poll. James Reston likened the esteem the American people held for their President to "a national phenomenon, like baseball. The thing is no longer just a remarkable political fact but a kind of national love affair...."

Happy at this adulation but weary from the strain of the summit, Ike sought relaxation in a fishing-and-golfing vacation in Colorado. On September 23, he spent two hours in his temporary office at Lowry Air Force Base, and then rushed off to nearby Cherry Hills Country Club for eighteen holes of golf. After a hearty lunch of hamburgers topped by raw onions, Ike played nine more holes, complaining briefly of indigestion, and then returned to Denver to join Mrs. Eisenhower for an early dinner. He woke in the night with violent pains in the chest; his personal physician, Dr. Howard Snyder, immediately diagnosed a massive heart attack. He gave the President morphine and sat with him through the night, and the next morning transferred him to Army's Fitzsimons General Hospital on the outskirts of Denver, telling reporters only that Ike was suffering "a digestive upset."

The nation did not learn of the President's heart attack until midafternoon September 24. For the next few days, Eisenhower remained in critical condition and then began a slow but steady recovery, leaving the hospital on November 11 and returning to the White House to resume his duties the following January. His ability to bounce back reassured the American people but left the Republicans in doubt about their political future. Eisenhower alone seemed capable of leading the GOP to victory in 1956. Despite his uneven domestic record, he had restored public confidence in American foreign policy by ending the Korean War, by avoiding military involvement in Asia, and by rekindling hopes for a break in the Cold War at the Geneva Conference. Eisenhower symbolized the new mood of tranquility that had replaced the frenzied anxiety of Truman's last years in office. With growing uneasiness, the nation and the Republican Party waited to hear his decision, unwilling to ask him to risk his life by running again yet uncertain of where else to turn for leadership. In less than three years, Eisenhower, the supposedly naive military hero, had become the indispensable man in American politics.

4

The Anxious Years

While Dwight Eisenhower lay recuperating in a Denver hospital, the world seemed deceptively calm. Dulles attended the fall 1955 foreign ministers conference and, though he failed to break the deadlock with the Soviets over either the future of Germany or nuclear disarmament, the meeting did not destroy the fragile spirit of Geneva. At least the two superpowers were still trying to solve their difficulties in direct negotiation, and the Russians in particular seemed ready to adopt a more conciliatory stance in diplomacy. In the fall of 1955, Khrushchev began a series of travels to Third World countries that signaled a new Soviet attempt to win support from the neutralist bloc by means of political flattery and economic inducement instead of aggressive threats. A more far-reaching change in Soviet policy became evident during the 20th Communist Party conference in Moscow in early 1956 when Khrushchev began repudiating the excesses of Stalin and outlining a new, more flexible policy toward the satellite empire in Eastern Europe. In fact, Khrushchev was mounting an ominous offensive designed to surpass the United States in global influence, but to contemporaries it seemed to forecast a period of relaxed tensions and possible detente in the Cold War.

At home, the mood was even more serene. McCarthy's decline had ended the worst extremes of the red scare; the people wanted to forget the wild charges and dangerous emotions that had bordered on hysteria. The 1954 school desegregation decision raised vital questions about the future of race relations, but a Supreme Court ruling in 1955 calling for implementation "with all deliberate speed" gave promise of a slow, gradual working out of a difficult problem. The economy, fully recovered from the post-Korean War slump, was booming, creating a sense of well-being for all groups in the nation except farmers, who began to experience a persistent price decline in the fall of 1955. Automobile sales hit a record high in 1955, and the Administration took advantage of the rising domestic prosperity to attain the balanced budget that Ike so badly wanted. A mood of contentment, almost of smug self-satisfaction, had taken hold as the American people looked forward to enjoying the twin blessings of peace and abundance under Eisenhower's beneficent and relaxed rule.

The President's health remained the one great source of anxiety. As soon as it became clear that his life was no longer in danger, Sherman Adams and John Foster Dulles teamed up to prevent Vice-President Richard Nixon from exercising the power of government. Adams carried on many of the presidential duties in Denver while Eisenhower regained his strength; Dulles stayed in Washington to conduct foreign policy and restrict Nixon's role to a purely ceremonial presiding over occasional cabinet meetings. After further rest at Gettysburg and Key West, Ike returned to the White House in January 1956 to face intense pressure from the leaders of the eastern Republican Establishment to run again. There seemed to be no other alternative for the GOP — men like Thomas Dewey and Earl Warren were too overexposed; relative newcomers such as Richard Nixon and Henry Cabot Lodge failed to command sufficient respect. After a crucial dinner meeting with a dozen of his most trusted associates, Eisenhower began to think seriously of a second term and, when the doctors gave their approval in mid-February, he made his decision public in a nationally televised speech. He confessed that he would have to rest at least ten hours each day and admitted candidly that he had been under great pressure to run again. The decision, he added, was his own, and he went on to declare, "As of this moment, there is not the slightest doubt that I can perform, as well as I ever have, all of the important duties of the Presidency."

In the course of a press conference in early March, the President opened up even more intense political speculation by refusing to say whether he wanted Richard Nixon as his running mate again, commenting that the Vice-President should "chart out his own course." Eisenhower had previously suggested to Nixon in private that he step down from the Vice-Presidency in favor of a cabinet post, and now the controversial Nixon was placed in an agonizing dilemma. Many reporters saw in Ike's words a subtle attempt to remove Nixon from the ticket; others thought the President was simply trying to force his Vice-President to demonstrate his political strength. After some solid support from party leaders and an impressive write-in vote in the New Hampshire primary, Nixon informed the President of his desire to serve as his running mate again. Ike, masking his inner feelings about Nixon, let Hagerty announce this news to the press. Later, the President permitted Harold Stassen to make an effort to replace Nixon with Governor Christian Herter of Massachusetts, but this clumsy attempt only solidified Nixon's position in the party and thus insured his place on the 1956 GOP ticket.

There was a much more hectic struggle for the Democratic nomination in 1956. Adlai Stevenson prevailed, but only after a long primary battle with Estes Kefauver in which Stevenson dropped his aloof stance and wooed the voters ardently if somewhat clumsily. The outlook for the Democrats was not very bright; the Republican slogan of peace and prosperity under Ike's benign countenance seemed to be unbeatable. But a sudden attack of ileitis forced Eisenhower to undergo emergency surgery in June that greatly improved the Democratic prospects. Eisenhower recovered quickly, but he remained pale and underweight for the next few months, creating the possibility, hinted at but rarely discussed publicly, that he might not survive another term in office.

The relatively calm international climate changed suddenly on July 27 when Egyptian leader Gamal Abdel Nasser nationalized the Suez Canal. This dramatic act climaxed a growing deterioration in the United States position in the Middle East since 1955, when Dulles had arranged the Baghdad Pact, a regional alliance consisting of Iran, Iraq, Turkey, Pakistan, and Great Britain. Although the United States was not formally a member, its key role antagonized Nasser, who began to form close ties with the Soviet Union, first with a major arms deal arranged through Czechoslovakia and then with an important trade agreement that mortgaged most of Egypt's cotton to the Soviet Union. The United States and Great Britain had offered to help underwrite the Aswan dam on the Nile, a grandiose project dear to Nasser's heart, but Dulles, after becoming angered by Egypt's recognition of Red China and dismayed by rising Congressional opposition to the Aswan project (especially by southerners who objected to financing competitive Egyptian cotton), decided, with Eisenhower's concurrence, to rescind the commitment. The Secretary of State brusquely informed the Egyptian ambassador of the change on July 19, casting highly undiplomatic, though probably valid, aspersions on his country's economic condition. Nasser gave his answer a week later with the canal seizure, thereby touching off a grave international crisis.

England and France, whose citizens were the chief stockholders in the company that owned the Suez canal, reacted violently. Both nations depended heavily on Middle Eastern oil and both viewed Nasser as an upstart who had to be disciplined immediately. The French wanted to strike at Nasser for the aid he gave Algerian rebels; Anthony Eden, who had recently replaced Churchill as Prime Minister, saw the Egyptian leader as another Hitler who must not be appeased. Worried by his allies' desire to use force, Eisenhower quickly sent messages counseling restraint and then dispatched Dulles to London to arrange for an international conference to find a way to restore peace to the troubled

Middle East. This prompt action by Eisenhower and Dulles prevent a hasty Anglo-French attack on Egypt, but the Americans failed to understand the depth of British and French resentment at the Egyptian action. With an eye on the coming presidential election, Dulles pursued a policy of procrastination with an endless series of negotiations. Meanwhile, as Emmet Hughes noted, the crisis went on with "the soft and rythmic ticking of a time bomb," threatening to explode the fragile peace Eisenhower had achieved and thus "shatter most Republican pretensions in foreign policy."

I

Stevenson faced a cruel dilemma in 1956. Convinced that Eisenhower's policies of drift at home and abroad were creating dangerous problems for the nation, he wanted to probe beneath the surface of the Administration's apparent success. Yet, faced with the prevailing image of peace and prosperity, he accepted the advice of professional politicians and tried to hammer away at gut political themes — sagging farm prices, pockets of unemployment, and GOP favoritism to large corporations. He ignored the complex and sensitive race issue (in part, at least, to placate the South) and he sidestepped the Suez crisis for fear of interfering with the Administration's quest for peace.

He did raise two new issues in the campaign — the possibility of replacing the draft with an all-volunteer professional army and a proposal for a nuclear test ban with the Soviet Union. Eisenhower quickly used his reputation as a military leader to denounce both suggestions as unsound and dangerous. Stevenson abandoned his selective service reform but, when West Coast audiences began to react favorably to his test ban idea, he made radiation perils arising from hydrogen bomb tests a major campaign theme. Many scientists supported his contention that the atmospheric tests of nuclear weapons posed a serious threat to human health, both in polluting the environment and in creating hazardous genetic mutations. Eisenhower struck back by insisting that only a complete nuclear disarmament agreement that included the inspection safeguards the Russians refused to accept could solve the problem. A crude Soviet attempt to meddle in the campaign, in the form of a letter to Eisenhower from Premier Bulganin backing Stevenson's test ban, embarrassed the Democrats and prevented them from gaining many votes on a very delicate issue.

The sudden outbreak of violence abroad, though contradicting the Republican peace theme, overshadowed Stevenson's efforts to awaken the nation and ensured Eisenhower's reelection. The first sign of trouble came in mid-October when a group of Polish leaders, headed by Wladislaw Gomulka, challenged tight Soviet control of their country and won out in a tense showdown with Khrushchev. A week later, restless young freedom fighters in Hungary overthrew the repressive Communist government and, after bloody fighting in

Budapest, won a deceptive Soviet promise to evacuate the country. The Hungarian rebels, unlike the Poles, went too far by proclaiming their intention of withdrawing from the Warsaw Pact and embracing genuine neutrality in the Cold War. On November 4, just two days before the American election, the Soviets stormed back into Budapest, crushing the brave resistance of the freedom fighters with utter disdain for world opinion. Eisenhower and Dulles watched in despair, paralyzed by the realization that any attempt to help the Hungarians might touch off a nuclear holocaust. With real liberation out of the question, they had to be content with an ineffective UN resolution condemning Soviet action and private expressions of regret for the Hungarian's fate. "Poor fellows, poor fellows," Eisenhower commented. "I think about them all the time. I wish there were some way of helping them."

The Suez time bomb, ticking ominously since July, finally exploded in late October when Israeli forces struck suddenly into Egyptian territory in the Sinai and drove for the canal. England and France immediately issued an ultimatum calling for Israel and Egypt to stop fighting or face armed intervention to safeguard the Suez waterway. As many suspected at the time, the Israeli invasion had been carefully coordinated in advance to serve as the excuse for Anglo-French intervention. Eisenhower cut short a campaign trip in the South when he learned of the blowup in the Middle East and, back in the White House, he vented his anger at the allied action, saying, "I've just never seen great powers make such a complete *mess* and *botch* of things." In a speech to the American people, he made clear his opposition to the Suez adventure, asserting, "There can be no peace – without law," and announced that he would work through the UN to end this act of aggression. Secretary of State Dulles performed the unpleasant task of aligning the United States with the Soviet Union in securing a General Assembly resolution condemning the Anglo-French resort to force and calling for a cease-fire. Adlai Stevenson, belatedly taking up the Suez issue, blasted Eisenhower and Dulles for "incredible blunders" that resulted in the United States standing before the world "with Soviet Russia and the dictator of Egypt against the democracies of Britain, France and Israel." Ike did not bother to reply, but Nixon answered for him, claiming that the Democratic candidate was too weak to lead the nation in a time of grave crisis, explaining, "the butchers of the Kremlin would make mincemeat of Stevenson over a conference table."

Election day, November 6, marked the tensest moment in the Cold War since the Berlin blockade in 1948. British and French troops had landed near Port Said the day before and were advancing on the canal; Russian tanks patrolled the silent streets of Budapest as the freedom fighters fled for the Austrian frontier; Nikita Khrushchev made reckless threats to launch rockets against British and French cities and to send Soviet "volunteers" to aid Egypt; Eisenhower put American armed forces on a worldwide alert, telling Emmet Hughes, "if those fellows start something, we may have to hit'em – and, if necessary, with *everything* in the bucket." At midday, as voters streamed to the polls, the crisis broke when Eden telephoned Eisenhower to inform him that England and France had agreed to a cease-fire. That evening, the early election returns revealed a strong trend for the President; by morning, Ike had won an even greater victory than in 1952, taking all but seven states and winning 58 percent of the popular vote.

Most observers felt that events overseas added several million votes to Eisenhower's total as the people rallied behind their President in a time of great uncertainty. Ike's continuing personal popularity and the record of four years of peace and prosperity undoubtedly underlay his impressive triumph. Yet the Republican party did not share fully in the victory, as the Democrats carried both houses of Congress to maintain their control of the legislative branch. This curious outcome was due partly to the ineffective campaign Stevenson waged, one that failed to generate substantial issues and that prevented the candidate from capitalizing on the last-minute international crisis. Stevenson had placed his greatest emphasis on the test ban proposal, with the premise that the Soviet Union could be trusted to cooperate on efforts to control the awesome nuclear weapons. Soviet ruthlessness in crushing the Hungarian revolt and Russian threats against England and France made his whole approach appear unrealistic to the American people and discredited his claim to Cold War leadership. Yet one can understand the bitterness of the Stevenson aide who commented, "Apparently all you have to do to win elections is to make fatal mistakes in foreign policy." One of the Democratic candidate's biographers summed up the irony of the 1956 election best when he wrote that "it was impossible to defeat a president whose aces in the hole were peace, prosperity — and war."

II

Eisenhower's popularity was never higher than when he began his second term in office on January 20, 1957; 79 percent of those surveyed by the Gallup poll approved his conduct of the presidency. Fresh from his triumphant reelection, he seemed in full command and yet there were already signs of the difficulties that would gradually overwhelm him during the next four years. The passage of the 22nd amendment, limiting Presidents to two terms in office, made Eisenhower a lame duck in the White House; the resentment of GOP right wingers who complained of his failure to help regain Republican control of Congress further weakened his power of leadership. Minority Leader William Knowland was often at odds with the White House and Eisenhower could rely more on the cooperation of the two Texas Democrats who dominated Congress, House Speaker Sam Rayburn and Senate Majority Leader Lyndon Johnson. The Texans slipped quietly into the White House at least once a month to have a late afternoon drink with the President and to work out legislative problems with him. But the Democratic leaders, sensitive to liberal charges that they were too cooperative with a Republican President, frequently used their power to block Eisenhower's program in Congress. Johnson, who had presidential ambitions of his own, took pleasure in keeping the Administration on a short leash and constantly letting the Republicans know who controlled Congressional action without ever risking a showdown with the popular Eisenhower.

Within the Administration, the President still relied heavily on John Foster Dulles and Sherman Adams. Dulles had been stricken with severe stomach cramps during the Suez crisis; he underwent surgery for an abdominal cancer just before the election and, though he returned to office in early 1957, he was a dying man who bravely served as Secretary of State until a month before his death in May 1959. Adams remained as efficient as ever in handling domestic problems for Ike, but his determination to protect the President from minor squabbles made him the Administration's hatchet man whose list of enemies kept growing. The cabinet gradually changed in composition. Oveta Culp Hobby dropped out as Secretary of Health, Education and Welfare in 1955, replaced by Marion Folsom, a former Eastman-Kodak executive. After the election, William Rogers, a close friend of the Vice-President, succeeded Herbert Brownell as Attorney General and later in the year the controversial Charles Wilson gave way to Neil McElroy, the more diplomatic president of Proctor and Gamble, as Secretary of Defense. The most significant change came in mid-1957 when George Humphrey stepped down as Secretary of the Treasury to return to private life. Eisenhower missed Humphrey's ebullient charm and candid advice, but he came to rely heavily on his equally conservative successor, Robert B. Anderson, a Texas banker and former Secretary of the Navy who was Ike's private choice to succeed him in the White House.

These changes did not reflect any fundamental shift in the political character of the Administration. Despite Eisenhower's adoption of the phrase "Modern Republicanism," coined by speech-writer Arthur Larson, the President did not actively seek to transform the GOP along liberal or progressive lines. He kept calling for new, young leadership, but he continued to surround himself with middle-aged business executives who displayed enlightened but essentially moderate views on the nation's domestic problems. The President's legislative program — federal aid for school construction, a major interstate highway system financed by users' taxes, a modest civil rights law to protect Negro voting rights, extension of social security, and the raising of the minimum wage suggest a distinctly middle-of-the-road approach that had characterized the Administration from the outset. Ike wanted to alleviate some of the more pressing economic and social concerns without engaging in any deep-seated reforms.

A balanced budget, the issue closest to his heart, touched off a major battle with Congress in 1957 and caused the President great anguish. Bent on curbing

deficit spending when he came into office, Eisenhower finally achieved that
goal in fiscal years 1956 and 1957, with surpluses of $4.5 and $2 billion, respectively. Heavier expenditures for defense and foreign aid, however, led Ike
to give his reluctant consent to a budget of $72 billion for fiscal year 1958,
an increase of $3 billion in federal spending. National defense accounted for
$45 billion of this sum, and Eisenhower had kept a tight rein on outgoing
Defense Secretary Wilson to prevent an even sharper rise. In explaining his
budget to Republican leaders, Ike complained of the insatiable demands of
the Pentagon, saying, "This country can choke itself to death piling up military
expenditures just as surely as it can defeat itself by not spending enough for
protection." In a New Year's Day conference with the Congressional leadership, the President promised to "do everything possible to keep down federal
expenditures" and asked Congress not to exceed his limits in appropriations.

In a press conference two weeks later, Secretary Humphrey stressed the
same economy theme and then, apparently fearful of excessive spending by
liberal Democrats, added an off-the-cuff warning. "If we fail to economize
over a longer period of time," he commented, "I will predict that you will
have a depression that will curl your hair...." Newspapers responded with
headlines proclaiming that the Treasury Secretary viewed Eisenhower's increased
budget as likely to lead to a serious depression, suggesting a major rift within
the Administration. A few days later Eisenhower compounded the problem
by telling reporters that he would welcome cuts in his budget. If Congress
can find places to save dollars, Ike concluded, "it is their duty to do it."
Right-wing Republicans immediately embarrassed the President by claiming
they could easily lop off $2 or $3 billion; conservative Democrat Harry Byrd
topped them by proposing cuts amounting to $6½ billion. Lyndon Johnson
led the resulting economy drive in Congress against what he termed the Administration's "swollen budget." Realizing belatedly that he had invited Congress
to engage in the politicially attractive game of budget cutting, Eisenhower
fought hard to resist cuts in both defense and foreign aid. In a showdown,
however, Congress held all the high cards, and Rayburn and Johnson were
finally able to pare $4 billion, including a whopping $1.6 billion from foreign
aid funds. The outcome of the battle of the budget, as Sherman Adams confessed, was "a serious and disturbing personal defeat" for the President.

The economy drive in Congress ended quickly when Humphrey's prediction
of a hair-curling depression came true with the onset of a recession in the fall
of 1957. A sharp drop in private investment and a slump in durable goods
manufacturing led to an economic decline marked by rising unemployment
and falling factory production. The President and Congress responded by
vigorous federal spending that helped counterbalance the decline in the private
sector and finally overcame the recession by the middle of 1958, though unemployment, which reached a high of over 5 million, continued to remain a

problem for the next three years. As a result of this prompt governmental action, as well as new spending for the arms race, Congress made up the $4 billion cut and added an additional $4.5 billion to Eisenhower's original budget. Thus the President not only was forced by Congress to assume the stance of opposing economy in government but had to face the continuation of heavy deficit financing, something he deeply resented. The ultimate embarrassment came in fiscal year 1959, when the accelerated rate of spending led to a deficit of more than $12 billion, the greatest ever reached in the United States in peacetime.

III

Civil rights remained the most disturbing domestic issue facing the Eisenhower Administration in the latter half of the 1950s. The President and his advisers placed their faith in gradual change in attitudes and customs, but the Negroes of the South, encouraged by the Supreme Court desegregation decision, refused to wait passively any longer. A new mood of black militancy first manifested itself in Montgomery, Alabama, a city of 50,000 Negroes and 70,000 whites, where both tradition and local ordinances had kept the two races apart. On the evening of December 1, 1955, Mrs. Rosa Parks, a black seamstress, violated a local law by taking a seat in the front of a city bus and refusing to move to the rear. Police quickly arrested her but, unlike past incidents, the Negro community refused to accept the outcome. Under the leadership of Reverend Martin Luther King, a young Baptist minister who had recently taken a church in the city, the Montgomery blacks decided to band together and boycott the bus system in protest over segregated seating. Since Negroes had formed the majority of riders, the buses began to run virtually empty, at great cost to the city. Despite intense pressure and harrassment, the blacks clung to their boycott, organizing car pools to take people to work and to shop. Eleven months later, the Supreme Court ruled the Alabama segregation laws unconstitutional, giving the blacks a great victory, not only by enabling them to sit where they pleased in Montgomery buses, but proving that through united action they could begin to achieve their full rights as American citizens. Martin Luther King summed up the feelings of millions of black Americans when he voiced his belief that "God had decided to use Montgomery as the proving ground for the struggle and triumph of freedom and justice in America."

Both the Supreme Court ruling and the black militancy gave rise to a predictable movement of southern whites to hold the line on the race issue. In 1955, White Citizens Councils sprung up across the South as racists vowed their determination to keep the schools their children attended lily-white and to deny blacks any meaningful form of social equality. The Councils usually relied primarily on moral and economic pressure to carry out their segregationist policies, but they occasionally hinted at more violent means. A handbill distributed in Montgomery in 1956 aped the Declaration of Independence by asserting, "When in the course of human events it becomes necessary to abolish the Negro race...." and affirming among the truths that were self-evident, "life, liberty and the pursuit of dead niggers." Southern political leaders carefully avoided references to violence, but they made clear their opposition to the mingling of the races in a Southern Manifesto in 1956 signed by 101 members of Congress, including every southern senator except Estes Kefauver and Albert Gore of Tennessee and Lyndon Johnson of Texas. This document denounced the 1954 Supreme Court decision as "a clear abuse of judicial power" and pledged "to use all lawful means to bring about a reversal of this decision which is contrary to the Constitution." Meanwhile, on the state level, governors and legislatures adopted the policy of massive resistance, passing laws to interpose the power of the states to prevent the integration of schools. These tactics, which ranged from creating private schools supported by state tuition payments to the total closing of all public schools in a region, as happened in Prince Edward County in Virginia from 1959 to 1964, brought the actual process of integration to a halt across the South after 1956.

The Eisenhower Administration gave very little leadership during this confusing period of social change. The President's reluctance to interfere in state activities became clear when Autherine Lucy, a black graduate student, tried to attend classes at the University of Alabama and was finally suspended by university officials to protect her from mob violence. Asked if the Justice Department would intervene to protect Miss Lucy's rights, Ike replied, "I certainly hope that we could avoid any interference as long as the state, from the Governor on down, will do its best to straighten it out." The local authorities then proceeded to "straighten it out" by expelling Miss Lucy for bringing suit against the university's board of trustees. Eisenhower sincerely believed in local autonomy in social and racial matters, but he failed to realize how vital federal action was to overcome deep-grained southern attitudes and traditions.

Some of his advisers, notably Attorney General Herbert Brownell, believed that the Administration should take a stronger stand on civil rights. Accordingly, in March 1956, the Administration presented a civil rights bill to Congress that proposed steps to protect Negro voting rights in the South through the creation of both a bipartisan Commission on Civil Rights and a special section of the Justice Department devoted to civil rights matters. The House passed this relatively mild measure in July but, with the election coming up, Majority Leader Lyndon Johnson sent it to the Senate Judiciary Committee chaired by James Eastland of Mississippi, an arch segregationist. In 1956, neither party was anxious to secure action on civil rights legislation; both were simply maneuvering for support from both northern blacks and southern whites.

After Eisenhower's reelection, both parties began to reconsider their stands on civil rights. Ike cut into the normal Democratic monopoly over Negro votes with important gains in northern cities such as New York and Chicago. In 1957, Brownell again persuaded the President to submit the earlier civil rights bill to Congress, and this time a change in attitude by Lyndon Johnson greatly improved its chances. With an eye on 1960, LBJ wanted to transform himself from a regional politician, who had always opposed civil rights measures in Congress, into a national leader with a broader outlook. Accordingly, he set out to avoid the southern filibuster that had doomed previous civil rights legislation by working behind the scenes to make the measure as innocuous as possible. He concentrated on two amendments. One would strike out Part III of the bill, which gave the Justice Department broad power to file civil rights injunctions not only in voting disputes but in school cases as well. The other dealt with insisting on the right of trial by jury for southerners found guilty of contempt of court in violating the rights of blacks to vote. With help from Eisenhower, who told a surprised press conference that it was "a mistake...to go too far too fast in laws in this delicate field," Johnson succeeded in getting the Senate to strike out Part III. There was a much greater fight over jury trials, which northern liberals felt would result in almost certain acquittal for southern defendants, and thus emasculate the whole bill. The Senate voted in favor of jury trials, and the Administration finally worked out a compromise in conference committee that permitted a federal judge to decide in each case whether a jury trial would be suitable.

The Civil Rights Act of 1957, the product of lukewarm Administration support and Johnson's shrewd backroom tactics, marked at best only a small step forward with the creation of the Civil Rights Commission and the new Justice Department division to protect Negro voting rights, but it stood as the first Congressional action in this field since 1875. The southern Negro, long systematically excluded from the electoral process, would now have the assistance of the federal government in his fight to reach the ballot box. A second Civil Rights Act in 1960 remedied some of the weaknesses in the 1957 legislation and helped increase the growing numbers of blacks who voted in the South, and thus began to have an impact on wary southern politicians. But throughout the 1950s, neither Congress nor the Administration would advocate action in the far more important and sensitive areas of public accommodations and economic opportunities. The Negro traveling in the South could still not stay at downtown hotels nor eat in the restaurants, and the economic disparity between the black and white worker throughout the country remained a huge gap that symbolized how far the nation had to go to realize the goal of first-class citizenship regardless of race.

The first real showdown between federal and state power over desegregation came in September 1957, just after Congress passed the Civil Rights Act. A federal judge had ordered the Little Rock school board to begin integrating its system, starting with Central High School. When school opened in September, Governor Orval Faubus, who had recently defeated an avowed segregationist in the Democratic primary, announced that the Arkansas National Guard would prevent the Negro students from attending Central High School, justifying his step as necessary to keep order and block expected mob action. The school board kept the nine Negro young people involved away from the school the first day of classes, and President Eisenhower showed no inclination to intervene, telling a press conference that "you cannot change people's hearts merely by laws." But the judge ordered the school board to proceed with integration "forthwith," and the next day the nine young blacks approached the doors of Central High, where 270 guardsmen were drawn up and a crowd of several thousand jeering whites had assembled. When fifteen-year-old Elizabeth Ann Eckford walked quietly up to the school door, a trooper barred her path and then the crowd hurled insults as she walked away.

Speculation now centered on how Eisenhower would respond to Governor Faubus' flagrant attempt to undermine a federal court order. Back in July, Ike told reporters that he could not imagine a situation requiring him "to send federal troops. . .into any area to enforce the orders of a federal court." Now he took a sterner position, telling Faubus that "the Federal Constitution will be upheld by me by every legal means at my command." But he still hoped to avoid a direct confrontation and, when Sherman Adams and Arkansas Congressman Brook Hays, a moderate on the race issue, arranged for a meeting with the defiant governor, Ike agreed to see him in Newport, Rhode Island, where the President was vacationing. Eisenhower and Faubus met alone for twenty minutes, and then Brownell joined them to outline in clear terms the Administration's determination to enforce the court's decision. Faubus returned to Arkansas and, when the court ordered him to remove the National Guard on September 20, he complied. When the nine teenagers then tried once again to enter Central High, a crowd of over 500 gathered around the school chanting, "Two, four, six, eight, we ain't gonna integrate." The blacks entered the building, but the mob grew in size and became increasingly uglier in mood, until at midday the Mayor of Little Rock ordered the Negroes home to prevent violence. The Mayor then sent a telegram to the President describing the tense scene and pleading with him to send federal troops "in the interest of humanity, law and order and because of democracy world wide." On September 21, the President acted, placing 10,000 Arkansas National Guardmen on federal status and ordering 1000 paratroopers into Little Rock to enforce the court order. The next day the nine Negroes returned for a third time and, under armed protection, began attending classes. The mob jeered, but it obeyed the troops' orders to move back, one man being cut slightly by a bayonet when he tried to hold his ground.

The federal troops remained in Little Rock for the rest of the school year, but the high school was closed from 1958 to 1959 and only opened again, with three black students, after another court order in 1959. Similar incidents occurred in Mansfield, Texas, and Clinton, Tennessee, though neither led to direct federal intervention. Eisenhower succeeded in maintaining the principle of federal supremacy in Little Rock, but his action, taken with such obvious reluctance (Sherman Adams called it "the most repugnant to him of all his acts in his eight years in the White House"), did not serve to speed the cause of school integration. By the end of his second term, only 765 of the nearly 7000 school districts in the South had ended segregation, and only 7 percent of all black students in the South were receiving an integrated education. Even in those communities where the races were mingled, the process usually followed the Little Rock formula, with integration of the high schools first, then the junior high schools three years later, and the elementary schools, one grade at a time, after another three years. The result was a slow and frustrating process that added greatly to the level of racial tension without providing southern blacks with the superior education they so desperately needed to compete more equally in American society.

IV

On October 4, 1957, with the Little Rock crisis fading from the headlines, the Soviet Union amazed the world by launching Sputnik, the first artificial earth satellite. The United States had announced plans to send up such a satellite as part of its observance of the International Geophysical Year from July 1957 to December 1958, but the Russians had struck first, gaining a great propaganda victory that they were quick to exploit. Americans reacted in shocked disbelief that was heightened when the first attempts to duplicate the Russian feat at Cape Canaveral ended in humiliating failure. The United States, which had always prided itself on technical leadership, now had to take second place to the once backward Soviet Union.

The public outcry in the United States came close to hysteria. Lyndon Johnson spoke out for the Democrats by asserting that "the Soviets have beaten us at our own game — daring scientific advances in the atomic age." He began to put pressure on the Administration to step up its space program, as did the American Aviation Publishers, who proclaimed, "The nation that first controls space will control the world. The choice is democracy or slavery." Eisenhower tried to quiet the uproar by claiming that the Sputnik "does not raise my apprehensions, not one iota." Former Defense Secretary Charles Wilson dismissed the Russian feat as "a nice technical trick," while Sherman Adams warned against getting involved with the Russians in "an outer-space basketball game." Privately, Eisenhower admitted he was concerned about the Russian achievement, and he responded by appointing MIT President James Killian to the new post of Special Assistant to the President for Science and Technology. He also asked Arthur Larson to prepare a series of speeches designed to reassure the American people, but a slight stroke the President suffered in November, which left him with a temporary speech impediment, forced him to give up this effort. He did order a speedup in American efforts to launch a satellite and finally, in January, the Army succeeded in sending the tiny Explorer into orbit, to the great relief of both the President and the American people.

The real significance of Sputnik lay in its military implications. Both the United States and the Soviet Union were trying to perfect an Inter-Continental Ballistic Missile (ICBM), a rocket powerful enough to hurl a hydrogen warhead some 5000 miles across the earth's surface. The Russians had tested an ICBM in August 1957, and the Sputnik gave proof that they possessed a rocket engine of far greater power than anything the United States was developing. The United States was trailing the Soviets in testing its Atlas ICBM, and vocal dissidents within the Pentagon criticized the Administration for refusing to approve a crash program in missiles. In the fall of 1957, Rowan Gaither, head of the Ford Foundation, delivered the secret report of a blue ribbon private panel on the state of the nation's defenses to the National Security Council. The Gaither Report claimed that the Russians were capable of surpassing the United States in nuclear striking power and warned of a possible Soviet first-strike against the United States as early as 1959. Gaither recommended a massive fallout shelter program that Eisenhower quickly rejected. At the same time, a Rockefeller Brothers report, written largely by Henry Kissinger, took an equally pessimistic view of American defenses and advocated a $3 billion increase in defense spending for the next ten years. In early 1958, Lyndon Johnson released the report of his Senate Defense Preparedness Subcommittee. Though the report avoided direct criticism of the Administration, it urged a rapid increase in spending for the nation's missile and space programs and led the President to create, later in the year, the National Aeronautics and Space Administration (NASA) to supervise American efforts to match the Russian achievements in space.

Johnson avoided a head-on clash with President Eisenhower, but other Democrats now began a partisan attack on the Administration with talk of a missile gap. Senator Stuart Symington of Missouri, who had served as Secretary of the Air Force under Truman, criticized the President for failure to spend all the funds Congress appropriated for missiles, and Senator John F. Kennedy joined in the assault, prophesying that "The deterrent ratio during 1960-1964 will in all likelihood be weighted against us." Symington and Kennedy, who both had presidential ambitions, used data supplied by disgruntled Pentagon sources, as did columnist Joseph Alsop, who warned that by

1962 the Soviet Union would have 1000 ICBMs to only 130 for the United States. Eisenhower refused to take these estimates seriously. He knew from American U-2 reports that the Soviets had stopped testing ICBMs after the first one in 1957, and he knew that there had been no actual missile deployment in Russia, which suggested the Soviets had run into unexpected difficulties in their program. Meanwhile, he refused to commit large sums to the building of first-generation, liquid-fuel missiles such as the Atlas, which were both unreliable and extremely vulnerable to enemy attack. Instead he devoted the bulk of the missile money to the second-generation weapons, the solid-fuel Polaris launched from submarines and the Minuteman ICBM, which could be buried deep beneath the surface in a concrete silo.

Eisenhower proved right about the missile program. By the end of his Administration, no gap had opened up. The Russians deployed a handful of ICBMs, while the United States had three Atlas missiles operational by early 1960 and the first Polaris submarine already on patrol. He had not gambled with national security, and he was furious at what he considered irresponsible attacks from the Democrats. "The idea of *them* charging *me* with not being interested in *defense*!" he exclaimed to Emmet Hughes. "Damn it, I've spent my whole life being concerned with defense of our country." Yet Ike had failed to convey to the nation the wisdom of his defense policies and thus had contributed to a growing sense of insecurity and anxiety. Acting on the simple conviction that the people should trust him in national security matters, and perhaps fearful of compromising the secret U-2 flights, he had not given Americans the assurances that they so desperately wanted.

V

The difficulties that beset Eisenhower during his second term seemed to reach their peak with the mild stroke on November 25, 1957. At first he felt only a slight dizziness, but then he began to have trouble speaking, especially in searching for the right word and having it come out properly. Doctors prescribed rest, and once again Sherman Adams tried to shield Ike from the burdens of office. "This man is not what he was," Adams told Arthur Larson in early December. But the President insisted on continuing with his duties and went ahead with a planned trip to Paris for a major NATO conference in mid-December. He carried off this arduous task effectively and then came back to deliver his State-of-the-Union message to Congress with hardly a slip. He made a private agreement with Vice-President Nixon in regard to stepping down if his health deteriorated suddenly but, although he still experienced mild difficulty with certain words, he recovered quickly and ended doubts as to his ability to remain in office.

Two major foreign policy crises in 1958 tested both Eisenhower's vitality and his capacity for leadership. The first came in the Middle East, which had remained tense following the Suez fiasco in 1956. British and French forces had left Egypt under UN supervision, and the Administration had tried to fill the power vacuum by securing a Congressional resolution authorizing the President to extend American military and economic aid to any Middle Eastern nation threatened by Communist aggression. The Eisenhower Doctrine, as the new policy was known, depended on the willingness of countries in this area to ask for American assistance and, by 1958, the tide seemed to be moving in the opposite direction. Early in the year, Egypt and Syria merged to form the United Arab Republic (UAR) and then Nasser launched a concerted propaganda effort to force pro-Western Jordan and Lebanon to join the new Arab confederation. Frightened by growing rebel activity within his country, President Camille Chamoun of Lebanon began to seek American support in the spring, but Ike preferred not to intervene, favoring instead an investigation under UN auspices.

The situation became critical on July 14 when news arrived in Washington of a bloody coup that had overthrown the government of Iraq, a staunch American ally and member of the Baghdad Pact. Officials in Washington feared that the new Iraqi leader was a puppet of Nasser (actually he proved to be an independent nationalist) and, when President Chamoun asked for American military intervention to save his beleaguered regime, Eisenhower and Dulles decided it was time for the United States to move. The President met that morning with the National Security Council and came away convinced that only a prompt American response could restore order to the Middle East. He explained his intentions to Congressional leaders in an early afternoon meeting and then gave General Nathan Twining, Chairman of the Joint Chiefs, the signal to go ahead. "We're going to send in everything we've got," the President commented confidently, "and this thing will be over in forty-eight hours if we do so."

The next day 1700 marines splashed ashore and moved quickly to secure Beirut and the nearby airport. Reinforcements soon arrived to build up the American forces to over 14,000, including troops armed with tactical atomic artillery, but Eisenhower kept a tight rein on the military. When some Pentagon officials said they wanted to occupy all Lebanon, Ike insisted on limiting American troops to the capital, explaining that if the Lebanese army could not control the remainder of the country, "I felt we were backing up a government with so little popular support that we probably should not be there." Eisenhower did not hesitate, however, in redeploying units of the Strategic Air Command to serve as a warning to the Russians not to interfere with the American operation. Bolstered by this show of force, President Chamoun was able to restore order in Lebanon and thus permit the last American troops to leave in late October. This prompt use of force served to quiet the Middle

East, easing fears of either a Communist or Arab nationalist takeover of the whole area. Above all, Ike had demonstrated once more his capacity for wise but restrained leadership in international affairs, the quality that so endeared him to the American people.

The sudden resumption of Chinese Communist shelling of Quemoy and Matsu in August 1958 created a more ominous showdown in Asia. The Formosa Straits had been quiet since 1955, when Eisenhower and Dulles had made clear the American determination to defend the offshore islands if they considered an attack on them threatened the Nationalists on Taiwan. In the intervening years, the Peking regime had bolstered its forces on the mainland, particularly by building up a series of airfields from which MIG fighters could operate. At the same time, Chiang had placed more than 100,000 troops, one third of his entire army, on these small islands and used them for commando raids against the Reds. The Communist barrage, aimed primarily at Quemoy and designed to cut off the island from Nationalist supplies and reinforcements, created a serious problem for the President. On the advice of the Joint Chiefs, he wanted to pursue an ambiguous policy, keeping both the Communists and the Nationalists guessing. If he took a strong stand to defend the islands, Chiang might decide to launch an attack against the mainland. If he refused to defend the outposts, however, he would invite a Communist takeover.

For the next month, Eisenhower tried to keep this complex and dangerous situation under control. To restrain the Chinese Communists, he permitted American naval vessels to escort relief convoys to within three miles of the islands and he let it be known that eight-inch atomic howitzers had been deployed on Quemoy and Matsu. He also permitted Dulles to issue a statement in early September reiterating the Administration's commitment to defend the islands and making them appear to be intimately related to the defense of Formosa itself. At the same time, he resisted military efforts to delegate authority over the use of the tactical atomic weapons in the field, and he reassured the nation in a special television address on September 14. "There is not going to be any appeasement," he told the American people, and then added, "I believe there is not going to be any war."

Eisenhower's mixture of firmness and restraint eventually defused the crisis. In September, the Chinese signaled their desire to reduce tension by resuming informal diplomatic talks in Warsaw and a month later the Peking regime stopped the artillery barrage for a week. When they resumed firing, the Communists did so only on the odd days of the month, letting the Nationalists resupply the island outposts on the even ones and leading Eisenhower to wonder "if we were in a Gilbert and Sullivan war." Though intermittent firing continued to take place in the Formosa Straits, the situation gradually subsided and the fear of war ended.

Like the Lebanon intervention, the offshore island flare-up showed Eisenhower at his best, acting judiciously in a perilous international situation. At the height of the crisis, the Joint Chiefs suddenly recommended a total withdrawal from Quemoy and Matsu, a step that made military sense but that would have had disastrous political consequences. Ike ignored the suggestion, though he did send Dulles to Taiwan to try, unsuccessfully, to have Chiang reduce the level of his forces on the islands. Eisenhower's ability to assess every aspect of a problem, unshaken by the emotions of those around him, stood out as his greatest asset. "It was good to see him so relaxed," commented one close associate. "There was no hurling of thunderbolts. . . .I realized as never before why a President is so important — to be able to give others, at such a time, an impression of unruffled assurance and confidence."

VI

At home, things continued to go badly for Eisenhower and the Republicans. The recession deepened in the early months of 1958, hitting its low point in April when over 5 million workers, 7 percent of the nation's labor force, were unemployed. Though the President resisted the most sweeping Democratic proposals for energetic spending to curb the economic decline, he abandoned his hopes for a balanced budget and accepted a heavy deficit for fiscal year 1959. The Democrats kept harping on the missile gap, forcing the Administration on the defensive and securing larger military appropriations than Eisenhower thought were necessary. And then scandal hit the White House as Sherman Adams, the President's trusted right-hand man, became the center of a political controversy.

Conflict of interest had haunted the Administration since 1952, when Nixon had been forced to explain his secret fund. Secretary of the Air Force Harold Talbott had resigned under fire in 1955, charged with using his position to favor a private company that he partly owned, and GOP National Chairman Wesley Roberts had been replaced after he had engaged in some questionable real estate transactions. But these scandals were minor compared to the revelation of the House Legislative Oversight Committee in June 1958 that Bernard Goldfine, a New England industrialist, had not only paid more than $3000 of Adams' hotel bills but had given him a luxurious oriental rug and a $700 vicuña coat (described by Arthur Larson as "a spectacularly unattractive garment"). In return, Sherman Adams had contacted both the Federal Trade Commission and the Securities and Exchange Commission on behalf of Goldfine and, though he had not done more than express an interest in the cases, these federal bodies had quickly dropped punative actions against Goldfine's companies. Adams appeared in person before the House committee to explain his actions and, while admitting to no impropriety, he confessed that he might have acted with "a little more prudence." The next day, Eisenhower read a statement to the press regretting his aide's "imprudence" but defending his basic honesty. The President greatly weakened his own position, however, by asserting: "I personally like Governor Adams. I admire his abilities. I respect him because of his personal and official integrity. I need him."

Reporters had a field day suggesting that Adams virtually ran the country for Eisenhower, referring to him variously as the "Rasputin" of the Administration and as the "abominable no-man" who performed all the unpleasant tasks for the White House. With his flinty personality, Adams had won few friends and made many enemies during his five years in Washington, and he found his position rapidly becoming untenable. Fellow Republicans, especially conservatives who had carried on a running battle with the White House staff, led the assaults, claiming that Adams would doom the GOP to defeat in the fall elections. Vice-President Nixon became the chief funnel for these right-wing complaints, reporting to Eisenhower in mid-July that the vast majority of Republicans felt Adams should resign. Ike hated to wield the hatchet himself, and he finally relied on Nixon and GOP National Chairman Meade Alcorn to explain the situation to Adams. On September 22, Adams flew to Newport, where the President was vacationing, and submitted his resignation, which Ike quickly if regretfully accepted. Later the President gave Adams a silver bowl with the inscription, "For Tireless Service to the Public, Brilliant Performance of Every Duty and Unsurpassed Dedication to his Country." In a more cynical vein, Emmet Hughes commented to Adams, "Well, the vultures of the Grand Old Party finally descended," and received a tight smile and the laconic response, "That's the great game of politics."

The Adams controversy threw the Republicans off stride as they entered into the 1958 Congressional elections, but it was not the decisive factor. The recession, though gradually tapering off in the summer, left unemployment at a high level and thus gave the Democrats a powerful issue. Republicans contributed to their own predicament in six states, including Ohio, by advocating right-to-work laws that brought out a massive labor vote for Democratic candidates. Eisenhower sent Richard Nixon out to try to stem the tide, but his charges that "the Acheson foreign policy resulted in war" hardly reassured voters in 1958. The President abandoned his traditional aloofness to campaign for GOP candidates; he made little headway with his denunciation of Democrats as "political radicals...self-styled liberals...with the irresistible impulse... to squander money – your money." Given this kind of campaign, it is hard not to agree with Emmet Hughes' assertion that in 1958 "the Republicans raced toward disaster."

The election resulted in an even greater setback than Republicans had feared. The Democrats picked up 47 seats in the House and an incredible 13 in the Senate to give them commanding majorities in both branches of Congress. Nationwide, Democrats outpolled the Republicans by nearly 6 million votes;

the sole major GOP victory came in New York, where Nelson Rockefeller won the governorship. Yet even this event provided Eisenhower with little solace, since Rockefeller had become a vocal critic of both the Administration's domestic and defense policies. The election meant that the President would face a hostile Congress during his final years in office with his own power of leadership crippled by the cumulative impact of Sputnik, continuing unemployment, the Adams scandal, and his status as a lame duck.

VII

Ending the Cold War remained Eisenhower's greatest goal and, during his last two years in the White House, he devoted nearly all his time and energy to this noble quest. He made one decisive stride forward in the crucial nuclear arms race when he announced on August 22, 1958 that the United States would suspend nuclear testing. This step came after a successful preliminary technical conference between American and Russian scientists on methods of detection and inspection, and the American test ban was conditioned on both a reciprocal Russian suspension and progress in further negotiations on methods of supervision and enforcement. After one final series of tests in early November 1958, the Russians refrained from further explosions in the atmosphere. There were no more nuclear tests for the remainder of Eisenhower's term in office, thus alleviating the dangerous problem of atmospheric fallout that Adlai Stevenson had called to the nation's attention in 1956.

In Europe, however, Ike's hopes for peace received a severe setback in late 1958 when Khrushchev suddenly reopened the perilous issue of Berlin. In a Moscow speech on November 10 the Soviet leader deplored the continuing occupation of the German city, and announced his intention of signing a peace treaty with the East German government that would have the effect of terminating allied rights in Berlin. In a formal diplomatic note on November 27, Khrushchev proposed that West Berlin be made into a free city while East Berlin would be incorporated into Communist-controlled East Germany. Ominously, Khrushchev gave the West a six-month deadline; if negotiations had not proved successful by that time, he planned to proceed with a separate peace treaty for East Germany, turning over Soviet rights in Berlin to a regime that the Western nations refused to recognize. When the United States quickly responded by stating that it would discuss the idea of a free city only if all Berlin were involved, everyone prepared for a diplomatic and possibly a military showdown by late May, when Khrushchev's deadline was due to expire.

On January 1, 1959, the Cold War came much closer to home with the emergence of Fidel Castro as the new ruler of Cuba. Throughout the 1950s, the United States had largely ignored Latin America in its concern with the threat of Communism in Asia and the Middle East. Only a tiny fraction of foreign aid went to the nations of the Western Hemisphere, whose loyalty was taken for granted. Dulles became concerned about the leftist Arbenz regime in Guatemala in 1954 and, after he failed to secure hemispheric sanctions against it, the CIA helped carry out a coup that brought a conservative military group to power and ended whatever danger of Communist penetration had existed in Central America. Four years later, the demonstrations and mob violence that greeted Vice-President Nixon on a good will tour of South America, culminating in an ugly car-rocking incident in Caracas, brought home to the American people the deep hatred felt by many Latin Americans toward the United States. Yet, when Castro climaxed his long guerrilla struggle with a tumultuous entry into Havana, most Americans expressed sympathy and even admiration for his cause, seeing him as a much more democratic leader that the deposed Fulgencio Batista. Sentiment in the United States soon turned against the new Cuban government, however, as a result of the brutal vengeance wrought on Batista's supporters, complete with hasty trials and mass executions that smacked of the Russian purges of the 1930s, and the gradual but unmistakable drift of Cuba into the Russian orbit in foreign policy. The Eisenhower Administration treated Castro with remarkable patience and restraint during 1959, but a future showdown seemed more and more likely as the Cuban leader found anti-Americanism to be his most successful rallying cry.

As Eisenhower faced the dilemmas posed by Khrushchev's Berlin ultimatum and Castro's growing hostility, he lost the services of the man he trusted most in foreign policy. The cancer that first attacked John Foster Dulles during the Suez crisis returned in early 1959; in April, after a gallant attempt to hang on, Dulles resigned as Secretary of State and the next month he died. The two men had worked closely together for six years and, though at times they had disagreed, Dulles had always subordinated his own views to those of the President and had served him with the greatest loyalty and devotion. Eisenhower quickly appointed Christian Herter as Secretary of State and, though Herter proved to be a competent replacement, the President never placed the same degree of confidence in him that he had in Dulles. Herter flew to Geneva four days after taking office to participate in a Foreign Ministers Conference on Berlin, which made little headway but permitted Khrushchev to allow his May 27 deadline to pass without a confrontation.

Eisenhower now began to play a new and more active role in American foreign policy, one that he had been contemplating since late 1958. At a meeting with Emmet Hughes in December, the President talked of a memorandum he and Jim Hagerty had prepared that called for Ike to assume the role of "the Man of Peace" by embarking on world travels and by seeking the personal meetings with Khrushchev that Dulles had always opposed. Eisenhower became excited as he spoke to Hughes about his resolve to engage in personal diplomacy, outlining with growing enthusiasm the "positive offers" he wanted to make to the Soviet leaders. "I'd like to lay before them things that would make clear to all the world our good intentions – things with no strings attached – things positive – things no one could suspect or attack," the President explained. "We should be – generous without surrendering...."

Ike put his ideas into practice in mid-1959 after the death of Dulles. In July, he announced that Khrushchev had accepted an invitation to visit the United States and confer with Eisenhower in September (a visit that Khrushchev had been eager to make and that Ike had been reluctant to offer without some prior sign of Russian agreement on Berlin). Then, in late August, Eisenhower began his personal travels with a trip to Western Europe to reassure the NATO allies that he would not appease Khrushchev when the two leaders met. Huge crowds greeted Ike in Germany, France, and England; Eisenhower returned home with a sense of elation and accomplishment, determined to made additional trips abroad as a way to use his popularity for the cause of peace.

Eisenhower even convinced himself that the Khrushchev visit would be worthwhile, despite the Soviet leader's intransigence on Berlin. "What we are talking about now is finding some little bridge," he told skeptical reporters, "some little avenue yet unexplored, through which we can possibly move toward a better situation." The Soviet leader arrived in an amiable mood in mid-September and, after receiving a formal welcome from Ike in Washington, engaged on a wild twelve-day tour of the country that included a stormy debate with the Mayor of Los Angeles, a denunciation of bourgeois morality on the Hollywood set of the movie *Can-Can,* an angry outburst at being barred from visiting Disneyland on security grounds, and a bucolic visit to an Iowa corn field. He spent the last three days in conference with Eisenhower at the President's Camp David retreat in the Maryland mountains. The two leaders emerged from their talks to announce that they had reached an understanding; the next day, Eisenhower explained that in return for the Soviet leader's withdrawing any time limit, he had agreed to a future summit conference to try to resolve the Berlin dispute. In fact, no real progress had been made on Berlin. The only result of the meeting was an agreement to keep negotiating, but the press dubbed the resulting relaxation in tension as "the spirit of Camp David," and the world breathed a sigh of relief.

The President capped his experiment in personal diplomacy by undertaking a 22,000-mile trip to eleven nations in December 1959. He flew first to India, where his twelve-mile motorcade into New Delhi drew fantastic crowds. He went on to Turkey where a half-million people lined Ataturk Boulevard to cheer Ike, to Morocco to be greeted by thousands of Berber tribesmen at Casablanca, to Rome where the rain failed to dampen the enthusiasm of Italians who raised their cry of "Viva Eek-ay," and finally to Paris, where he engaged in serious diplomacy with Charles de Gaulle, Harold Macmillan, and Konrad Adenauer.

The allied leaders finally agreed to hold a summit conference with Khrushchev in Paris in the spring, thereby fulfilling the promise of the Camp David conference and raising hopes for an ultimate solution to the Berlin crisis.

Ike returned home after a last stop in Spain, where he enjoyed a leisurely visit with Generalissimo Franco and a relatively cool reception from the people of Madrid. He had been gone for three weeks, and along the way he had symbolized the purpose of his travels by handing out hundreds of gold medallions with the inscription "In Appreciation, D.D.E." on one side and "Peace and Friendship in Freedom" on the other. "I talked with Kings and Presidents, Prime Ministers and humble men in cottages and mud huts," he reported to the nation. "Their common denominator was their faith that America will help lead the way toward a just peace." Foreign policy commentators remarked on the failure of the President to resolve the hard issues of the Cold War through his personal diplomacy, citing the continuing Berlin crisis and the ongoing arms race, but the American people responded enthusiastically to his endeavors. A Gallup poll taken in January 1960 showed popular confidence in his leadership at a remarkable 71 percent, the highest in three years. Ike's obvious sincerity and unstinted effort had convinced a majority of Americans that he was indeed "the Man of Peace."

VIII

Despite the President's continuing personal popularity, the Democrats looked forward confidently to the 1960 election. For the first time in eight years, Dwight Eisenhower would not be a candidate, and the Democrats, still the majority party as congressional elections in the 1950s had shown, hoped to win back the millions of voters Ike had lured away. The mood of the nation also seemed to confirm their optimism. Eisenhower had succeeded in relieving the tensions of the early 1950s by ending the Korean War and easing the red scare, but new dilemmas had emerged that created a feeling of national inadequacy. Sputnik had shaken the people's confidence in American superiority. A lagging rate of economic growth, only 2.5 percent in the late 1950s compared to 5 percent for the Soviet Union, Khrushchev's threats to "bury" the United States in peaceful economic competition, and his boast that "your grandchildren will live under Communism" hit home to millions of Americans. Walter Lippmann voiced the growing concern about the loss of American vitality, and even President Eisenhower appointed a special Committee on National Goals, charging it "to sound a call to greatness."

The Democrats had an abundance of potential candidates. Senator Hubert Humphrey of Minnesota entered the race early as the liberal contender; Majority Leader Lyndon Johnson avoided formal candidacy but worked hard behind the scenes to line up support for the nomination. Senator Stuart Symington of Missouri was a dark horse who staked his chances on the single issue of the missile gap. Two-time loser Adlai Stevenson still had a loyal following in the party, but he refused to seek the nomination actively, though he clearly would have welcomed another draft. The front-runner was wealthy Massachusetts Senator John F. Kennedy, who hoped to transform his two apparent handicaps, youth and Catholicism, into political assets.

Kennedy had begun to seek the nomination at the end of the 1956 convention, where he had lost a close race for the vice-presidential spot to Kefauver and, by early 1960, he held a commanding lead in the Gallup poll. Kennedy keyed his effort to the issue of lethargy, offering himself as an energetic and dynamic alternative to the stagnant Eisenhower Administration. He planned to take the same primary route that Kefauver had tried, but with a far more attractive public image and unlimited funds. He swept through the New Hampshire primary in March and then won a narrow victory over Humphrey in Wisconsin, where there was a substantial Catholic vote. West Virginia proved the real test on the religious issue. Stumping this predominantly Protestant state intensively, Kennedy waged a massive, expensive, and well-organized campaign that buried Humphrey, who withdrew from the race with the sardonic comment, "You can't beat a billion dollars."

Vice-President Richard Nixon had virtually no opposition for the Republican nomination. His one possible opponent, Governor Nelson Rockefeller of New York, ended his candidacy in late 1959 when polls showed him trailing the Vice-President by a huge margin among the party's rank and file. Nixon's great handicap lay in his controversial reputation as an emotional and unforgiving partisan, dating back to the Alger Hiss case and savage electioneering tactics in California. He had served as the Administration's political hatchet man in the early Eisenhower years but, by the late 1950s, he was cultivating a new image as a man of experience, wisdom, and judgment who had absorbed Ike's qualities of leadership through years of close association. Pure chance, however, had given Nixon his greatest boost. In July 1959 Eisenhower sent him on a good-will trip to Russia where Nikita Khrushchev, angered by a Captive Nations Resolution just passed by Congress, engaged him in a furious debate before television cameras at an American trade fair in Moscow. Nixon held his ground before Khrushchev's tirade, and the cameras caught him answering back, his finger in the Russian leader's face, in a picture that was worth more than a thousand words. From that time forward, Nixon was known as the man who could stand up to the Russian bully and defend his country, a priceless asset in American politics at the height of the Cold War.

Dramatic world events during the spring of 1960 suddenly overshadowed domestic political maneuvering. On May 1, the Soviets had shot down a U-2 spy plane piloted by Francis Gary Powers on a high-altitude surveillance flight over central Russia. Khrushchev shrewdly withheld information about this feat while the American government put out a cover story to the effect that a "weather plane" had strayed off course and was missing over Russian territory. When the Soviets then informed the world that they had not only shot down the U-2 but held Powers as living proof of American duplicity, Eisenhower finally admitted the truth, taking full responsibility and justifying the overflights on grounds of national security. The Administration, declared Secretary of State Herter, would be "derelict to its duties" if it did not do everything necessary to overcome the "danger of surprise attack." In a press conference on May 11, Eisenhower indicated that the overflights, which many felt should have been halted on the eve of the forthcoming Paris summit conference, would continue in the future as he commented, "Our deterrent must never be placed in jeopardy."

The U-2 flights had been taking place regularly since 1956, despite secret Russian protests over the violation of their air space. Khrushchev evidently felt he had ended them by shooting down Powers' plane; he found Eisenhower's insistence on continuing them intolerable. The Russian leader flew to Paris for the summit conference, but he boycotted the first formal session on May 16, demanding that Eisenhower condemn the U-2 flights and promise to discontinue them as his price for holding the conference. As an added insult, Khrushchev announced that he was withdrawing his previous invitation for Eisenhower to visit Russia later in the year. With great dignity, Eisenhower refused to engage in a shouting match with the Russian leader. He offered no apology, but he did state that he had already suspended U-2 missions and had given orders that they "are not to be resumed." Khrushchev, who realized that the West was not likely to back down on Berlin, the main item on the summit agenda, then left Paris after a stormy news conference with 3000 members of the world's press in which he berated Eisenhower and the West. The Soviet leader, however, was careful not to issue any new ultimatums over Berlin, evidently preferring to await the outcome of the American election before renewing that sensitive issue.

The U-2 fiasco and the collapse of the summit conference suddenly made foreign policy a major consideration in American politics. Though the setbacks would seem to have an adverse effect on the party in power, such was not the case. Eisenhower received a heart-warming reception when he returned home, as more than a million people lined the streets of Washington to cheer him. Nixon, already identified as a man who could stand up to Khrushchev in debate, suddenly forged ahead of Kennedy in the Gallup poll for the first time. Among the Democrats, Adlai Stevenson boosted his chances by condemning the Administration for its clumsy handling of the U-2 flight by which, as he charged, "we handed Khrushchev the crowbar and sledgehammer to wreck" the Paris summit. John Kennedy echoed Stevenson by telling an Oregon audience that he thought that Ike might have offered "an apology" to Khrushchev, but Congressional leaders, guided by Lyndon Johnson, rallied to the President's support. There may have been mistakes, Johnson admitted, "but one mistake that we cannot afford to make right now is to weaken the free world by division within our own ranks."

Political experts predicted that the U-2 incident would slow Kennedy's drive for the nomination, since his youth and inexperience weakened his claim to leadership at a time of grave international tension. But the Kennedy bandwagon, efficiently managed by the candidate's brother Robert, rolled on impressively, sweeping all before it when the Democrats convened in Los Angeles. A last minute attempt to stampede the delegates for Stevenson failed; crowds outside the Sports Arena demonstrated for their eloquent hero, but inside the hall the Kennedy forces kept their lines firm. JFK won easily on the first ballot, and then the next day stunned many of his liberal supporters by choosing Lyndon Johnson as his running mate. Despite the ideological differences, which were not as great as many supposed, the ticket gave the party a chance to retain the South, the area of greatest Republican inroads in the 1950s. In his acceptance speech, Kennedy coined the phrase "New Frontier" in stressing the need for "a new generation of leadership — new men to cope with new problems and new opportunities." Sounding a note that would echo through the coming campaign, Kennedy declared, "All mankind waits upon our decision....We cannot fail their trust; we cannot fail to try." Youth, fervor, enthusiasm, dedication — these were the qualities Kennedy offered the nation as he began his quest for the Presidency.

The world seemed indeed to be in dire straits in the summer of 1960. In June, Eisenhower suffered the most humiliating setback of his entire presidency when 10,000 rioting Japanese students forced the Japanese Prime Minister to cancel the President's forthcoming visit to Japan. Closer to home, Castro became more and more truculent, finally forcing Eisenhower to retaliate by securing Congressional authorization to curtail the Cuban sugar quota drastically. Castro responded by embracing the Soviets, who supplied both economic assistance to his regime and the promise of rocket support in case of American attack. The Monroe Doctrine, Khrushchev proclaimed in July, "has outlived its time,...has died so to say, a natural death." In Africa the newly independent Congo exploded with violence when black soldiers rebelled against their white officers and began a reign of terror in Leopoldville that finally led to UN intervention. The Soviet shooting down of an American reconnaissance plane in the Barents Sea threatened briefly to create another U-2 incident, but this time the United States hit back strongly with evidence that the episode took place over international waters. In the UN, Ambassador Henry Cabot Lodge accused the Russians of engaging in "an act of piracy over the high seas" and impressed American television viewers with his angry denunciation of the Soviets for the "cold-hearted," "cynical," and "brutal" way they waged the Cold War.

These international crises dominated the headlines when the Republicans met in Chicago to confirm their choice of Nixon. The Vice-President, aware that he needed the full backing of the eastern wing of the party, made a last minute deal with Nelson Rockefeller to liberalize that platform on domestic issues and toughen it on foreign policy (Rockefeller was a leading advocate of heavier defense spending). GOP conservatives grumbled at these concessions (Arizona Senator Barry Goldwater labeled the deal "the Munich of the Republican party"), but the convention quickly adopted the amended platform and then nominated Nixon overwhelmingly. The candidate chose Henry Cabot Lodge as his running mate in the belief that Lodge's experience at the United Nations and his reputation as a man who could stand up to the Russians would give the Republicans an unbeatable edge in the all-important foreign policy field. In his acceptance speech, Nixon met the Democrats head on by flatly asserting, "America is the strongest nation militarily, economically and ideologically in the world." Nixon clearly meant to answer Kennedy's challenging call for new leadership by standing on the Eisenhower record and stressing the maturity, experience, and judgment that he and Lodge had gained from serving the man who had presided over eight years of peace and prosperity.

IX

The theme of a deteriorating international situation runs through the 1960 campaign. The Congo remained tense as the UN sought to prevent renewed acts of violence, Castro made increasingly defiant gestures toward the United States, and in September Nikita Khrushchev returned to the United States uninvited to attend the UN General Assembly meeting in New York City. Khrushchev launched a series of bitter tirades against both the United States and the UN, culminating in a dramatic shoe-pounding scene that shocked the American people. Kennedy sought to take advantage of the foreign policy difficulties of the Republicans by constantly reminding voters of declining American prestige in the world and the fact that Cuba had become "a Communist satellite ninety miles off the coast of the United States." Nixon fought back, associating himself with Eisenhower by asserting, "we have ended one war, we have kept out of other wars and we have kept the peace without surrender for eight years."

The two rivals went to extremes in presenting their cases to the American people. Nixon took the position that all was well in the nation and in the world. Ike had brought peace and prosperity out of the mess he inherited from Truman and, as his hand-picked successor, Nixon would continue the same wise policies. Experience, moderation, stability — these were the values the GOP stressed in 1960. The Democrats, on the other hand, portrayed the nation as being mired down in stagnation, with Kennedy hammering away at the necessity of "getting the country moving again." He cited the missile gap, the Russian lead in space, the lagging rate of economic growth, and the sense of national drift in arguing that it was time for new leadership. Kennedy's youth and charm attracted large crowds, especially notable for the women who jumped to catch a glimpse of him and reached out to touch his clothes. Nixon, suffering from an infected knee that hospitalized him for ten days, seemed less dynamic, though he could still bring a partisan audience to its feet, roaring with approval at his sharply barbed attacks on the Democrats.

Two unusual features of the campaign added greatly to the uncertainty of what promised to be very close race. The first was the religious issue, which Kennedy met head-on at the outset in a nationally televised speech to a group of Protestant ministers in Houston. JFK promised not to let religion influence him as president, saying he wanted to be "a Chief Executive whose public acts are responsible to all and obligated to none," but he also appealed shrewdly to the people's sense of fair play by adding, "If this election is decided on the basis that 40 million Americans lost their chance of being President on the day they were baptized, then it is the whole nation that will be the loser." The backlash of sympathy Kennedy evoked helped offset the prejudice many Americans still held against a Catholic candidate and thus went far toward neutralizing the religious issue. The televised debates added the second new dimension to the 1960 contest. Nixon unwisely agreed to them in the belief that he possessed both the skill in verbal confrontation and the mastery of the medium to score an impressive victory. Kennedy prepared carefully for the first exchange, which took place in late September, and he came off extremely well, displaying a quick mind and a sure grasp of national issues as he put Nixon on the defensive. A poor makeup job and the recent loss of ten pounds hurt the Vice-President's visual image and, although in subsequent debates he performed much more effectively, the damage was done. By besting Nixon in the first encounter, Kennedy cut deeply into the GOP claim to experience and maturity and won the respect of many who previously had doubts about his youth and intelligence.

By late October, Kennedy was clearly in the lead, despite a foolish call for evacuation of Quemoy and Matsu, which Nixon promptly labeled appeasement, and an equally rash statement urging aid for Cuban exiles and implying United States support for the return of these "fighters for freedom" to their home-land. A recession that had been building slowly since April hurt Nixon, as unemployment, which had remained high since 1958, rose even more. LBJ, campaigning extensively in the South, began to win back traditional Demo-cratic votes in that area as Nixon's southern strategy suffered a major setback when Henry Cabot Lodge promised northern Negroes that the Republicans would appoint a black cabinet member. At the outset, Nixon had asked Pre-sident Eisenhower to play a passive role in the campaign but, in late October, he appealed to Ike to help reverse the political tide. The popular President, who may have resented his earlier exclusion, drew huge crowds in New York City as he called on voters to support Nixon and Lodge, men who "have advised and helped me well for 8 years," and who "will always be proudly standing for every principle that has made the United States great." Aware of Ike's enormous appeal, Kennedy redoubled his efforts during the last week and pitched his rhetoric uncomfortably high. In his final television speech, JFK referred to the United States as "the sentinel at the gates of freedom around the world," and then proclaimed, "If we succeed, freedom succeeds. If we fail, freedom fails."

The next day the American people went to the polls and gave Kennedy the narrowest of victories. Running well behind Democratic Congressional candidates, JFK carried 23 states with 303 electoral votes, to 26 states with 219 for Nixon (conservative Virginia Senator Harry Byrd picked up 15 electoral votes in Mississippi, Alabama, and Oklahoma), and barely nosed out his Republican opponent in popular votes. The Democratic victory reflected the party's traditional pattern — a combination of heavily populated urban states in the Northeast and Middle West with a smattering of smaller states from the rural South and West. The religious issue cut both ways as postelection surveys indicated that a large gain in Catholic votes almost cancelled out a drop of 18 percent among Protestants who normally voted Democratic. Kennedy appealed strongly to Jewish and Negro voters (a phone call by Bobby Kennedy that led to a quick release for Martin Luther King from a four-month jail sentence in Georgia helped enormously) and, in general, he succeeded in reestablishing the old New Deal coalition that Eisenhower had wrecked in 1952 and 1956.

The outgoing President viewed the results with dismay. Never too fond of Nixon (he had hurt him badly early in the campaign by telling a reporter that if he had "a week" he might be able to cite one idea the Vice-President had contributed to his Administration), Ike had come to resent deeply Kennedy's attacks on his domestic and foreign policies. He viewed his successor as a young upstart who had a great deal to learn about the complex and sensitive issues facing the President of the United States. Above all, he regretted the fact that Kennedy stood for heavier federal spending for space exploration and nation defense. In a farewell address on January 17, 1961, Eisenhower delivered a somber warning to the nation. "In the councils of government," he observed, "we must guard against the acquisition of unwarranted influence, whether sought or unsought, by the military-industrial complex. The potential for the disastrous rise of misplaced power exists and will persist."

There was much that Eisenhower could take pride in as he left office. The nation was far better off than it had been in 1952. He had ended the Korean War, with its serious domestic implications, presided over the passing of McCarthy and the red scare, held down the military's insistent demands for heavier defense spending, and had made the first, halting moves toward detente with the Soviet Union by suspending nuclear testing and meeting with Khrushchev at Geneva and Camp David. At home, he worked cooperatively with a Democratic-controlled Congress to achieve a more modest record of accomplishment. During his two terms in office, Congress had adopted the National Defense Education Act, a limited but important first step toward federal aid to education, admitted Hawaii and Alaska to statehood, approved the long-sought St. Lawrence Seaway, and had enacted a sweeping, $30 billion interstate highway program.

Ike's place in history now seems secure. It is unlikely that he will ever be regarded as a great President; his sense of moderation and restraint kept him from playing the dynamic role in the White House that we associate with the nation's most outstanding leaders. In domestic affairs, his refusal to take an active part in challenging McCarthy's demagogery and in carrying out the full implications of the Supreme Court desegregation decision marred his record. But, in foreign policy, this same quality of restraint served the country extremely well. Eisenhower proved unable to end the Cold War, but he used his great prestige and experience in international affairs to resist pressures from military and diplomatic hawks to escalate the conflict with the Soviet Union. Thus he avoided intervention in Vietnam, limited the confrontation with Communist China in the Formosa Straits, and kept the arms race under control despite the furor touched off by the Soviet Sputnik. Emmet Hughes notes that Ike was at his most decisive when he displayed "a steely resolve *not* to do something that he sincerely believed wrong in itself or alien to his office." This remarkable quality kept him from abusing the power inherent in the presidency and enabled the nation to enjoy a period of relative tranquillity before the onset of the hectic 1960s.

5

The Kennedy Years

John F. Kennedy was a young man in a hurry. He spent little time in the 73 days between his election and inauguration bemoaning the closeness of his victory. Instead he concentrated on the job that lay ahead, building up a team of young, dynamic men who could fulfill his promise of getting the nation moving again. Activity became the hallmark of the Kennedy Administration. During the campaign, the candidate had appointed seven task forces to prepare reports on the vital national problems he would confront as President, ranging from reorganization of the defense establishment to the disposal of agricultural surpluses abroad. In December, he set up nineteen more groups, eleven on foreign policy and eight on domestic issues. By the time he took office in January, Kennedy had more than 100 of the nation's leading experts submitting reports on the problems the New Frontier hoped to solve.

Kennedy approached other aspects of the transition with the same reliance on expert advice. In November, he asked Clark Clifford, Truman's former aide and a prominent Washington attorney, and Richard Neustadt, a political scientist and specialist on the presidency, to prepare reports on the transfer of power, and he appointed Clifford to handle the formal transition with the Eisenhower Administration. The President-elect spent most of his time on the crucial matter of appointments. He accepted suggestions and ideas from a wide range of sources, but he made a special effort to tap the judgment of the eastern Establishment, the tightly knit and powerful legal and financial community centering in New York City that had viewed his election with considerable skepticism. Robert Lovett, a leading banker and former official in the Truman Administration, became Kennedy's chief contact, suggesting the appointment of men who would enjoy the confidence of the Establishment. Lovett's urbane realism contrasted sharply with the liberal idealism of many of Kennedy's supporters, and JFK gave increasing weight to this elder statesman's shrewd advice.

Lovett's influence could be seen in Kennedy's three major cabinet selections. National security had long been the new President's major concern, and thus it was surprising that he chose Robert McNamara, a man he had never met or worked with, for the vital post of Secretary of Defense. Lovett recommended McNamara, the young president of the Ford Motor Company who had the reputation of using computer techniques and systems analysis with ruthless efficiency and, after a careful scrutiny of his credentials, Kennedy offered him the choice of either Treasury or Defense. McNamara had worked in the War Department under Lovett during World War II and, though he had little recent experience with military issues, he accepted Defense after a meeting with Kennedy. Tough-minded and pragmatic, McNamara was an ideal choice for a New Frontier post and, with his enormous energy and supreme confidence in statistics, he would soon become the master of the Pentagon, awing the military with his efficient methods and presiding over a massive buildup in American striking power. Despite his intelligence and dedication, however, McNamara lacked an understanding of human and emotional drives and, in the course of his relentless stewardship, would become the victim of his own narrow approach.

Kennedy's two other top cabinet choices were equally unorthodox. For Treasury, he selected Douglas Dillon, a Republican who served as Under Secretary of State for Eisenhower and had close ties with the Establishment. Dillon, the son of a prominent New York investment banker, held relatively liberal economic ideas, yet his appointment was designed to reassure worried conservatives. The man JFK finally selected for Secretary of State was even more obscure. He offered the post to Lovett, who turned it down for reasons of age and health. Kennedy then disposed of two eager suitors, Adlai Stevenson and Chester Bowles, by appointing them Ambassador to the UN and Under Secretary of State, respectively. After briefly considering Senator William Fulbright, JFK finally decided on Dean Rusk, the quiet, intelligent, but colorless head of the Rockefeller Foundation who had been suggested to him by Lovett and Dean Acheson. Rusk had served in the State Department under Acheson, where he had displayed both competence as a diplomat and a rigid Cold War mentality, and he had recently published an article extolling the idea of vigorous presidential leadership in foreign policy. Kennedy, who planned to direct American diplomacy personally, saw in Rusk a man who could administer the State Department without challenging White House dominance in international affairs.

The President-elect filled the remaining cabinet posts with able but not exceptional men. He pleased important constituencies within the party by appointing Senator Abraham Ribicoff, a Jew, as Secretary of Health, Education, and Welfare and Governor Luther Hodges of North Carolina, an older southern moderate, as Secretary of Commerce. Liberals, upset by Kennedy's attempts to placate the Establishment in his major appointments, received solace with Stewart Udall in Interior, Orville Freeman in Agriculture, and Arthur Goldberg in Labor. Goldberg, a labor lawyer from Illinois, would prove to be an especially good choice as he became the articulate and effective spokesman for urban liberalism on the New Frontier. J. Edward Day, a Stevenson Democrat, became the Postmaster General, leaving only the Justice Department to fill. At the intense urging of Joseph Kennedy, the new President finally selected his brother Robert for this key post, despite the fact that he lacked the legal experience the position seemed to demand. Bobby Kennedy had served on the staff of several Senate committees, beginning with McCarthy and ending with the Rackets Committee, where he had begun a vendetta against Teamster Union boss Jimmy Hoffa. The President-elect wanted to avail himself of Bobby's shrewd advice and utter loyalty; he jokingly commented that he gave his brother the job to give "him a little experience before he goes out to practice law" but, in truth, JFK moved to maintain tight control over the most politically sensitive of all government departments.

The new cabinet compared favorably with Eisenhower's, but it hardly represented a bold new departure. Kennedy had observed the usual tradition of picking a balanced and moderate team to run the government. He rarely met with the entire group, dispensing with Eisenhower's regular cabinet meetings and, instead, dealt directly with each department head in the area of his special concern. JFK placed his greatest emphasis on White House leadership, and it was his staff that reflected his overriding commitment to action. Several of the key members were long-standing Kennedy aides who had proved their ability and loyalty under pressure: Kenneth O'Donnell as appointments secretary, Theodore Sorenson as special counsel, Larry O'Brien as liaison man with Congress, Pierre Salinger as press secretary. Others came from the academic world, such as McGeorge Bundy, the Harvard Dean who would head up a small but highly effective and influential National Security Council staff, Arthur Schlesinger, Jr., the prolific historian and liberal propagandist who became the intellectual in residence, and Richard Goodwin, a brilliant but brash young lawyer and speech writer. For economic advice, Kennedy chose Walter Heller, an outspoken professor from the University of Minnesota, who advocated bold, innovative policies to invigorate the sluggish American economy.

The New Frontiersmen, as the press soon dubbed the Kennedy staff, quickly built up a mystique based on youth, intellect, and above all, decisiveness. In studied contrast to the cautious, deliberate tone of the Eisenhower Administration, the Kennedy men believed in action, in quick, bold, decisive steps to restore America's world position and to regain the nation's sense of self-confidence. They prided themselves on being cold and pragmatic decision makers who would not let false sentiment hold them back; they displayed an arrogant belief in their own ability and an immature conviction that all problems could be solved through intense study and the proper application of government power.

John F. Kennedy personified the activist spirit of his Administration. Long meetings bored him, and he viewed the normal bureaucratic process, with its inevitable delays and compromises, with deep suspicion. So he dispensed with cabinet meetings (what could the Postmaster General contribute to a discussion of Castro, he scoffed), dismantled the elaborate National Security Council structure built up under Eisenhower in favor of McGeorge Bundy's small but highly qualified staff in the White House, and sought to place Kennedy men within the existing departments who could move forward with his programs and report back to him on any roadblocks. He liked *ad hoc* interdepartmental committees that could bypass the vested interests of the traditional departments, and he wanted to assert direct Presidential authority to make a sluggish federal government alive and humming with activity.

Despite the slimness of his mandate, he hoped to exercise fully the implied powers of the Presidency by playing the role of advocate for change. He believed in using the White House as a "bully pulpit" in the tradition of Theodore Roosevelt and of leading the American people as Franklin Roosevelt had done. Just as FDR had made radio his most effective weapon, Kennedy relied on television, a medium that seemed ideally suited to his cool charm. He scheduled frequent press conferences before live cameras, an innovation that shocked veteran reporters who resented becoming actors in a carefully stage-managed production, and he prepared intensively for these televised encounters, memorizing mountains of trivia in order to impress an awed public with his detailed grasp of public affairs. He realized that his youth, fervor, and promise of change were his greatest assets as he set out to convince the American people that he was opening a new era in the nation's history.

I

"And so, my fellow Americans, ask not what your country can do for you," proclaimed John F. Kennedy on January 20, 1961; "ask what you can do for your country." The remainder of that memorable inaugural address spelled out in quite clear terms the very great demands that Kennedy planned to place on the American people in the continuing Cold War with the Soviet Union. Ignoring the many pressing domestic problems he had identified in the campaign, Kennedy spoke exclusively of world issues. "Let every nation know, whether it wishes us well or ill, that we shall pay any price, bear any burden, meet any hardship, support any friend, oppose any foe to assure the survival and the success of liberty," he declared. He spoke of his willingness to negotiate, his determination to build up the nation's arms "beyond doubt," and the pride he took in "defending freedom in its hour of maximum danger."

The rhetoric was extravagant, but apparently quite sincere. Kennedy really believed that the world had reached a crossroads and that the policies the United States pursued in the next few years would make a vital difference. He worried most about the momentum Khrushchev had built up in the late 1950s with the Russian breakthrough in missiles, the challenge over Berlin, and the appeal of Communism to the rising Third World. In part, Kennedy's speech was a reply to a very truculent address that Khrushchev had delivered in Moscow on January 6. The Russian leader boasted of Soviet technological progress and its rate of economic growth as he predicted the triumph of socialism throughout the world. Khrushchev ruled out a world war as too destructive in the nuclear age, but he spoke approvingly of wars of national liberation in which colonial peoples used guerrilla tactics to win their freedom. Kennedy took careful note of these words in his State-of-the-Union Address on January 30 by reminding the American people that the Communists had not yielded "their ambitions for world domination." "Our task," the President affirmed, "is to convince them that aggression and subversion will not be profitable routes to pursue these ends."

The state of the American armed services was crucial for Kennedy. On taking office, he found that the situation was both better and worse than he realized — the United States had not fallen behind the Soviet Union in nuclear striking power, but its conventional forces were woefully inadequate. Robert McNamara first revealed the mythical character of the missile gap in a background press briefing in February and, though Kennedy continued to insist that such a gap existed, he took steps to insure a significant American nuclear advantage for the years ahead by stepping up the production of both Polaris and Minuteman missiles. By the mid-1960s the United States would have a decisive nuclear advantage over the Soviet Union; Kennedy denied any intention of creating a first-strike force, but his goals of 1000 ICBMs and 656 submarine-launched missiles would serve to offset superior Soviet conventional strength.

The major preoccupation, however, was with the relatively weak American ground forces. McNamara found that only eleven of the fourteen Army divisions were ready for combat, with only 10,000 troops available in the United States as a strategic reserve that could be dispatched to world trouble spots. The Air Force lacked the planes and equipment to lift even this small number into battle quickly, and there were serious shortages in personnel carriers, self-propelled howitzers, and other combat material. The new Defense Secretary agreed with Eisenhower's critics, notable former Army Chief of Staff Maxwell

Taylor, that the economy drive and reliance on massive retaliation had robbed the United States of the ability to meet the threats of limited and brushfire wars. McNamara and Kennedy immediately drew up plans to strengthen conventional forces. In a special message to Congress on March 28, the President asked for additional funds to build up balanced forces "to prevent the steady erosion of the free world through limited wars." "Any potential aggressor... must know that our response will be suitable, selective, swift and effective," he concluded.

Over the next three years, the Kennedy Administration remedied the weaknesses in the nation's defense posture, thereby reversing Eisenhower's attempt to limit excessive military spending. The defense budget rose from $43 to $56 billion from 1960 to 1962; the armed services increased by 300,000 men in 1961 alone. McNamara won the respect and praise of liberal intellectuals by bringing order, efficiency, and civilian control to the Pentagon, but they only belatedly realized that he had created an enormous reservoir of military power that was available for use abroad. Kennedy displayed a personal fondness for the Special Forces, flying to Fort Bragg, North Carolina, to watch their maneuvers and even intervening to overrule the generals in permitting them to wear the distinctive green berets. Kennedy saw this elite group as the counterinsurgency force that would frustrate Khrushchev's efforts to triumph over the United States through wars of national liberation.

Before this defense buildup could be completed, however, Kennedy faced critical problems in the Caribbean and in Southeast Asia. Castro posed the most immediate danger. Throughout 1960 the Cuban leader had drifted steadily into the Russian camp and, just before Kennedy took office, Castro had provoked Eisenhower into severing diplomatic relations between the two nations. Kennedy learned after his election that the CIA was training an exile army in Guatemala for an invasion of Cuba. After a review by the Joint Chiefs of Staff, the President authorized the CIA to proceed with the plan, though he received contrary advice from his liberal advisers. Senator Fulbright spoke out most bluntly, telling JFK, "The Castro regime is a thorn in the flesh; but it is not a dagger in the heart." Even Dean Acheson called the scheme "a wild idea," but Kennedy went ahead, aware that he had committed himself to a strong course of action by his criticism of Ike's failure to stop Castro.

The landing at the Bay of Pigs on April 17 proved to be a disaster. Without air power, the 1500-man exile force was pinned down on the beaches by Castro's troops; the hoped-for spontaneous uprising of the Cuban people never took place. Within two days, Castro had wiped out the threat to his regime, taking over a thousand prisoners and humiliating a bewildered Kennedy. The President immediately assumed full responsibility for the fiasco; he admitted his miscalculation but defended the decision not to use American troops in Cuba on grounds that Khrushchev could then have moved against West Berlin.

He told the Russians that he had no intention of invading Cuba, but he warned that any Soviet move into the hemisphere would meet with a swift American response. He promised the American people that he would prevent further "communist penetration" into the Western Hemisphere and then stated his personal conclusion from the tragedy: "Only the strong, only the industrious, only the determined, only the courageous, only the visionary who determine the real nature of our struggle can possibly survive." Thus Kennedy seemed to be saying that the real lesson of the Bay of Pigs was that harder work, greater sacrifice, and even more reliance on military force were needed to win the Cold War.

Communist aggression in Indo-China provided an even sterner test of Kennedy's skill at crisis management. In Vietnam, a civil war was under way by 1960 as Viet Cong terrorists sought to overthrow the American-backed regime of Ngo Dinh Diem in Saigon. With help from North Vietnam, the Viet Cong were beginning to control the countryside and to threaten Diem's grip on South Vietnam. Some six hundred American military men had been advising the South Vietnamese army since the Geneva agreement in 1954, but their emphasis on halting aggression from the north had not prepared their charges for the guerrilla war they now faced at home. In Laos, independent since 1954, a tug of war between rival groups backed by the United States and North Vietnam had led to a dangerous situation in which the Communist forces were occupying the strategic Plain of Jars. Since the main infiltration route from North to South Vietnam ran through southern Laos, the outcome in that country was crucial for the Saigon regime.

Kennedy turned first to Laos. The Joint Chiefs of Staff recommended against a proposed air strike against the Communist troops in the Plain of Jars. Such a move, the military leaders warned, would not succeed unless the United States committed at least 250,000 men and was prepared to use nuclear weapons if China or Russia intervened. Sobered by this advice, Kennedy decided to seek a peaceful solution instead by sending veteran diplomat Averell Harriman to Geneva to negotiate with the Communists. Over a year later, in July 1962, Harriman signed an agreement backing a coalition regime under Prince Souvanna Phouma and providing for the neutrality of Laos. In succeeding years, both sides violated the agreement as the Communists continued to use the Ho Chi Minh trail through Laos to reinforce the Viet Cong in the south, but at least Kennedy had avoided full-scale American military involvement in a remote area.

Kennedy was not willing to yield so easily on South Vietnam. Though he never subscribed to the simplistic domino thesis, the President viewed the Asian civil war as a crucial test of Khrushchev's tactic of supporting wars of national liberation. If the Communists won, the West would face similar challenges throughout the world while, if the tide could be turned in Vietnam, the Soviets might desist from further challenges. At the same time, he recognized the great difficulty the United States faced in trying to carry on a struggle that the French had lost so badly only a few years before. At a White House luncheon in mid-May, General Douglas MacArthur reminded Kennedy of the folly of placing American troops against the Asian hordes by saying, "we couldn't win a fight in Asia." Later in the month, Charles de Gaulle made an even more somber comment. "For you," he told Kennedy, "intervention in this region will be an entanglement without end." "I predict to you," de Gaulle continued, "that you will, step by step, be sucked into a bottomless military and political quagmire...."

Despite these prophetic warnings, Kennedy decided he could not abandon Diem. He sent Vice-President Johnson to South Vietnam as a gesture of American support (LBJ came back to tell Kennedy not to "throw in the towel in the area and pull back our defenses to San Francisco and a 'Fortress America' concept"). On May 11, the President adopted revised recommendations of a special task force on Vietnam that included the dispatch of 400 Green Berets to help train the South Vietnamese in counterinsurgency and the beginning of covert operations against North Vietnam — infiltration, sabotage, commando raids, and even occasional air attacks. The goal of American policy, according to National Security Memorandum #52, was "to prevent Communist domination of South Vietnam" and "to create in that country a viable and increasingly democratic society." Kennedy had retreated in Cuba and Laos; in South Vietnam he had decided to take a stand.

II

Despite his preoccupation with the world crisis, Kennedy tried hard in 1961 to make good his pledge to get the nation moving again at home. During the campaign, he had advocated a series of domestic measures that harked back to the Truman years — aid to education, health insurance for the aged, expanded minimum wage coverage. In the 1950s, the Eisenhower Administration had moved gingerly on these issues; Kennedy hoped to end the logjam and pass what many considered long overdue reforms.

On the surface, the outlook seemed bright. The Democrats enjoyed substantial majorities in Congress, 262 to 174 in the House and 64 to 36 in the Senate, and for the first time in eight years they controlled the White House. But, in reality, the chances for legislative achievement were slim. In the recent election, the Democrats had lost twenty House seats, nearly all held by northern liberals, as well as two Senate votes. The situation was particularly crucial in the House, which was divided three ways: 174 Republicans, 160 northern and western Democrats, and 101 southerners who held the balance of power and who often voted with conservative Republicans. To carry out his program,

Kennedy would have to secure the support of sixty to seventy southern Democrats. Realizing his dilemma, the President tried hard to woo the South. He deliberately refrained from asking for any new civil rights legislation in 1961; he moved quickly to raise cotton-support prices; and he channeled as much patronage and federal construction to the South as he could. Yet he operated with a serious disadvantage. Despite fourteen years on Capitol Hill, JFK had never ingratiated himself with the powerful southern committee chairmen who controlled the legislative process. In the disdainful judgment of Lyndon Johnson, Kennedy "had the minnows but not the whales" on his side. Men such as Speaker Sam Rayburn of Texas and Senators Robert Kerr of Oklahoma, John Stennis of Mississippi and Richard Russell of Georgia held the real power in Congress and they viewed the new President as an interloper who had yet to prove his ability.

In January 1961, Kennedy enlisted the support of Sam Rayburn to remove the most threatening roadblock to his legislative program, a deadlocked House Rules Committee. There were eight Democrats and only four Republicans on this body, which had to pass on all measures before they could be debated on the House floor, but Democratic Chairman Howard Smith of Virginia and one other southern member regularly voted with the Republicans to create a 6-6 voting pattern. Unless Kennedy could break this stalemate, his measures would never reach the House floor or the Senate, where their chances for passage were much better. The solution Rayburn offered was to enlarge the Rules Committee by adding three members, two loyal Democrats and one Republican, and thereby create an 8-7 margin for the Administration.

Rayburn worked for two weeks to line up a majority for his proposal but, by late January, he confessed to Kennedy that he was a handful of votes short. The Administration entered directly into the battle, with Larry O'Brien and cabinet members Stewart Udall and Luther Hodges appealing directly to wavering Democrats. Rayburn postponed the vote for several days while the pressures built up; the veteran Speaker, his own prestige at stake, twisted every arm that he could to ensure a favorable outcome. When the roll was called on January 31, the Administration prevailed by the exceedingly narrow margin of five votes. Twenty-two Republicans had voted to increase the Rules Committee; this liberal GOP support had barely offset the loss of 64 southern Democrats who stood with Howard Smith against Rayburn and Kennedy.

The President understood the meaning of the vote. "There is no sense in raising hell," he told Arthur Schlesinger, "and then not being successful. There is no sense in putting the office of the Presidency on the line on an issue, and then being defeated." He did not protest when Wilbur Mills kept the medicare bill bottled up in the Ways and Means Committee, because he knew he lacked the votes to win House passage. He did try to secure favorable action on an ambitious plan to increase the minimum wage and to expand its coverage to include 4.3 million retail, laundry, restaurant, and hotel workers who labored for far less than the prevailing $1 an hour. The House substituted a much more restrictive bill by a margin of one vote; only Senate passage of a liberal version finally forced the House to concur in a modest expansion of the minimum wage program. Kennedy suffered his greatest defeat on aid to education when he backed legislation that would have excluded parochial schools from receiving federal assistance on constitutional grounds. The Catholic hierarchy decided to fight for the inclusion of church-operated schools and, in a stunning surprise, Representative James J. Delaney, a Catholic from New York City and one of the two loyal Democrats appointed by Rayburn to the expanded Rules Committee, joined with Howard Smith to refuse to send the Administration's education bill to the House floor. With this defeat, in the words of Tom Wicker, "Kennedy had lost Congress." The Administration's tactic of packing the Rules Committee had backfired with Delaney's defection and, from this point on, Kennedy would have great difficulty in passing any controversial legislation in the House.

The setbacks in Congress, along with the Cuban fiasco, drove Kennedy to take a bold new departure in space exploration in an effort to recoup his lost prestige. The American space effort had continued to lag behind the Russian one since Sputnik, and the Soviets scored another impressive propaganda victory on April 12 when they sent Yuri Gagarin into orbit around the earth, the first man to achieve that feat. Kennedy angrily asked Vice-President Johnson to take stock of the American program and explore the possibility of sending a man to the moon. "Is there any other space program which promises dramatic results in which we could win?" Kennedy wanted to know. "Are we working 24 hours a day on existing programs?...Are we making maximum effort? Are we achieving results?" Johnson, a long-time space enthusiast, quickly came back with an affirmative answer: the United States should embark on a crash program to send a man to the moon ahead of the Russians. Others in the Administration disagreed. Jerome Weisner, Kennedy's thoughtful science adviser, questioned the scientific value of a manned moon-launch, though he supported it reluctantly for diplomatic and military reasons. Dwight Eisenhower, in retirement at Gettysburg, commented bluntly, "Anybody who would spend $40 billion in a race to the moon for national prestige is nuts."

Kennedy announced his decision to send a man to the moon before the end of the 1960s in a nationally televised address to Congress on May 25. In somber tones, he declared that it was "time for this nation to take a clearly leading role in space achievement, which in many ways may hold the key to our future on earth." The costs would be staggering, up to $9 billion in the next five years, Kennedy admitted, but it was necessary to beat the Russians to the moon because, "whatever mankind must undertake, free men must fully share." The Apollo program that Kennedy launched in 1961 would eventually cost

more than $30 billion, and this heavy expenditure would have a highly stimu-
lating effect on the sluggish American economy, a by-product that Kennedy
had counted on in making his decision. Most Americans were not swept off
their feet; a Gallup poll showed that 58 percent of those questioned were opposed to the moon flight. Scientists continued to bemoan the huge expendi-
ture on what was essentially a massive engineering enterprise, with one calling
it "the smallest but most expensive pyramid in history." But Kennedy pressed
on, hoping to find in space the success that so far had eluded him in foreign
and domestic policy.

III

Berlin remained the most pressing and dangerous issue confronting Kennedy
in the spring of 1961. The German city symbolized a major American Cold
War victory and the presence of a Western outpost deep within Communist
East Germany infuriated Khrushchev. Earlier he had threatened to sign a peace
treaty that would end Allied occupation rights in Berlin and make West Berlin
a free city. Eisenhower had refused to accept there terms, and Khrushchev
had allowed the issue to drift after the abortive Paris summit conference while
he awaited the outcome of the American elections. Soon after Kennedy took
office, the Russians indicated that they viewed a Berlin settlement as their
highest priority.

Kennedy preferred to delay. A firm believer in the Acheson formula of
negotiation from strength, the President hoped to build up American armed
forces to high levels of readiness before sitting down to discuss Berlin with
Khrushchev. But, when the Soviet leader suggested that the two men hold an
informal exchange of views, Kennedy accepted and made arrangements to meet
with him in Vienna in early June. The two men ranged widely over the differences between their two countries, but inevitably the conversations narrowed
down to Berlin. From the outset, Khrushchev took a blustering, aggressive
line that caught Kennedy by surprise, despite the warnings about the Russian
leader's bullying tactics from American experts. Khrushchev took a hard line
on Berlin, describing the West German government as a threat to mankind and
insisting on a settlement within six months. "The conclusion of a peace treaty
with Germany cannot be postponed any longer," Khrushchev informed Kennedy.
"A peaceful settlement in Europe must be attained this year." When the President declared that the United States would insist on asserting its wartime
rights in Berlin regardless of such a treaty, Khrushchev responded, "I want peace,
but if you want war, that is your problem." "It is you, and not I, who wants
to force a change," Kennedy replied, and then commented, "it will be a cold
winter."

Shaken by his confrontation with Khrushchev, Kennedy felt he had been too weak. Believing that the Soviets respected only firmness, he decided to take a strong stand on Berlin with actions that were unmistakable. Toning down somewhat the recommendations of a Berlin task force headed by Dean Acheson, Kennedy presented his program to the nation in a speech on July 25. He stressed the determination of the United States to defend the German city, citing the airlift of 1948 and the traditional American commitment to this outpost of freedom. He made a series of specific requests from the Congress, including a $3.2 billion boost in military spending (on top of an earlier increase requested in March), authority to expand the draft, and the activation of 250,000 reservists as well as the immediate mobilization of two full divisions and 54 air squadrons. At the same time, he outlined a comprehensive civil defense program designed to signal to the Russians his willingness to run the risk of nuclear war over Berlin. Nor did the President shrink from mentioning the fact that "in the thermonuclear age, any misjudgment on either side about the intentions of the other could rain more devastation in several hours than has been wrought in all the wars of human history."

Kennedy did everything but make a new negotiating offer to the Russians on Berlin. Apparently, he hoped that by escalating the Berlin crisis with a show of force, he could make Khrushchev withdraw his ultimatum. For the next two weeks, the Russians gave no sign of backing down. Then, on August 13, they responded with a totally unexpected move by building a wall to seal off their sector of Berlin from the Western occupied sections of the city. During the 1950s, Berlin had become the escape hatch for hundreds of thousands of young, ambitious East Germans who sought a freer, more attractive life in the West. The wall stopped the vital drain on trained East German manpower and thus enabled Khrushchev to achieve a unilateral solution to the German problem. The Kennedy Administration regretted the human tragedy the wall created, separating people with concrete and barbed wire and leading to the needless slaughter of those who tried to flee across it, but the President wisely accepted reality and refrained from taking any military countermeasures. Relieved perhaps that Khrushchev had not taken any bolder or more dangerous steps, JFK authorized Secretary of State Rusk to begin negotiations over Berlin with Soviet Foreign Minister Gromyko and, though these talks dragged on without success, in October Khrushchev called off his December deadline on an East German peace treaty.

The Berlin crisis, created in large part by Kennedy's belligerent July 25 speech, thus gradually faded away. The American acceptance of the wall indicated a willingness to live with the status quo, including a de facto policy of two Germanys, which was essentially what Khrushchev had wanted all along, but Kennedy continued to view the outcome as an American victory. Two years later, he received a tumultuous reception when he visited West Berlin. The huge crowds and the shouts of encouragement touched him deeply, and he gave vent to his feelings when he spoke to the people from in front of the City Hall. He praised the population for standing "in the front line for almost two decades," and he invited those who claimed not to understand "the great issue between the free world and the Communist world" to "come to Berlin." He then ended with his assertion that all free men were citizens of Berlin to proclaim, "as a free man, I take pride in the words *'Ich bin ein Berliner.'*"

IV

Two issues — the state of the economy and a new approach to civil rights — headed Kennedy's domestic agenda in 1961. In his campaign promise to get the nation moving again, JFK had bemoaned the economic stagnation of the Eisenhower years and had called repeatedly for raising the annual increase in the gross national product from 3 to 5 percent. When he took office, he found the nation mired down in a recession that had resulted in an unemployment rate of over 8 percent by February 1961. Consequently, the President postponed his quest for long-term economic growth in favor of measures to deal with the immediate emergency.

His advisers were divided into two opposing groups. One, representing the Federal Reserve System and the major government departments, perceived the problem of employment and economic stagnation as essentially structural. In this view, the lack of skilled labor, inadequate technical education, and the existence of large depressed areas such as Appalachia prevented the emergence of the skilled, sophisticated work force needed for industrial expansion. To overcome this manpower drag, the structuralists advocated fundamental social and educational reforms, particularly job training programs and area redevelopment. The second group, headed by Walter Heller, chairman of the Council of Economic Advisers, viewed the problem in fiscal terms. In the 1950s, Eisenhower's attempts to balance the budget had kept taxation too high and public spending too low; as a result, each time the nation emerged from a recession, conservative budget policies created a fiscal drag that blocked full recovery and renewed economic growth. For Heller and other advocates of the "new economics" the solution lay in deliberately unbalancing the budget in times of recovery as well as recession. Heller favored a tax reduction as the quickest way to achieve rapid growth; others advocated the more traditional remedy of increased federal spending, particularly on public works.

Faced with the recession in early 1961, Kennedy chose a structuralist course. In February he asked Congress to pass a series of measures to provide for aid to depressed areas, a temporary boost in unemployment benefits, increased Social Security payments, and a comprehensive housing and community development program, measures that both Houses enacted by June. At the same time, the President accelerated government spending by speeding up projects already approved and by securing Congressional authorization for increased funds for space and defense. Kennedy refused, however, to consider either a tax cut (which seemed to contradict his call for self-sacrifice in the inaugural address) and a massive public works program for fear of unbalancing the budget drastically. The extra appropriations for the Apollo moon-shot and the partial mobilization during the Berlin crisis did lead to a modest deficit, but the President, aware of conservative concern for fiscal orthodoxy, refused to go further, leading Walter Lippmann to comment, "It's like the Eisenhower administration thirty years younger."

The recession ended by mid-1961, much to Kennedy's relief, yet the economy failed to achieve the desired 5 percent rate of growth. Unemployment remained high, at nearly 6 percent of the work force, and the GNP advanced only by 3.5 percent, little better than the average for the 1950s. Despite this disappointing performance, the President continued to resist Heller's arguments for a tax cut and Arthur Goldberg's pleas for extensive public works. He placed his reliance instead on a 7 percent investment credit designed, along with new depreciation schedules, to induce corporations to increase capital spending dramatically and thus lift the entire economy forward. Businessmen viewed the tax credit skeptically, however, and Congress failed to enact it until 1962, thus insuring another year of only modest economic advance.

In the civil rights field, Kennedy moved just as cautiously. In his Congressional career, he had never played a prominent role in the fight for equal rights and, though he subscribed generally to the effort to achieve full citizenship for blacks, he had never embraced it as a cause close to his heart. Civil rights was one of the few domestic areas in which he failed to appoint a task force after the election and, when he found himself dependent on the support of southern Congressmen to enact his program, he decided not to seek passage of any civil rights measures in 1961. This prudent course, dictated as it was by Congressional realities, angered black leaders who knew the importance of Presidential gestures, even those doomed to failure, and who recalled the overwhelming support blacks had given Kennedy in 1960.

The President and his brother, the Attorney General, hoped to move toward racial justice by pursuing less dramatic but, in the long run, more effective tactics. Kennedy did follow the tradition of appointing the Vice-President to head the Committee on Equal Employment Opportunity, giving Johnson broadened power to make sure that Negroes had a fair chance at the 20 million jobs involved in federal contracts, and he appointed many blacks to high government posts, including an unprecedented five federal judges. But the real departure came in the Justice Department, where Robert Kennedy chose the strategy of litigation to give Negroes full political rights. The Civil Rights Acts of 1957 and 1960 had provided for federal intervention to help blacks overcome the many southern roadblocks to the ballot box, but the Eisenhower Administration had only filed six suits on behalf of southern Negroes who were denied the right to register. Convinced that voting was the key to all other rights for blacks, the Attorney General appointed Burke Marshall, an outstanding Washington lawyer, to head the Civil Rights Division and secured the cooperation of FBI Director J. Edgar Hoover in using his agents to gather information on southern attempts to deny Negro political rights. In the next three years, scores of federal officials appeared in the South to help the Negro exercise the right to vote; the Justice Department eventually filed 37 suits and succeeded in enabling Negroes to register in counties where no black had voted since the days of reconstruction.

The quiet revolution in voting patterns that the Kennedys sought to achieve failed to take into account the far more explosive change that was taking place among southern blacks. In early 1960, young Negro college students in Greensboro, North Carolina pioneered a new tactic by sitting in at a Woolworth lunch counter and demanding to be served along with whites. The sit-in movement, in keeping with Martin Luther King's stress on nonviolent means of protest, swept across the South as young blacks displayed remarkable patience, restraint, and courage as they challenged the institution of segregation in lunch counters, bus stations, hotels, and movie theaters across the South. White racists reacted in predictable fashion, threatening to use violence to keep the blacks in their place. The situation became critical in the spring of 1961 when the Congress of Racial Equality (CORE), under the vigorous leadership of James Farmer, sent a series of "freedom riders" into the South to force integration of all public facilities in interstate bus terminals. When the protesters reached Alabama, white mobs began to gather, at first just hurling insults, but then beating up the riders and even burning one of the buses. When Alabama officials failed to maintain order, the Attorney General sent a force of 600 federal marshals into the state, who by their presence finally shamed local officials into ending the violence.

The freedom riders, by publicizing the prevalence of segregation in the South, forced the Kennedys to take effective action to end discrimination in interstate travel. In the summer of 1961, the Justice Department asked the Interstate Commerce Commission to rule on this point; on September 22, the ICC ordered the major rail and bus lines to desegregate all their facilities. The government achieved the same result in 15 southern air terminals by threatening to withhold federal aid. By 1962, blacks could travel freely through the South without having to use separate waiting rooms, restaurants, and restrooms, thereby exercising rights that the Supreme Court had decreed back in 1950.

The President and the Attorney General hoped that the advances they had achieved in voting rights and interstate travel would satisfy black leaders. But these small successes served only to intensify Negro aspirations. Martin Luther King voiced the growing demand for more and more action. "For years now

I have heard the word 'Wait,' " King declared. "It rings in the ear of every Negro with piercing familiarity. This 'Wait' has always meant 'Never.' " Other black leaders, while showing appreciation for the Kennedys' limited gains, expressed disappointment with the Administration's "essentially cautious and defensive" approach to the plight of black Americans. The demand for desegregation was only the beginning of a great Negro upheaval that aimed ultimately at securing full equality in American life.

V

The most significant decision Kennedy made in 1961 was barely noticed at the time. By September the situation in Vietnam had become critical. The influx of American advisers during the late spring and summer had failed to halt the Viet Cong insurgency; the Diem regime, losing out in the countryside, now appealed to the United States for combat troops. Aware of the disastrous French experience nearly a decade earlier, Kennedy was reluctant to order American soldiers into Vietnam but, at the same time, he did not want the Communists to win a decisive war of national liberation. And he was under intense pressure from the Joint Chiefs of Staff, who saw the Viet Cong as puppets controlled not by Hanoi but by Peking and Moscow, carrying out "a planned phase in the communist timetable for world domination."

The President decided to send two trusted aides, General Maxwell Taylor and Walt W. Rostow, to assess the situation in Vietnam and offer their recommendations for action. Taylor had become Kennedy's personal military adviser in mid-1961; his reputation as an intellectual set him apart from the Pentagon brass, and the President found his hawkish but dispassionate views quite congenial. Rostow, an economic historian from M.I.T. who served as Bundy's deputy on the White House national security staff, was an impassioned Cold Warrior who shared Kennedy's enthusiasm for counterinsurgency. No comparable State Departmen official took part in this crucial mission, and thus diplomatic considerations could not influence its findings.

Taylor and Rostow spent two weeks in South Vietnam in October and then returned to Washington to present their report to President Kennedy. Accepting the basic Cold War proposition that "the Communists are pursuing a clear and systematic strategy in Southeast Asia," they described the deteriorating situation in the countryside, admitted the corruption and inefficiency of the Diem government, but on balance saw South Vietnam as a still viable cause for the United States to embrace. To reverse the tide of war, the report recommended extensive American air operations and the dispatch of eight to ten thousand combat troops (to be disguised at first as flood control workers repairing recent ravages of the Mekong River!). The authors recognized the danger of possible United States involvement, but Taylor assured the President that "the risks of backing into a major Asian war by way of SVN are present but are not impressive." "NVN," he explained, "is extremely vulnerable to conventional bombing, a weakness which should be exploited diplomatically in convincing Hanoi to lay off SVN." In other words, if American combat troops failed to halt the Viet Cong, the United States could still control the situation by threatening to devastate North Vietnam from the air.

Kennedy received the report skeptically. "...it will be just like Berlin," he told Arthur Schlesinger. "The troops will march in; the bands will play; the crowds will cheer; and in four days everyone will have forgotten. Then we will be told we have to send in more troops. It's like taking a drink. The effect wears off, and you have to take another." Secretaries Rusk and McNamara, however, endorsed the Taylor recommendations: "The loss of South Viet-Nam would make pointless any further discussion about the importance of Southeast Asia to the free world....The loss of South Viet-Nam to Communism would not only destroy SEATO but would undermine the credibility of American commitments elsewhere." Their classic restatement of the domino thesis may not have convinced Kennedy, but he was certainly impressed by this sober reminder that the loss of Vietnam to the Reds "would stimulate bitter domestic controversies in the United States and would be seized upon by extreme elements to divide the country and harass the Administration...." Kennedy remembered all too vividly how the fall of China had discredited the Truman Administration and paved the way for the Republican return to power under Eisenhower in 1952. Domestic political concern made some form of military response imperative.

The President finally decided on a compromise. He extended the American commitment to South Vietnam but stopped short of sending in combat troops. In an exchange of letters with Diem in December 1961, the President, in return for reforms that never took place in Saigon, promised to step up United States economic assistance, provide American air and helicopter teams to give the South Vietnamese the mobility to seek and destroy the Viet Cong guerrillas, and increase the level of American military advisers, including an additional 600 Green Berets. In short, the United States would take over direction of a major counterinsurgent effort, supplying everything except the combat troops, who would still be provided by the Vietnamese themselves. Kennedy had avoided full-scale intervention in Vietnam yet, by escalating the level of American support, he had irrevocably engaged the nation's prestige in the Vietnamese civil war.

VI

The dismal science of economics absorbed more and more of Kennedy's attention in 1962. In addition to the slow rate of economic growth, he worried about the adverse balance of payments and the accompanying outflow of gold. These problems had developed in the late 1950s as a result of extensive American foreign aid, heavy spending by American tourists, businessmen and soldiers abroad, and increasing resistance to high-priced United States goods in overseas markets. By 1960 the United States was spending and investing $4 billion more abroad than foreigners did in this country, thereby creating a deficit that led to a massive export of gold — $2 billion in 1960 alone. Kennedy checked the gold drain by a series of technical measures, but the balance of payments deficit continued, causing the President to heed Secretary of the Treasury Dillion's advice and avoid both heavy budget deficits and lower interest rates, measures that would complicate the foreign economic problem even though helping on the domestic side.

By the end of 1961, the President had decided to seek relief by stimulating American exports — a sharp increase in the sale of United States goods abroad would reduce the deficit and restore worldwide confidence in the American economy. The Reciprocal Trade Agreements Act, originally passed in 1934, was coming up for renewal, and Kennedy decided to seek a major overhaul by asking Congress to enact new legislation giving him broad powers to reduce American tariffs in order to gain advantages in foreign markets. His chief concern lay in Europe, where Britain, in an historic reversal, had asked to be admitted to the Common Market. Kennedy wanted to encourage this move toward European economic unity and at the same time prevent a trade war between the United States and the potentially powerful combination of European nations. Accordingly, he announced what Joseph Kraft termed "a grand design," a trade expansion act that would empower the President to reduce tariffs by as much as 50 percent to gain reciprocal advantages for American exports, and even to do away with duties entirely on some goods in agreements with an expanded European Common Market.

The President gave his trade bill top priority in Congress in 1962. The White House launched a massive lobbying campaign, lining up support from industries that hoped to gain from the bill and deluging Congressmen with facts and figures on the potential advantages for the United States. Kennedy, who normally left legislative programs to others, took a personal role in the drive for the trade bill, stressing it in press conferences, public appearances, and formal speeches. Often the rhetoric became excessive. If the bill failed, declared one enthusiast, "the United States will have to default on power, resign from history"; the President himself asserted in a New Orleans speech: "We must either trade or fade. We must either go backward or go forward." This intense pressure finally prevailed as Congress enacted the trade expansion bill in October 1962 by the topheavy margins of 298 to 125 in the House and 78 to 8 in the Senate.

Kennedy hailed this victory as "the most important international piece of legislation...affecting economics since the passage of the Marshall plan." Events failed to bear out this judgment. Many of the expected gains disappeared when Charles de Gaulle blocked English entry into the Common Market in 1963; in later negotiating sessions, the Europeans refused to grant the liberal trade concessions Kennedy had been counting on. American exports did rise, but the balance of payments deficit also continued to climb as did the movement of gold abroad. Equally important, the price the President paid in Congress for this dubious achievement proved quite high. The priority he gave trade expansion injured his other legislative proposals, notably aid to education, which continued to languish in committee, and medicare, which lost by a single vote in the Senate. If Kennedy had spent as much time and attention on these domestic reforms as he did on the trade bill, he might have achieved more lasting results. As it was, by the end of 1962 he had failed to gain passage of a single measure that he had originally identified as necessary to get the nation moving forward again.

Another economic problem, the specter of inflation, haunted Kennedy and, as the nation passed out of the recession in late 1961, he acted to insure price stability. At Walter Heller's suggestion, the President relied mainly on "jawboning," repeated exhortations to labor and management to keep wages and prices down and thus prevent an inflationary spiral that would prevent real economic growth. Lacking any statutory authority in this area, Kennedy hoped to persuade both businessmen and union leaders to act with restraint by appeals to their patriotism. The Council of Economic Advisers cooperated by outlining wage and price guidelines in January 1962 and, though this body set no precise figures, its report recommended that wage increases be limited to the rise in productivity, generally thought to be about 3 percent a year. Realizing the key role of steel in the economy, Kennedy and Secretary of Labor Arthur Goldberg concentrated on convincing both the industry and the United Steelworkers of America to negotiate a contract that would not lead to higher steel prices. David McDonald, the steelworkers' leader, proved cooperative, meeting several times at the White House with Kennedy, Goldberg, and U.S. Steel executive Roger Blough and, in March, the union accepted an extremely modest contract that provided for no increase in wages and only a ten-cents-an-hour raise in fringe benefits. The President, pleased by his efforts and the restraint shown by labor, hailed the new contract as "noninflationary."

On April 10, only a few weeks after the settlement, Roger Blough came to the White House to inform Kennedy that U.S. Steel was raising its prices by $6 a ton, effective immediately. The President, shocked by this news, called in Goldberg, and the two men tried unsuccessfully to persuade Blough to reconsider his decision. Kennedy was furious at what he considered a betrayal of trust. He and the Secretary of Labor had used their influence to prevent a wage increase on the understanding that prices would remain unchanged;

Blough's action had completely undercut the President's position with labor and threatened to touch off a major inflationary movement. Conferring with his economic advisers later that day, JFK remarked as much in sorrow as in anger, "My father always told me that all businessmen were sons-of-bitches, but I never believed it till now." This comment quickly leaked to the press and, though Kennedy later claimed he referred only to steel men, he never denied the description, and a few days later he remarked to Schlesinger, "They *are* a bunch of bastards...."

The President decided to mount a full-scale offensive against Roger Blough and the steel industry. When other large steel firms, led by Bethlehem, announced similar price rises the next day, Kennedy called a news conference to denounce the action as "a wholly unjustifiable and irresponsible defiance of the public interest." Reminding the nation of the critical situation in places like Berlin and Vietnam, he voiced his belief that the American people would find it difficult to understand how "a tiny handful of steel executives...can show such contempt for the interests of 185 million Americans." The President combined his verbal blast with more practical measures. He ordered Secretary of Defense McNamara to shift government purchases to firms that had not yet raised their prices and asked the Justice Department to investigate possible antitrust action against the steel companies for acting in collusion. A White House task force considered other possibilities, including government price and wage controls, and a host of federal agencies explored ways of putting pressure on big steel. The most embarrassing action came when two FBI agents roused a puzzled reporter at three in the morning in Philadelphia to check on a story about Bethlehem Steel acting at the request of Roger Blough. Businessmen, already furious at Kennedy for interfering with private economic decisions, viewed the postmidnight incident as an example of police-state tactics.

Despite the intense political pressure, economic considerations proved decisive in ending the steel crisis. Several smaller companies who supplied about 25 percent of the nation's output, notably Inland and Kaiser, refused to go along with the price rise at first, hoping to expand their share of the market at the expense of the big corporations. When Kennedy learned of this development, he contacted the executives of Inland and Kaiser to reinforce their decision and he urged McNamara to favor these cooperating companies with defense purchases. Meanwhile Clark Clifford negotiated secretly with Roger Blough, who finally realized that he had gone too far. On April 12, less than 72 hours after the initial price rise, Bethlehem announced cancellation of the increase, and U.S. Steel quickly followed. Though critics accused Kennedy of overreacting to the steel price boost, he had forced private enterprise to recognize that the public interest, as defined by the President, could not easily be flouted.

The rollback in steel prices left serious strains in the relations between the Kennedy Administration and the business community. Executives began to sport lapel-buttons proudly proclaiming membership in the "S.O.B. Club" and to display bumper stickers reading "Help Kennedy Stamp Out Free Enterprise." Businessmen felt that the federal government had become an antagonist and, after the years of close partnership under Eisenhower, they resented the new feeling of alienation. Politically, the antagonism probably helped Kennedy win popular support, recalling as it did the feud between FDR and business in the New Deal years. But the young President, though enjoying the lighter side, such as the *New Yorker* cartoon showing one tycoon telling another, "My father always told me that all Presidents were sons-of-bitches," regretted the hostility that now prevailed and the potentially negative impact it might have on his efforts to achieve economic advance. When stock prices, which had been steadily bullish since Kennedy's inauguration, suddenly collapsed on May 28 with the sharpest one-day fall since the Great Crash in 1929, business leaders began speaking ominously about "the Kennedy market," implying that the President had destroyed investor confidence by his actions in the steel crisis. The reasons for the decline were primarily economic (a delayed effect of the recession as well as a growing realization that inflation had been halted), but Kennedy worried about the charges. He consulted with Robert Lovett and other Establishment leaders and, in June, he tried to reopen direct communication with the business community by devoting a Yale University commencement speech to an elaboration of the new economics in an attempt to discredit the prevailing myths. But despite his call for cooperation between government and business, most executives received his economic prescriptions coolly and critically.

In mid-1962 the President, disturbed by the sluggish nature of the economy, began to consider a temporary income tax cut of from $5 to 10 billion on both individuals and corporations. Walter Heller pressed hard for such a move, arguing that it was necessary to sustain rapid growth and prevent another recession. Treasury Secretary Dillon, worried over the balance of payments and foreign confidence in the dollar, opposed a "quickie" tax reduction and argued instead for a comprehensive bill that would stress tax reform. When Congressional leaders voiced objections to any immediate cut, Kennedy shelved the proposal and, instead, began consideration of a broader tax bill for 1963. By fall, the President was moving toward acceptance of Heller's ideas, and now Dillon agreed that tax reduction as well as tax reform was needed to stimulate the economy. The lone holdout was economist John Kenneth Galbraith, who still advocated massive public spending instead of tax reductions to encourage private investment, but Kennedy, realizing that Congress was far likelier to vote for tax cuts than increased spending, overruled his objections.

When Congress convened in 1963, Kennedy presented a tax measure that combined modest reforms with a $10 billion cut. Business leaders reacted suspiciously, even though the legislation was designed to stimulate private spending, and Republicans expressed outrage at the idea of deliberately unbalancing the budget. Former President Eisenhower wrote to House GOP leader Charles Halleck to express his indignation, calling the plan "fiscal recklessness" and warning that it would lead to "a vast wasteland of debt and financial chaos." But gradually business leaders began to find the idea of reduced taxes attractive and, when Kennedy acquiesced in House demands that the reform features be trimmed, the chances for passage improved. The President gave a televised speech citing the need to create 10,000 new jobs a day to provide employment for the 7 million young Americans who would enter the labor market in the 1960s. The economy was finally moving forward, JFK maintained; "We need a tax cut to keep this present drive from running out of gas."

The House finally acted on September 25, 1963, passing the bill by a vote of 271 to 155. The Senate would delay action until after Kennedy's death, but the ultimate passage did lead to impressive results. In 1964, the economy finally achieved the desired 5 percent rate of growth; businessmen reaped the greatest advantage as corporate profits increased by 70 percent between 1960 and 1965. Unemployment gradually receded, dropping to 4 percent by March 1966, but the problems of inadequate skills and depressed areas continued to plague the United States throughout the decade. Thus, despite the sharp antagonism Kennedy had aroused in the business community, he served corporate interests far better than he did other groups in society, notably organized labor, who had stood so solidly behind his new economics.

VII

The Cold War reached its most ominous moments in the fall of 1962 when Nikita Khrushchev took the daring risk of placing 42 intermediate range ballistic missiles in Cuba. The American intelligence community realized by midsummer that the Soviets were engaging in a major arms buildup on the island. With the off-year Congressional elections coming up soon, Republican candidates began to criticize the Kennedy Administration for its failure to respond to the Soviet moves, suggesting that the United States should impose a blockade around Cuba. JFK preferred a more cautious response, sending a private warning to the Soviet ambassador through his brother Robert and declaring publicly that America would tolerate defensive weapons, including surface-to-air missiles, but could not accept the presence of offensive arms, presumably ground-to-ground missiles, so close to the United States. The Russians ignored this clear warning. Apparently Khrushchev wanted to redress the unfavorable balance of nuclear power with the Cuban missiles; he may well have hoped to use them to pressure the United States diplomatically in Berlin or elsewhere in the world.

On October 14, an American U-2 took high-altitude photographs of western

Cuba for the first time in more than a month. The next day, photo analysts discovered the telltale signs of missile sites under construction; on the morning of October 16, national security adviser McGeorge Bundy informed the President. Kennedy decided immediately to keep the news secret while he explored the situation with his advisers. He convened an informal group known as the Executive Committee of the National Security Council and, for the next six days, this body, which included Robert Kennedy, McGeorge Bundy, Dean Rusk, Robert McNamara, and about ten others, discussed the various alternatives. At first a majority favored an immediate air strike to knock out the missiles but, when the Air Force could not guarantee complete success for such a surgical strike, the group began to splinter. Some favored an invasion of Cuba, others less drastic measures, and one, Ambassador to the UN Adlai Stevenson, suggested the most peaceful alternative of all, a diplomatic negotiation with Russia whereby the United States would swap its missile bases in Turkey for a Soviet withdrawal from Cuba. President Kennedy finally settled on a compromise course, though he never ruled out entirely the possibility of invasion if Russia proved unyielding.

The President informed the nation of the crisis in a special televised address on Monday evening, October 22. He described the bases under construction, warned that the missiles could deliver nuclear warheads to cities deep within the United States and then described his twofold response. First, the United States would impose a quarantine around the island of Cuba, hopefully with the consent of the Organization of American States, to block delivery of any additional missiles to Cuba. In this way, the American Navy could seal off the island without engaging in overt acts of aggression. Second, Kennedy escalated the missile crisis to the level of a nuclear confrontation. "It shall be the policy of this Nation," the President declared, "to regard any nuclear missile launched from Cuba against any nation in the Western Hemisphere as an attack by the Soviet Union on the United States, requiring a full retaliatory response upon the Soviet Union." Kennedy then called on Khrushchev to end "this clandestine, reckless, and provocative threat to world peace" and "to move the world back from the abyss of destruction" by withdrawing the missiles. The United States could not accept the presence of nuclear missiles in Cuba, Kennedy was saying, and was prepared to use force, up to the point of nuclear war, to secure their removal.

The next day Khrushchev called the American quarantine an act of "outright banditry" and accused Kennedy of taking mankind "to the abyss of a world missile-nuclear war." Meanwhile nearly a hundred ships of the U.S. Navy began to take their stations in a cordon five hundred miles from Cuba as more than 20 Soviet vessels continued on their way toward the island. Work continued day and night on the missile bases in Cuba; the largest invasion force ever assembled in the United States began to form in Florida. The first break in the mounting tension came on Wednesday, October 24, when the Soviet ships suddenly stopped dead in the water and then changed course away from Cuba. "We're eyeball to eyeball," Dean Rusk commented, "and I think the other fellow just blinked." Millions of Americans breathed a sigh of relief at the Russian decision to respect the blockade, but Kennedy realized that the crisis had now entered its most dangerous phase. The Russians were speeding completion of the missile bases in Cuba; unless they stopped work on them soon, the President would have to go ahead with the invasion of the island.

On Friday evening, October 26, Khrushchev sent JFK a long, rambling message in which the Russian leader expressed his fear of nuclear holocaust and then seemed to propose a way out. The Soviet Union would withdraw the missiles from Cuba, Khrushchev suggested, if the President would give a public promise not to invade the island in the future. Kennedy felt a great sense of relief. He could easily make the pledge, since he had no intention of using force to overthrow Castro, and he realized that Khrushchev needed a face-saving agreement to cover his retreat. But before the President could act, the next morning a new note came in from Moscow, written in stiff, bureaucratic prose and much more ominous in tone. The Soviet Union, the note stated, would not remove its weapons from Cuba until the United States pulled its missiles out of Turkey. Though Kennedy had ordered the removal of the obsolete American Jupiter missiles several months earlier, and was angry to discover during the crisis that Turkish objections had led to State Department procrastination, he was unwilling to remove them under direct threat from the Russians. The military, who had chafed under Kennedy's compromise course of action, now claimed that Khrushchev was stalling for time and urged an immediate invasion of Cuba.

Robert Kennedy then spoke up and shrewdly suggested one final move to avoid the use of force. Why not, he said, ignore the second Soviet note and instead respond affirmatively to Khrushchev's first proposal. The President agreed to this idea, and later on Saturday, October 27, sent a message to Khrushchev promising not to invade Cuba if the Soviets would withdraw their missiles. In order to make clear that this was the last chance for a peaceful solution, the President asked his brother to meet that evening with Soviet Ambassador Anatoly Dobrynin. Robert Kennedy informed Dobrynin of the note that had just been sent and then said the United States must have a reply by the next day. The Attorney General later recalled telling the Ambassador, "that if they did not remove those bases, we would remove them....Perhaps his country might feel it necessary to take retaliatory action; but before that was over, there would be not only dead Americans but dead Russians as well." Robert Kennedy then went back to the White House, where he found the President in a despondent mood. "He ordered twenty-four troop-carrier squadrons of the Air Force Reserve to active duty," the Attorney General wrote. "The expectation was a military confrontation by Tuesday and possibly tomorrow."

At nine o'clock Sunday morning, the Moscow radio began broadcasting Khrushchev's reply; by the time the third paragraph had been translated, it was clear that the crisis was over. Khrushchev accepted Kennedy's proposal and began withdrawing the missiles. Castro tried to disrupt the arrangement by refusing to allow UN supervision of the pullout, but the United States was satisfied with aerial inspection of the missiles on the decks of Russian freighters. For a brief time the world had been poised on the brink of nuclear war. Kennedy emerged from the crisis with his reputation enhanced; he had proved his courage under fire. His ranking in the Gallup poll, which had been dropping throughout 1962, suddenly spurted to new highs and in the Congressional elections that took place two weeks later, the Democrats held on to their margins instead of suffering the usual off-year losses. Yet, despite the outcome, thoughtful critics wondered if the risk of nuclear war had really been necessary. In the midst of the crisis, Walter Lippmann suggested precisely the course Stevenson had advocated, a quiet negotiation to exchange the missiles in Cuba for those in Turkey. Such a resort to traditional diplomacy would have prevented Kennedy from gaining his public victory but, if it had been successful, the world would have been spared the agony of a nuclear confrontation. As it was, the United States quietly removed its obsolete missiles from Turkey a few months after the Russians so ostentatiously took theirs out of Cuba. These doubts would grow in time but, in 1962, Kennedy basked in the nearly universal praise for his handling of the crisis, confident that he had finally displayed the qualities of leadership he most prized.

VIII

Kennedy applied the same techniques of crisis management he had employed in Berlin and Cuba to the civil rights problem. Intent on carrying out a slow program of executive action, primarily by working quietly through the courts to expand Negro voting rights in the South, the Administration tried to contain the wrath of black activists and keep on good terms with southern segregationists. Civil tranquillity, not civil rights, appeared to be the desired goal. But the black revolution was gathering force, leading to demonstrations that threatened violence and finally forced Kennedy to abandon his passive approach.

The reluctance of the President and Attorney General to play an active role in the civil rights movement was apparent throughout 1962. They offered no new legislation in this area until February 1963, and then only sponsored a modest measure to strengthen voting rights and extend the Civil Rights Commission. Though they continued to appoint Negroes to important federal posts in the North, they bitterly disappointed black leaders by selecting five judges for the Fifth Judicial Circuit, which included most of the South, who held strongly segregationist views and who, according to Alexander Bickel, "exhibited a distinct tendency to exercise all available discretion against Negro plaintiffs." Kennedy's reluctance to fulfill his campaign pledge to end discrimination in federally financed housing programs proved even more frustrating to civil rights activists. Though he had criticized Eisenhower for failing to take this step, claiming it required only "a stroke of the pen," the President refrained from acting throughout 1961 for fear of antagonizing southern Congressmen whose votes he needed. The next year, he delayed while Congress discussed his proposal to create a new Department of Housing, which would enable him to appoint Robert Weaver, the present housing commissioner, as the first black cabinet member. Southern Congressmen blocked action on this measure and finally on, November 20, 1962, after the great jump in his prestige with the Cuban missile crisis, Kennedy signed the long-awaited order. Even this step proved disappointing, however, since he limited the ban on discrimination to dwellings owned or directly financed by the federal government, and thus excluded 85 percent of the nation's housing.

Bold actions by Negroes themselves finally forced the Administration to come directly to grips with the nation's most pressing domestic issue. In May 1961 James Meredith, a slight but determined black Air Force veteran, filed suit to gain entry into the previously all-white University of Mississippi. Over a year later, the courts ruled in his favor, but racist Governor Ross Barnett vowed that he would not let "that boy to get to Ole Miss" and defied a federal court order to admit Meredith. It seemed to be Little Rock all over again, but the President and his brother hoped to avoid the use of troops by negotiating with the Governor. For three days, they conferred with Barnett by telephone, threatening to use force if he did not back down, and eventually they worked out a compromise. Meredith would slip quietly into the campus at Oxford on Sunday while Kennedy gave a nationally televised speech stressing his insistence on upholding the law; the Governor, while maintaining a public stand of resistance, would use the state police to keep outside troublemakers away from Oxford and to preserve order on the campus.

The hastily contrived arrangement quickly broke down and led to the violence the President had hoped to avoid. An ugly crowd of roughnecks, many of them clearly not students, surrounded Meredith and his bodyguard of federal marshalls, shouting "2-4-1-3, we hate Kennedy" and "Kill the nigger-loving bastards." Instead of breaking up the mob, the state police suddenly withdrew and, by evening, a riot swept over the campus as protesters hurled bottles, rocks, and bricks at the beleaguered marshalls. The President, furious at Barnett, called in both Mississippi national guard units and federal troops from Memphis. The soldiers restored order by morning, but two men had died in the violence and several hundred had been injured. Surrounded by the marshalls, Meredith registered and began attending classes under the protection of 23,000 troops. His courageous behavior won the sympathy of millions of white Americans, but Kennedy's vacillating handling of the episode served only to embitter the South without winning the respect of the nation's black leaders.

A far more serious confrontation developed the following spring in Birmingham, Alabama. The black community, led by ministers Martin Luther King and Fred Shuttlesworth, began a massive protest designed to force the city's white leaders to end segretation in downtown lunch counters and restrooms and to provide equal opportunity for blacks in retail employment. With remarkable unity, 150,000 Negroes, 40 percent of the city's population, supported the demonstrations that began in April 1963. Practicing the tactics of passive resistance, the protestors staged sit-in's in downtown eating places and arranged huge marches that forced the police to arrest hundreds of blacks, who went off to jail peacefully chanting the movement's powerful hymn, "We Shall Overcome." By May, as the authorities were arresting as many as 500 blacks a day, President Kennedy urged King and Shuttlesworth to tone down their demonstrations and adopt less provocative tactics. The black leaders went ahead with the protest, finally causing Eugene "Bull" Connor, the bigoted police commissioner, to overreact by setting loose trained dogs on the crowds and dispersing demonstrators with massive jets of water from fire hoses. Newspaper photographs and television scenes of Negro women being attacked by police dogs and children being bowled over by streams of water led to a nationwide feeling of revulsion. "The civil rights movement should thank God for Bull Connor," Kennedy commented privately. "He's helped it as much as Abraham Lincoln."

The President came under intense pressure to intervene in Birmingham, but he held back, since the local authorities were not violating any federal statutes. Robert Kennedy finally sent Burke Marshall to the city in early May to arrange for negotiations between the black leaders and the local white establishment. On May 10, the businessmen finally agreed to desegregate public facilities in their stores and employ a number of blacks. The next day, however, two bombs exploded in the Negro section of the city, one destroying the home of Martin Luther King's younger brother. After rioting broke out, the President rushed troops to several Alabama bases, but order was gradually restored and the demonstrations ended as the negotiated desegregation agreement took effect.

The rising public indigation over the treatment of blacks in the South made the President realize it was time to take a bolder stand. George Wallace, the strongly segregationist Alabama governor, provided the occasion when he tried to duplicate Barnett's tactics in vowing to stand in the schoolroom door to prevent the integration of the University of Alabama. This time Kennedy did not negotiate; he federalized the Alabama national guard and sent the Deputy Attorney General to the campus with orders not to tolerate any interference by Wallace. On June 11, the Governor gave way after offering only token opposition to the admission of two black students. That evening, Kennedy delivered an eloquent appeal to the nation's conscience. Announcing that he was preparing new legislation on civil rights, he declared, "We are confronted primarily with a moral issue. It is as old as the Scriptures and is as clear as the American Constitution." He went on to affirm that "the time has come for this nation to fulfill its promise" of full equality for all citizens. "Those who do nothing are inviting shame as well as violence," he concluded. "Those who act boldly are recognizing right as well as reality."

At last Kennedy had taken up the cause of black equality and made it his own. The brutal assassination a few hours later of Medgar Evars, leader of the NAACP in Mississippi, only underscored the urgency of the situation. A week later, Kennedy sent a comprehensive civil rights bill to Congress that went far beyond his modest February proposals. Now the President advocated an end to segregation in public facilities — restaurants, hotels, theaters — that had any connection with interstate commerce and the delegation of power to the Attorney General to withhold funds from state programs that practiced discrimination and to institute suits to seek integration of public schools in areas where blacks were either too poor or too intimidated to act on their own. Civil rights enthusiasts wanted even broader legislation, particularly authority to create a Fair Employment Practices Commission to narrow the economic gap between black and white workers, but the measure was strong enough to infuriate the South and insure a bitter fight in Congress.

Tactics now became all important. Kennedy hoped to rely on national indignation and judicious legislative compromise to build a majority for the Administration's bill and, when he learned that black leaders, led by A. Philip Randolph, were planning a massive march on Washington to pressure Congress, JFK tried to dissuade them from such direct methods. The movement's leadership refused to give up the proven technique of peaceful demonstration; they did finally agree to move their rally from the capitol grounds, where it might appear threatening to Congress, to the broad mall in front of the Lincoln Memorial. Robert Kennedy succeeded in gaining other changes, such as persuading black activist John Lewis to drop from his speech the embarrassing question, "I want to know, which side is the federal government on?" The March on Washington took place on August 28, and it proved a tremendous success. A quarter-million Americans assembled peacefully before the Lincoln Memorial to take part in a day-long ceremony filled with song and oratory, culminating in Martin Luther King's moving description of his dream — the ultimate equality of blacks in American society.

The March on Washington marked a symbolic triumph for the civil rights movement. Murray Kempton caught its significance when he wrote that "it represented an acceptance of the Negro revolt as part of the American myth, and so an acceptance of the revolutionaries into the American establishment." The demonstration did little to speed passage of the civil rights bill; Kennedy told the leaders afterwards that the oratory had not changed a single vote and, at the time of the President's death in November, the legislation was still making its way slowly through the Congress. Yet, by assisting the black leaders in finding a peaceful outlet for their anger, Kennedy had helped the movement gain the respectability it needed for ultimate success.

John F. Kennedy's own record on civil rights remains curiously mixed. His aloofness from the movement, his reluctance to act, and his belated embracing of its goals antagonized black leaders who knew how heavily their people had voted for him in 1960. Yet they marveled at his continuing appeal to black Americans. Roy Wilkins told of giving a speech to a Negro group and attacking Kennedy for ten minutes. "...everyone sat on their hands," Wilkins noted. "Then I said a few favorable words about the things he had done, and they clapped and clapped." When a national poll asked Negroes in mid-1963 to rank those they felt had done the most to advance the black cause, they responded the NAACP, Martin Luther King, and John F. Kennedy. Even if events had forced him to take up the cause of civil rights, the President won the loyalty and affection of black America by aligning the federal government against Ross Barnett, Bull Connor, George Wallace, and the whole outmoded system of segregation for which they stood. It was his most enduring victory.

IX

Two developments, one with ominous implications and the other with far greater promise for the future, took place in American foreign policy in 1963. The disturbing events occurred in South Vietnam. For a brief time, the massive infusion of American aid and advisers approved by Kennedy in late 1961 helped turn the tide in favor of Saigon. Helicopters gave the South Vietnamese forces greatly needed mobility, and the Green Berets helped develop a strategic hamlet policy that gave promise of winning back the countryside from the Viet Cong. But, by 1963, the war was going badly again. Diem failed to carry out the political reforms necessary to unify the people around his leadership; instead, under the influence of his brother Ngo Dinh Nhu, he became more and more autocratic, finally touching off a grave political crisis when he tried to repress the Buddhists in the spring and summer of 1963. An elderly monk in Saigon shocked the world on June 11, 1963 by setting himself on fire. Madame Nhu clapped her hands in delight at this human "barbecue," but repeated acts of self-immolation underlined the unpopularity of the Saigon regime and led JFK and his advisers to begin a painful reassessment of their commitment to Diem.

By the fall of 1963, Kennedy was genuinely torn over the situation in South Vietnam. He listened carefully to the advice of Averell Harriman and others in the State Department who kept telling him the conflict was essentially a civil war in which democratic reforms that would win the confidence of the South Vietnamese people, not military force, were the keys to victory. The President reflected his appreciation for this point of view in a television ·interview with Walter Cronkite on September 2. "In the final analysis, it is their war," he commented. "They are the ones who have to win it or lose it. We can help them...but they have to win it, the people of Viet Nam, against the Communists." But only a week later, Kennedy told Chet Huntley and David Brinkley that he could never abandon the South Vietnamese. "I think we should stay," he asserted. "We should use our influence in as effective a way as we can, but should not withdraw." Privately, he told aide Kenneth O'Donnell that he hoped to negotiate an American withdrawal in the future, but that he could not act until after the 1964 elections, which suggests that the memory of Truman and the fall of China still haunted him.

Diem's increasingly dictatorial policies, climaxed by a brutal raid on Buddhist temples and pagodas, forced the President to alter his policy. He took two significant steps in August. The first was to appoint Henry Cabot Lodge, a skilled and tough-minded diplomat, to replace Frederick Nolting, the American ambassador in Saigon who had become an advocate for Diem. As soon as Lodge arrived in South Vietnam, he began taking a hard line with the government, insisting on reforms as the price for continued American aid. The second step came in a famous cable sent to Lodge by the State Department on Saturday, August 24, when many government leaders, including Robert McNamara and Maxwell Taylor, were out of Washington. In effect, the cable instructed Lodge to encourage a group of South Vietnamese generals who were planning a coup. The United States would not take part in such a conspiracy, but Lodge was to inform the generals that they could count on American support if they were successful. Lodge clearly understood the new policy, since he cabled back on August 29, "We are launched on a course from which there is no respectable turning back: the overthrow of the Diem government." The agony continued for two more months, but finally on November 1, the generals stormed the palace in Saigon. Lodge offered to intervene to insure Diem's personal safety, but Diem and his brother were caught trying to escape and were immediately executed by the new ruling junta.

The assassination of Diem led to a period of chaos in Saigon that resulted in an ever-increasing American participation in the war. Though Kennedy did not live to observe this process, his policies led directly to the Americanization of the conflict. By encouraging the overthrow of Diem, he had committed the United States to the defense of the new government in Saigon, making inevitable the rapid buildup of American forces in South Vietnam, forces that had grown from less than 1000 in 1961 to nearly 20,000 by the end of 1963. Despite his reservations and qualms, Kennedy had inextricably tied the nation's prestige and honor to the outcome of the Vietnamese civil war.

Kennedy's more hopeful achievement came in the arms race. The dangers of nuclear testing in the atmosphere had led to a voluntary suspension of tests by the United States and Russia in 1958 and to negotiations for a permanent ban that broke down on the difficult issue of inspection. The United States insisted on provisions for on-site checks to guard against secret underground nuclear blasts, which were difficult to differentiate from earthquakes on seismic recording devices. The Soviets, traditionally hostile to inspection proposals, refused to permit any outsiders to have free access within Russia. Then, in August 1961, at the height of the Berlin crisis, Khrushchev ended the voluntary moratorium by announcing a series of Soviet atmospheric tests that culminated in a massive 58 megaton explosion in late October. Though American scientists felt that similar United States tests were unnecessary, given the American technical lead over the Russians, Kennedy felt he could not permit the Soviet move to go unchallenged. He authorized a series of underground explosions and then, on March 2, informed the American people that despite the hazards of nuclear fallout, the United States would conduct a series of hydrogen bomb tests in the Pacific beginning in April.

The resumption of atmospheric nuclear testing, carrying with it the unknown radiation dangers to human life, troubled Kennedy deeply. At the end of the Cuban missile crisis, he suggested to Khrushchev that the United States and Russia "turn their urgent attention to the compelling necessity for ending the arms race and reducing world tensions." When the Soviet leader replied with a proposal to end all nuclear tests, new negotiations got under way that quickly broke down when the Soviets would accept only three inspections a year and not the minimum of seven the United States demanded. Kennedy sought to break the logjam by sending a high-level negotiating team to Moscow to bargain directly with Khrushchev. In a remarkable speech at American University on June 10, 1963, the President announced this decision and then went on to plead for a reexamination of American attitudes toward Russia. Avoiding the Cold War rhetoric he had used so often in the past, Kennedy expressed his admiration for the Russian people, citing their heroic resistance to Nazi Germany in World War II, and affirming the common interest both nations now shared in avoiding a nuclear holocaust. He admitted that differences were bound to persist, but "at least we can help make the world safe for diversity. For in the final analysis, our most common link is that we all inhabit this small planet," Kennedy continued. "We all breathe the same air. We all cherish our children's future. And we are all mortal."

Nikita Khrushchev called it "the greatest speech by an American President since Rossevelt" as he greeted Averell Harriman, the diplomat Kennedy sent to Moscow to negotiate the test ban treaty. In ten days, Harriman, Khrushchev and a British representative reached agreement by limiting the test ban to those areas that could be monitored without on-site inspection — the atmosphere, outer space, and under water. Kennedy hailed the agreement as a first step on "the path of peace"; the Joint Chiefs of Staff, far more skeptical of the Russians, accepted it only after Robert McNamara promised them an extensive program of underground nuclear tests to preserve America's technical superiority and gave them a written pledge to resume atmospheric explosions "should they be deemed essential to our national security." With the support of the military, the Administration secured quick Senate approval of the treaty by a sweeping margin of 80 to 19. Though in future years the United States would touch off more nuclear blasts underground than it had ever conducted in the atmosphere, the President had taken a major step toward controlling the arms race. The limited test ban treaty was Kennedy's finest legacy to the world.

X

In the fall of 1963, Kennedy was already looking ahead to reelection and a second term. The first three years in office had tempered the optimistic belief that will and determination alone could solve the nation's foreign and domestic problems. In a revealing televised interview in December 1962, Kennedy had confessed that "the problems are more difficult than I had imagined them to be. The responsibilities placed on the United States are greater than I imagined them to be, and there are greater limitations upon our ability to bring about a favorable result than I had imagined them to be." The last revelation is particularly important. Through hard experience, Kennedy had learned the very real limits on presidential power. By 1963, the lesson was even clearer. He had failed to move his program through Congress, suffering defeat on aid to education and medicare and delay on his tax cut and civil rights measures. His standing in the Gallup poll had slumped to 59 percent and, in foreign policy, his elation over the nuclear test ban treaty was tempered by the Vietnam fiasco. The economy was showing increasing signs of vitality, but Kennedy did not yet feel that he had gotten the nation moving forward dynamically.

It was in this mixed mood that JFK went to Texas on November 21 and met his untimely death from an assassin's bullet in Dallas the next day. His sudden passing shocked the nation and gave rise to the legend of the brilliant young President who was struck down in his prime, before he had a chance to display his great power of leadership.

The Kennedy myth stems from the personal charm and attractive style that marked the President's conduct in office. The youthful energy and zest for life, the articulate and often moving rhetoric, the saving sense of humor — these very human qualities endeared Kennedy to millions of Americans and tended to obscure his lack of accomplishment during nearly three years in the White House. The aura of romance that surrounded a young President with his attractive wife and handsome children haunted a nation stunned by a senseless act of violence. His loyal followers were quick to embellish his memory with one-sided accounts of his Presidency that minimized his failures and stressed instead the potential victories he did not live to achieve.

Undoubtedly Kennedy's greatest service was to give the nation a sense of direction after the apparent drift of the Eisenhower years and a new confidence in America's future. But in raising the level of aspiration, Kennedy promised too much. As Henry Fairlie points out so persuasively in his book, *The Kennedy Promise,* the young President offered himself to the American people as the answer to all their problems. Americans believed in Kennedy and in his ability to achieve the many goals he outlined for the nation. Unable to fulfill these exaggerated expectations, Kennedy instead guided the country from crisis to crisis in a desperate effort to demonstrate his ability to act coolly and courageously under pressure. Confrontation became Kennedy's technique for governing — Berlin and Cuba and Vietnam abroad and at home the steel crisis and the ugly incidents at Oxford and Birmingham. "In the administration of John F. Kennedy, activity was mistaken for action...," comments Fairlie. "Toughness was mistaken for strength, articulacy was mistaken for clarity, self-confidence was mistaken for character." The tragedy of John F. Kennedy was not that he failed to get the nation moving, but that he was unable to channel the hectic movement that he generated into solid and enduring achievements.

6

All the Way with LBJ

The nation was fortunate to have a leader of the stature of Lyndon B. Johnson to take over the Presidency in the days of shock that followed Kennedy's assassination. Chosen originally by JFK as his running mate for reasons of political expediency, Johnson possessed precisely the qualities needed — maturity, experience and, above all, skill in handling Congress, where Kennedy's legislative program still remained stalled. LBJ had first entered politics in the 1930s, serving in Congress as a staunch New Dealer and becoming known as a protégé of Franklin Roosevelt. He won a Senate seat in 1948 by the narrowest of margins, but only four years later his Democratic colleagues chose him as their spokesman. As Majority Leader in the 1950s, Johnson won a national reputation as an adroit and shrewd parliamentarian who worked effectively with the Eisenhower Administration. He alienated Democratic liberals by his cooperation with Republicans and southern conservatives and by his free-wheeling methods, but he won the respect of seasoned observers of Congress for his devotion to detail, his intimate knowledge of the strengths and weaknesses of his fellow Senators, and his solid record of achievement.

Johnson had virtually disappeared from sight after the 1960 election, relegated to the obscurity of the Vice-Presidency and eclipsed by the brilliance of John F. Kennedy. Although JFK was always careful to avoid bruising Johnson's ego, consulting him on all major decisions and sending him on several missions abroad, LBJ inevitably came to resent the glib, cocky, and often superficial style of the New Frontier. He had little in common with either the

140

Irish Mafia or the Ivy League intellectuals who surrounded Kennedy. Nor could he have been happy to observe the failure of the Administration to move its program through Congress or listen to the growing demand for institutional reform to break what James MacGregor Burns termed "the deadlock of democracy."

Whatever his inner feelings, Johnson carefully held them in check when he so unexpectedly became President in November 1963. He moved quickly and effectively to reassure the nation and capitalize on the grief for his fallen predecessor to secure his long-delayed legislative goals. Several of the Kennedy aides, notably Theodore Sorenson and Arthur Schlesinger, immediately offered their resignations, but LBJ insisted that they all remain, at least through the difficult transition period. Johnson realized the importance of continuity and he respected the intelligence, if not the loyalty, of Kennedy's close advisers. At the same time, he brought in a parallel set of men whom he could trust, including Bill Moyers, the youthful deputy director of the Peace Corps, Walter Jenkins, his long-time legislative aide, Horace Busby, a conservative journalist and speechwriter, and Jack Valenti, a combination valet, companion, and sounding board. In addition, LBJ turned to two Washington lawyers for advice and counsel. The first was Clark Clifford, the architect of Truman's upset victory in 1948, who had an unrivaled knowledge of national politics, a cool, analytical mind, and a warm respect for Johnson. The other informal Presidential adviser was Abe Fortas, a former New Dealer who had become an influential attorney commanding high fees representing corporations yet also arguing for the downtrodden before the Supreme Court. "He's as smart as they come," Johnson once commented about Fortas, "he has a heart, but he's no damn knee-jerk liberal." Both Clifford and Fortas were outsiders, men from the Middle West and South who had earned respect and power and yet had never been fully accepted by the Eastern Establishment. Like Truman, Johnson embodied a streak of rural populism that made him sympathetic to liberal causes but distrustful of the intellectual and aristocratic elites who championed them. Troubled by a deep sense of inferiority over his regional background and educational handicaps, Johnson found in Clifford and Fortas men who shared his values and who could provide advice he trusted.

In the first hectic days in office, Johnson decided to focus attention on Congress, the body he understood best. He asked Ted Sorenson and John Kenneth Galbraith to write a speech to be given to a special joint session, and then gave the draft to Abe Fortas, who confessed, "I corned it up a little." On November 27, only five days after Kennedy's death, Johnson spoke to members of both Houses. With a telling reference to Kennedy's inaugural call, "Let us begin," Johnson declared, "Today in the moment of new resolve, I would say to all my fellow Americans, let us continue." He then called on the Congress to pass the tax reduction and civil rights measures Kennedy had fought for in the months before his death. In addition to continuity, LBJ stressed the theme of consensus. "Let us turn away from the fanatics of the far left and the far right, from the apostles of bitterness and bigotry, from those defiant of law and those who pour venom into our nation's bloodstream." And then, playing on the emotions of his audience, he vowed, "Let us here highly resolve that John Fitzgerald Kennedy did not live or die in vain," and proceeded to recite the first verse of "America the Beautiful."

The waves of applause assured Johnson that he had struck the right note — sentimental and romantic, almost banal, but just what the Congress and the nation wanted to hear. At a moment of great self-doubt, a new leader was rallying the people to channel their grief for Kennedy along constructive lines by adopting his long-delayed program. The old image of Johnson as the Texas wheeler-dealer, the man who had built a fortune from a television monopoly while serving in Congress, who had originally won election to the Senate by 87 votes, with the decisive margin coming from a corrupt South Texas county, and who had manipulated the Senate with often cynical disdain for principle, faded from the national consciousness. The new Johnson, the man of moderation and dedication, seemed to promise the country the wise and experienced leadership it so badly needed.

I

Congress had been Lyndon Johnson's natural habitat for over two decades and in that time he had mastered its intricacies as few others have done. As Majority Leader of the Senate, he had made the Johnson "treatment" famous. In the hands of worshipping journalists, it sounded mysterious but, in practice, the treatment became a judicious mixture of enticement and fear. Johnson realized that members of Congress were insecure, constantly afraid of the next election and possible rejection by the voters. So in the Senate he had learned to play up to his colleagues, to flatter them excessively, and to offer them opportunities to look good to the people back home. At the same time, he learned what troubled them, where they were most vulnerable, and he was ready to play on their fears when he needed a few more votes. But he relied far more on persuasion than threats and, as President, he found he had even more to promise in winning over reluctant legislators — patronage, invitations to White House functions, or flights on Air Force One. He loved to cite his favorite quotation from Isaiah, "Come now, and let us reason together, saith the Lord." Above all, he used the force of his vibrant personality to overwhelm resistance and gain acceptance for his views. "At the climax of an LBJ persuasion," commented Eric Goldman, "the President might well be out of his chair, peering intently into the other man's eyes, literally grasping a lapel, a shoulder or an arm." Only the bravest Congressman had the determination to resist Johnson's relentless pressure.

In his first address to Congress, the new President had singled out the two measures he would seek action on immediately — the tax cut and civil rights. He deliberately deferred on other portions of Kennedy's program, notably Medicare and aid to education, realizing that these long-debated items would have to wait until after the 1964 election. His choice also reflected his opportunism — both the tax and civil rights bills were well on their way to passage and thus success would take relatively little new effort.

Johnson was a late convert to Walter Heller's new economics. He had always believed in the orthodoxy of a balanced budget and, as Vice-President, he had shown no enthusiasm for the idea of cutting back on taxes to stimulate economic growth. In his first meeting with his economic advisers after taking office, he announced his willingness to press for the $11 billion tax cut, but he laid down one vital condition — a substantial drop in federal spending in order to reduce the planned deficit in the 1965 budget. Secretary of the Treasury Douglas Dillon concurred, but Heller, chairman of the Council of Economic Advisers, and Budget Director Kermit Gordon protested, claiming that the budget of $101.5 billion that Kennedy had approved was the very least the nation could afford. Johnson then proceeded to give the dissenting economists a lesson in practical politics. The tax bill had passed the House in November but sat stalled in the Senate Finance Committee, chaired by Senator Harry Byrd of Virgina, whose devotion to economy in government was legendary. Unless the Administration could offer Byrd reduced expenditures to sweeten the tax cut, the chances for action were slight. When Heller claimed that the budget projections could be defended, Johnson shot back, "I can defend 101.5 billion dollars — you take on Senator Byrd." He then told his advisers that if they did not get the budget under $100 billion, "you won't pee one drop."

The economists had no choice but to go along and, under Johnson's stern eye, they finally pared the budget down to $97.9 billion, cutting the deficit for 1965 in half, much to the delight of Senator Byrd, who now agreed to let the tax reduction bill escape from his committee. Byrd voted against the measure but, after a late-night conference with Johnson, he told the President, "I'll be working for you behind the scenes." The Virginian honored this private commitment, helping Johnson turn back a Republican attempt to weight the bill down with unacceptable amendments. On February 26, 1964, Congress completed action on the bill, which resulted in an $11.5 billion tax cut and a sharp spurt in the rate of economic growth. Johnson signed the bill in a brief televised ceremony in which he praised Republicans as well as Democrats and urged, "Let us unite, let us close ranks." In just over three months, he had enacted a vital measure that had languished in Congress for over a year; his insistence on reduced expenditures had been the key to prompt Congressional action.

Civil rights provided an even tougher test for Johnson. His southern background and close friendship with Richard Russell of Georgia, the South's leading spokesman in the Senate, made liberals suspicious, despite Johnson's role in securing passage of the 1957 and 1960 Civil Rights Acts. Those in the movement remembered how he had compromised on these limited voting rights measures, and they were afraid he would give in again. Kennedy's comprehensive bill, which aimed at granting blacks equal access to public accommodations, had passed the House on November 20, but the Senate gauntlet still loomed. Russell and other southerners had vowed to fight to the bitter end for segregation and were threatening to engage in a filibuster. Critics of the President feared that in his desire for consensus and quick action he would compromise with the southern conservatives.

In his November 27 speech, Johnson had tried to make clear his commitment to Kennedy's civil rights bill, calling its passage the most fitting memorial the Congress could make for the fallen leader. "We have talked long enough about equal rights in this country," Johnson declared. "We have talked for one hundred years or more. It is time now to write the next chapter and to write it in the books of law." In the ensuing legislative struggle, Johnson stayed in the background, letting Hubert Humphrey manage the fight on the Senate floor. He insisted, however, that there be no compromises, no deals to weaken the legislation. When Russell led the southern Senators in a filibuster, Johnson refused to budge, allowing other measures to die as he backed Humphrey's plan to ask for cloture to end the debate. Johnson counted on Everett Dirksen of Illinois, the Republican leader in the Senate, to deliver GOP votes to pass a cloture motion by the necessary two thirds majority. The President conferred with Dirksen privately at the White House on several occasions and finally, on June 10, with the filibuster in its second month, Dirksen announced, "The time has come for equality of opportunity in sharing in government, in education, and in employment....That calls for cloture and for the enactment of a civil rights bill." For the first time in history the Senate voted to cut off debate on a civil rights bill and, on July 2, a triumphant LBJ signed the measure that effectively ended the segregation of Negroes in hotels, restaurants, and public places across the country.

Civil rights and tax reduction were Kennedy measures; in 1964 Johnson wanted to place his own stamp on the legislative process. In the early 1960s, there was growing concern over the existence of poverty in the midst of prevailing American affluence. Michael Harrington spotlighted this phenomenon with his influential 1962 book, *The Other America*. Harrington cited surveys that indicated that as many as 35 million Americans lived in poverty, and he vividly described the culture of the impoverished — the hand-to-mouth existence, the high incidence of physical disease and mental illness, the pervasive feeling of hopelessness, and the sense of entrapment as generation after generation stayed on the welfare rolls. Harrington's book brought what he termed "the invisible poor" to the attention of the American people and gave Johnson the issue he was seeking. LBJ remembered the abject living conditions of Mexican-Americans he had taught as a young man and the efforts he had made to help young people escape the "treadmill of poverty" when he had directed the National Youth Administration program in Texas during the depression years. When Walter Heller informed Johnson that Kennedy had been considering a program to combat poverty at the time of his death, the President decided to go ahead.

Johnson announced his intentions in the course of his State-of-the-Union address to Congress on January 8. "This administration, today, here and now, declares unconditional war on poverty in America," he affirmed. ". . . it will not be a short or easy struggle, no single weapon or strategy will suffice, but we shall not rest until that war is won." Six weeks later, he sent enabling legislation to Congress and then used all his legislative wiles to overcome the resistance of skeptical Representatives and Senators, even persuading a group of industrialists and businessmen to pressure members from their states. The Senate acted quickly, and the House finally concurred in early August by a vote of 228 to 190. Johnson appointed Sargent Shriver, Kennedy's brother-in-law and director of the Peace Corps, to head the new Office of Economic Opportunity (OEO).

Shriver began immediately to carry out the ten separate parts of the poverty program, which ranged from the Job Corps, designed to train poor urban youths with industrial skills in camps around the country, to the community action effort whereby the Administration tried to involve the impoverished in the design and control of measures to improve their way of life. The antipoverty measures suffered from inadequate study, relatively small funding, and intense political in-fighting between local government officials and federal bureaucrats who tried valiantly to carry out the mandate of participation by the poor themselves. The singling out of the poor for special government assistance angered lower-middle class working groups, who resented the way liberal intellectuals wanted to reward those just below them on the social scale, and the poverty program gradually lost support in Congress, ending up finally as a casualty of the war in Vietnam. Thus Johnson never fulfilled his proud boast that the United States had made "a commitment to eradicate poverty among its people," but he did succeed in reducing the ranks of the impoverished by 12.5 million during his five years in office.

II

The outcome of the 1964 election was never in doubt. The martyrdom of John F. Kennedy, the political skill of Lyndon Johnson, and the hopeless candidacy of Barry Goldwater ensured an overwhelming Democratic triumph. The real issues at stake lay beneath the surface — Lyndon Johnson's determination to move out of the Kennedy shadow by winning reelection on his own and the future course of the steadily worsening war in Vietnam.

The Republicans removed any element of suspense from the campaign in their weird preconvention maneuvering. Richard Nixon, the party's titular leader, temporarily removed himself from politics after a stinging defeat in the 1962 California governor's race, telling reporters, "You won't have Nixon to kick around any more...." The natural choice of the eastern Republicans who had dominated the party since the days of Willkie was Nelson Rockefeller, but he seriously injured his chances when he divorced his first wife and married a younger woman in 1963. Henry Cabot Lodge, who had served most recently as Ambassador to South Vietnam, came home for a brief but unsuccessful run for the nomination after a surprise victory in the New Hampshire primary, and William Scranton, the Governor of Pennsylvania, entered the contest after Rockefeller's defeat in the primaries only to find that Goldwater had the nomination locked up. The Arizona Republican, who had emerged as the party's most eloquent conservative spokesman in 1960, reflected the frustrations of many Republicans over the way the nation had been moving in the 1960s. An engaging man of limited intellect, Goldwater spoke out against big government, civil rights, social security, and arms control efforts. Sympathetic to the John Birch Society, a more extreme manifestation of right-wing discontent, Goldwater hoped to bring back the old American virtues of frugality, self-reliance, and rugged individualism. He received the nomination because many rank-and-file Republicans shared his longings and because he had a very effective grass-roots organization that concentrated on winning over the majority of delegates chosen through state caucuses and committees. He won only one contested primary, in California, where he nosed out Rockefeller with 51.6 percent of the vote, but he swept to an easy victory in the San Francisco convention and then evoked tumultuous applause from his worshipping admirers by declaring that "extremism in the defense of liberty is no vice!" as stunned liberals and moderates finally realized that they had lost control of the GOP.

Lyndon Johnson worried far more about the ambitions of Bobby Kennedy than the candidacy of Barry Goldwater. Faced with a vice-presidential write-in campaign for the late President's brother in the New Hampshire primary, Johnson ordered his aides to mount a similar effort for his own presidential aspirations and took great delight when he outpolled Bobby by 4000 votes. He yearned above all else for independence, fearing that his Administration would become simply an interregnum between the reign of the two Kennedy brothers. "I don't want to get elected because of the Kennedys," he commented in the spring of 1964. "I want to get elected on my own." Aware that he could not publicly rebuff the popular Attorney General, LBJ tried to suggest that Bobby voluntarily withdraw from the vice-presidential contest, but Kennedy refused to oblige. In an uneasy face-to-face meeting at the White House on

July 29, Johnson finally informed Bobby that he would not be his running mate in 1964. The Attorney General took the news calmly, saying wistfully as he left the oval office, "Well, I am sorry that you have reached this conclusion, because I think I could have been of help to you." The next day, Johnson announced his solution to what the press had dubbed "the Bobby problem" with a statement saying that he had ruled out his entire cabinet from vice-presidential consideration. Thus a clumsy, almost transparent maneuver created a furor in the press, with references to "a mass execution" of the cabinet, but it ended the Bobby problem without an open break with the Kennedy loyalists.

Johnson's remaining dilemma, the war in Vietnam, could not be handled so easily. The situation in South Vietnam had deteriorated steadily since the assassination of Diem in November 1963. A series of military juntas had come and gone in Saigon, while the Viet Cong gradually increased its grip on the countryside. By March 1964, Secretary of Defense McNamara was reporting that the VC controlled 40 percent of South Vietnam, that "large groups of the population are now showing signs of apathy and indifference," and that "in the last 90 days the weakening of the government's position has been particularly noticeable." McNamara informed the President that the Joint Chiefs favored a bombing campaign to carry the war to the North Vietnamese, but Johnson, concentrating on domestic issues in Congress and fearful of escalating the war in an election year, refused to broaden the American role significantly. Instead he agreed to covert operations, including air strikes in Laos, commando raids by South Vietnamese north of the 17th parallel, and American destroyer patrols along the North Vietnamese coast to gather intelligence and serve as a psychological threat to Hanoi. The President also agreed to permit the State Department to prepare a Congressional resolution giving him authority to wage war against North Vietnam, to be used in an emergency.

Neither the secret operations nor the contingency planning offset the growing charges by Barry Goldwater that the Administration was prepared to accept defeat in Vietnam. Johnson realized the danger of being outflanked by Goldwater's hawkish stand on Vietnam and, when news arrived on August 2 of a North Vietnamese torpedo boat attack on the American destroyer *Maddox,* he was ready to act. The *Maddox* and a sister ship, the *C. Turner Joy,* were conducting electronic eavesdropping operations in the Gulf of Tonkin; at the same time, South Vietnamese commando parties were carrying out raids nearby along the coast of North Vietnam. The United States sent a stern note of protest to Hanoi over the August 2 attack, but two days later Communist PT boats apparently attacked both destroyers at night. The reports were conflicting. The commander of the task force cabled back to Washington, "Review of action makes many recorded contacts and torpedoes fired appear doubtful. Freak weather effects and over-eager sonarman may have accounted for many reports.

No actual visual sighting by *Maddox*. Suggest complete evaluation before any further action." Johnson failed to heed this cautious advice. Instead he ordered reprisal air raids against both torpedo boat bases and oil storage tanks in North Vietnam and then requested Congressional action on the draft resolution the State Department had prepared in the spring.

Congress acted quickly to give Johnson the authority he desired. The resolution empowered the President to "take all necessary measures to repel any armed attack against forces of the United States and to prevent further aggression." As Johnson explained privately, the Tonkin Gulf resolution "was like Grandma's nightshirt – it covered everything." The House quickly passed the measure by a unanimous vote but, in the Senate, Wayne Morse of Oregon and Ernest Gruening of Alaska held up action as they asked William Fulbright, the chairman of the Foreign Relations Committee and sponsor of the resolution, some embarrassing questions about the implications for the future. Fulbright admitted that the Tonkin Gulf resolution gave the President power to wage full-scale war in Vietnam, but he assured his colleagues that "the landing of a large land army on the continent of Asia" was "the last thing we would want to do." The resolution then passed on August 7 by a vote of 88 to 2, with only Morse and Gruening voting against it.

Later investigation revealed the dubious nature of the attacks on the *Maddox* and *C. Turner Joy* and led to speculation that Johnson had deliberately arranged the entire incident to secure war authority from Congress under false pretenses. There is no evidence that the President rigged the episode, nor does it appear that Johnson had yet decided to escalate the Vietnam war. Rather the Tonkin Gulf affair reflects LBJ's political instincts at work in an election year. Worried by Goldwater's criticism of his Vietnam policy, Johnson was eager to seize on the torpedo boat attacks to launch a retaliatory strike to prove that he was as ardent a defender of American honor as his Republican challenger. He acted impulsively out of political expediency, not long-range conspiracy. The resolution was a natural follow-up, designed to give him secure Congressional backing for whatever future steps he might have to take in Vietnam.

After the Gulf of Tonkin resolution, Johnson played down the war as he campaigned for reelection. On several occasions, he promised not to send troops to fight in Indo-China ("We don't want our boys to do the fighting for Asian boys"), but he spent much more time attacking Goldwater than in defending his own policies. When the Republican candidate, who was known to favor sharing control of nuclear weapons with generals in the field, charged that LBJ had authorized military commanders in Vietnam to use tactical atomic bombs, the President issued a blistering repudiation. "Loose charges on nuclear weapons...by any candidate for any office, let alone the Presidency," Johnson declared, "are a disservice to our national security, a disservice to peace and for that matter a disservice to the entire free world." And then, to drive the point home, the Democrats produced a television commercial that portrayed a little girl picking the petals off a daisy, counting down toward zero as the camera faded to a massive nuclear explosion and the entire screen became enveloped in a mushroom cloud. It was only shown once, but the "daisy girl" helped drive home the message that Goldwater could not be trusted with the power of life and death in the nuclear age.

Only Johnson's desire to win the largest landslide in history can explain the magnitude of the effort he made in 1964. Though the pollsters predicted a substantial Democratic victory, the President traveled extensively around the country, campaigning as though the race would not be decided until the last minute. He directed an all-out attack on Goldwater, playing up the candidate's zealous but ill-advised opposition to civil rights legislation, the test ban treaty, and the Tennessee Valley Authority (Goldwater wanted to sell it to private interests). Johnson berated the Republican spokesman for his confused proposals to revise the Social Security system, and the Democrats scored heavily with another television commercial that showed two huge hands tearing a Social Security card in two. The result was exactly what LBJ had hungered for — a massive victory in which he received 61 percent of the popular vote (slightly more than Harding in 1920 and FDR in 1936) and carried 44 states, leaving Goldwater only five in the deep South and Arizona. At last, Johnson was President in his own right with a mandate to expand American influence abroad and carry out a sweeping program of reform at home.

III

It is surprising how few changes Johnson made when he began his new term in 1965. Several of the most dedicated Kennedy aides such as Sorenson and Schlesinger had left in 1964, and Bobby resigned as Attorney General to run successfully for the Senate in New York. McGeorge Bundy remained the President's National Security Adviser, and Larry O'Brien, who directed the 1964 campaign, was elevated to the cabinet as Postmaster General. In the major cabinet posts, Johnson kept both Dean Rusk, with whom he had a special bond as a southerner, as Secretary of State, and Robert McNamara, whose intelligence and dedication he admired greatly, as Secretary of Defense. When Douglas Dillon retired as Secretary of the Treasury, Johnson replaced him with Henry Fowler, a veteran Washington bureaucrat; John T. Connor, a drug company executive, took the place of Luther Hodges as Secretary of Commerce. Three Kennedy stalwarts, Stewart Udall, Orville Freeman, and Willard Wirtz stayed on in Interior, Agriculture and Labor and, after several months of delay, the President took Bobby Kennedy's advice and promoted New Frontiersman Nicholas Katzenbach to Attorney General. Only in the White House did the Kennedy influence wane as Douglass Cater, a liberal journalist, Marvin Watson, a Texas conservative, and Joseph Califano, a young lawyer who had served as McNamara's special assistant, replaced men like O'Brien, O'Donnell, and Sorenson in key staff positions. When Adlai Stevenson died in 1965, Johnson persuaded Arthur Goldberg, Kennedy's Secretary of Labor who had been appointed to the Supreme Court in 1962, to resign his position as a Justice and become the new Ambassador to the UN. Then LBJ prevailed on a reluctant Abe Fortas to take Goldberg's place on the Court. Despite his official position, Fortas, along with Clark Clifford, continued to serve as one of Johnson's most trusted private advisers, counseling the President on foreign as well as domestic policy decisions.

Well aware of how quickly an electoral mandate can vanish, Johnson moved swiftly to enact his Great Society program in 1965. He had first used the phrase, coined by speech writer Richard Goodwin, in May 1964, when he spoke of moving America "upward to the Great Society," which he explained "rests on abundance and liberty for all." "It demands an end to poverty and racial justice...," Johnson explained. "It is a place where the city of man serves not only the needs of the body and the demands of commerce but the desire for beauty and the hunger for community." Despite the rhetoric, the Great Society in fact was the New Frontier — Medicare, aid to education, civil rights — all the Democratic reform measures that dated back to the days of Harry Truman, with the single addition of the war on poverty. Thanks to Barry Goldwater, the time at last seemed ripe to enact this long-delayed program. The 89th Congress contained the largest Democratic majorities since the New Deal days of 1937, with a margin of 295 to 140 in the House and 68 to 32 in the Senate. The most dramatic changes had taken place in the House, where there were 91 new members, nearly one fifth of the entire body. Over seventy were Democrats who had ridden in on Johnson's coattails and were pledged to support the Great Society measures. The old coalition of southern Democrats and conservative Republicans had been shattered; the last obstacle to reform disappeared as the House voted to give Speaker John McCormack the power to call for floor action on any bill held for more than 21 days in the Rules Committee. "It could be better," LBJ confided to a friend, "but not this side of Heaven."

Johnson decided to make Medicare the first order of business in Congress. For nearly two decades, the idea of a federally sponsored program of medical aid to the elderly had been bottled up in Congress. The American Medical Association had blocked action on health insurance when Truman first proposed it in 1949, and the doctors continued to fight against it in the early 1960s, pouring huge sums into the lobbying effort. The most crucial opposition, however, came from Representative Wilbur Mills of Arkansas, the chairman of the powerful House Ways and Means Committee. Mills disliked the way that Medicare had been proposed as a system of compulsory medical insurance for those over 65 under the Social Security system; he feared that the heavy expenditures for hospital bills would undermine the fiscal soundness of the general pension fund. In the past, Mills had blocked action on Medicare but, in 1965, influenced by the size of Johnson's victory and the addition of pro-Medicare members to his committee, he agreed to give it a fair hearing. The AMA, fearful that Medicare would pass, sponsored a rival measure dubbed Eldercare that was a voluntary system of hospital insurance with the government paying the premiums for the indigent. The Republicans had offered a third alternative, called Bettercare, which was also voluntary but had the attraction of covering some doctors' services, and not just hospital costs (the original Medicare proposal omitted doctors' bills in an attempt to escape AMA charges of socialized medicine).

The Ways and Means Committee began consideration of the three measures in early March, with Assistant Secretary of Health, Education, and Welfare Wilbur Cohen representing the Administration. After some discussion, Cohen was startled when Mills suddenly expressed his liking for Bettercare. Then, to everyone's astonishment, Mills suggested that the Committee form a "three-layer cake" by merging features of all three plans: compulsory health insurance for those on Social Security from Medicare, government subsidy for the indigent not eligible for Social Security from Eldercare, and payment of some doctors' services from Bettercare. "Mills did it so fast," Cohen reported to LBJ, "the Republicans were dumbstruck." The AMA and the Republicans had no choice but to go along; "It was," Cohen commented, "the most brilliant legislative move I'd seen in thirty years."

The expanded Medicare bill still had to pass through the Senate Finance Committee, chaired by the skeptical Harry Byrd, but Johnson shrewdly maneuvered Byrd into promising speedy action on the measure on national television, and the Virginia Senator kept his word. The last threat came on the Senate floor, where attempts were made to liberalize the program that might have doomed it in the House but, through strenuous White House lobbying, the bill passed virtually unchanged in July. Immensely pleased with the outcome, Johnson decided it was only appropriate to fly to Independence, Missouri and hold the signing ceremony at the Harry S. Truman Library, in honor of Truman's original advocacy of health care. "That little fellow was pretty much always on the right track," LBJ confided to Eric Goldman, "and he was able to spot a bastard two hundred yards off." The 81-year-old ex-President, pleased by the honor Johnson had done him, voiced his appreciation and then commented, "I am glad to have lived this long and to witness today the signing of the Medicare bill which puts the nation right, where it needs to be right."

Lyndon Johnson took an even greater personal interest in aid to education, which became his major legislative goal in 1965. As a young man, he had taught school for several years in Texas, and he spoke fervently of his desire to go down in history as "the education President." The issue of federal aid to primary and secondary schools had been stalled in Congress for almost as long as Medicare. Kennedy's attempts to secure action had floundered in 1961 on the religious issue when Catholics had rebelled at his insistence that parochial schools not be included in the aid package. As a Protestant, Johnson could risk the charge of favoring Catholics, and he was prepared to include church-supported schools if an acceptable formula could be found. In 1964 he had asked John Gardner, a Republican and head of the Carnegie Corporation, to lead a task force on the education problem. Gardner's group came up with an ingenious way around the religious issue. Instead of aiding schools, the federal government would aid pupils, including those in private as well as public institutions. The child-benefit approach met a 1947 Supreme Court test on the separation of church and state, and thus removed the constitutional question. To make the program politically attractive, Gardner's task force tied it in with the war on poverty by allocating the federal funds on the basis of the number of impoverished children in each state.

Johnson immediately realized the appeal of the new approach and had legislation drafted to carry it out. The aid to education bill provided funds for library books, experimental teaching centers, and research into innovative instruction that benefited all school children. But the heart of the bill lay in the $1 billion that the federal government would distribute to the states for the improvement of primary and secondary education. The states could use the money both for local school districts and to provide services for children in church schools, such as new textbooks, foreign language instruction, and cultural activities. A complicated formula, combining both the number of disadvantaged students and the amount of existing state expenditures for education, insured that the funds would go to those who needed help most, although nearly 90 percent of the schools in the country received some measure of federal assistance.

LBJ threw himself into the legislative struggle to pass the education bill, directing the strategy from the White House and meeting frequently with members of Congress. He insisted that the measure be passed without any amendments, telling his aides he wanted it put through "without a comma changed." He regaled fascinated Congressmen with stories of his teaching days in Cotulla, Texas and convinced them of his personal commitment as he combined his arm-twisting with a patriotic appeal "to give these American kids what they deserve." His pressure paid off. Despite grumbling, the House passed the education bill without any significant change in March, with floor debate limited to only three days. The Senate proved equally docile, acting with record speed so that the final measure reached Johnson's desk in April, only 89 days after the opening of Congress. With his flair for the dramatic, LBJ decided to hold the signing ceremony in the one-room schoolhouse he had attended as a boy in the small Texas hill country town of Stonewall. Television cameras whirred as

Johnson signed the bill in the dingy room before assembled dignitaries, seven Mexican-Americans from his Cotulla teaching days, a group of high school debaters he had coached in Houston, and Miss Katie, the seventy-two-year-old schoolmarm who had taught him through the eighth grade. However corny the stage-managing, there could be no doubt about Johnson's sincerity when he declared, "As President of the United States, I believe deeply that no law I have signed or will ever sign means more to the future of America."

Civil rights provided a third major legislative goal, and one that Johnson had not originally intended to seek in 1965. Dramatic events in the South gave the race question a sudden urgency that compelled LBJ to add it to his program and give it high priority. Martin Luther King was once again the chief catalyst. In January 1965 he began a major effort to register the 3 million blacks in the South who had not yet gained the right to vote. To spotlight the issue, he chose the Alabama city of Selma, where 14,000 whites ruled the community, using a stringent literacy test to keep all but a few hundred of the 15,000 blacks from voting. King and his young volunteers began their campaign of peaceful demonstration, but they soon ran into the determined opposition of Sheriff James G. Clark, Jr., a prototype of the bigoted southern lawman who swaggered through the streets of Selma with a gold-braided cap, a huge pistol, and an electric cattle prod that he used to break up the crowds of demonstrators. The showdown between King's peaceful followers and Clark's armed posse came on Sunday, March 7 and, through television, the entire nation watched the encounter. The blacks set out on a freedom march from Selma to Montgomery, some 50 miles away, but as soon as they crossed the Alabama River just outside Selma, Clark and his men, using bullwhips and billy clubs, brutally attacked the marchers and dispersed them. Civil rights leaders called for federal intervention and, after a Unitarian minister was killed a few days later by a group of whites shouting, "Hey, nigger lover," the whole nation was aroused.

At first Johnson hesitated, reluctant to follow Eisenhower's example at Little Rock and intervene with federal troops, but the situation grew uglier, and young black demonstrators taunted him for his failure to act. So he met with Governor George Wallace at the White House in mid-March and thought he had wrung a promise from the arch-segregationist to call out the Alabama National Guard to preserve order. As soon as Wallace returned to Montgomery, however, he welched, claiming his state lacked the funds to protect the demonstrators. Johnson eagerly seized on Wallace's excuse as an invitation to step in; the next day he federalized units of the Alabama National Guard and thus insured the preservation of order without a showdown over states rights. A few weeks later, Martin Luther King and his growing band made the "March to Freedom," arriving in Montgomery with their arms locked together and singing the powerful Baptist hymn that had become the movement's anthem, "We Shall Overcome."

Still fearful that he had lost the initiative, the President decided to assert his leadership by appearing in person before Congress, the first time a Chief Executive had done so for a legislative request in nearly 20 years. "I speak tonight for the dignity of man and the destiny of democracy," Johnson began. He then proceeded to call upon the Congress to pass a new civil rights act that would insure Negroes the right to vote. In eloquent phrases, the southern President voiced his conviction that "it is wrong — deadly wrong — to deny any of your fellow Americans the right to vote in this country." The question, he insisted, was not a Negro problem, not a southern problem, not a northern problem, but "only an American problem." Then he spoke of those who had borne the struggle in Selma and affirmed: "Their cause must be our cause too. Because it is not just Negroes, but really it is all of us who must overcome the cripplying legacy of bigotry and injustice. And...we...shall...overcome." After a moment of silence, the applause came in rippling waves and then the Congressmen and Senators stood to give the President, as he proudly recalled in his memoirs, "a shouting ovation that I shall never forget as long as I live."

The Administration's bill provided for federal registrars in any county in which less than half those of voting age had actually gone to the polls in 1964. This automatic procedure would enable blacks to avoid the discriminatory literacy tests that so often were used to deny them the ballot, and hopefully would enable enfranchised Negroes to achieve further gains with their new political strength. Despite bitter resistance from southerners, the measure passed through the House and, after a brief filibuster, won grudging Senate approval. This time Johnson stayed in Washington for the signing ceremony, confining his taste for theatrics to the presence of Rosa Parks, the black seamstress who began the Montgomery bus boycott in 1955 and Vivian Malone, the first member of her race to graduate from the University of Alabama. Speaking in the rotunda of the Capitol, directly before a statue of Lincoln, Johnson expressed his belief "that we will move step by step — often painfully, but I think with clear vision — along the path toward American freedom."

Medicare, federal aid to education, voting rights for blacks — with these three measures, Johnson had brought to culmination the post-New Deal reform program that had languished in Congress under Truman, Eisenhower, and Kennedy. Yet this was only the beginning. Before the first session of the 89th Congress ended in October, it had passed 89 Administration measures, including bills to revise discriminatory national origins immigration quotas, establish a Department of Housing and Urban Development (HUD), add $2.4 billion in aid to higher education, and take the first tentative steps to improve the deteriorating American environment with water and air pollution acts and, at the special urging of the President's wife, Lady Bird Johnson, the Highway Beautification Act to limit billboards on the nation's new interstate highway system. It was the greatest burst of legislative activity since FDR's hundred days in

1933. Observers explained the outpouring by pointing to the continued re-
morse over Kennedy's death that helped speed passage of his original program;
they also cited the devastating impact of Goldwater's defeat on the Republican
membership in Congress. But above all else, there loomed the figure of Lyndon Johnson, the master of the legislative process who took advantage of the
favorable climate to drive his measures through Congress with his inimitable
mixture of guile and energy.

Johnson was at the very pinnacle of political success by the fall of 1965 —
he had won reelection by an overwhelming margin and had proved his match-
less skill in dominating Congress. Yet, despite a high standing in the Gallup
poll, he still felt he was being denied the recognition he deserved. The press
spent little time extolling his virtues; instead, journalists concentrated on his
personal idiosyncracies. A spate of accounts in 1964 of a bizarre episode in
which LBJ took a handful of reporters on a wild drive around the Texas hill
country in his white Continental convertible, hitting speeds of 90 miles an hour
and forcing other cars off the road as he drove with one hand grasping a cup
of beer and only one on the wheel continued to haunt the President. Reporters seized on other incidents that projected an unflattering Presidential image
— the time he picked up his beagle by the ears, bringing howls of protest from
dog lovers, and the way in which he bared his belly to show the press the scars
of a gall-bladder operation he underwent in 1965. Millions thought of him as
a crude Texan, a wheeler-dealer who bulldozed the men around him and lacked
the dignity and refinement many felt a President should display. When faithful
Jack Valenti tried to correct this impression by telling a group of advertising
men that Johnson was a "sensitive man, a cultivated man, a warm-hearted man,"
and that he himself slept "each night a little better, a little more confidently
because Lyndon Johnson is my President," he drew only expressions of stunned
disbelief and hoots of derision.

Johnson desperately wanted to receive the personal affection that JFK had
evoked — to be liked by the American people. Yet he knew that despite his
great ability and accomplishments, he lacked the Kennedy charisma. He could
overpower other politicians; he could master Congress; he could impress individuals in small groups, but he could not persuade his countrymen that he was a
great President. My support, he told Eric Goldman, "is like a Western river,
broad but not deep." As long as things were going well, this lack of rapport
made little difference, but if the tide of events ever turned against LBJ, he and
the nation would be in serious trouble. With all his virtues, he lacked the most
fundamental attribute of leadership in a democracy — the ability to inspire the
confidence and trust of the people.

IV

Foreign policy proved to be Johnson's downfall. In the more than three decades of his public service, he had focused almost exclusively on domestic issues. He had rarely traveled outside the United States before becoming Vice-President, and then his few ventures abroad for Kennedy had been carefully arranged tours that prevented him from gaining any firsthand knowledge of foreign cultures. Consequently his view of the world grew out of his reactions to contemporary events, from Chamberlain's appeasement of Hitler to Kennedy's tolerance of Castro. Like many Americans, he concluded that the lesson of history was clear — stop aggression as soon as it appears and display a firm determination to defend American interests throughout the world. Roosevelt had failed to impress the dictators with American resolve; Truman had permitted Acheson to leave Korea vulnerable and exposed; Kennedy had allowed Castro to remain in power in Cuba. LBJ set out to prevent another Pearl Harbor or Korean War; above all, he wanted to avoid another Cuba, telling an aide that "any man who permitted a second Communist state to spring up in this hemisphere would be impeached and ought to be." He hoped to achieve his goals by a calculated policy of strength and toughness, viewing world affairs in intensely personal terms and planning to intimidate potential aggressors much as he had manipulated rivals in domestic politics. In his memoirs, he summed up his approach to the world with the revealing comment: "The protection of American interests in a revolutionary, nuclear world is not for men who want to throw in our hand every time we face a challenge."

Johnson revealed his penchant for defending American interests aggressively in his first major foreign crisis — the Dominican rebellion in April 1965. The situation in this Caribbean nation had been unstable since the 1961 overthrow of Raphael Trujillo, the strongman who had ruled for nearly thirty years. Juan Bosch, an idealistic liberal, triumphed easily in elections held in early 1963, but his regime lasted only seven months, ending when his failure to govern effectively permitted conservative army officers to drive him into exile in Puerto Rico. The country suffered a severe economic decline under his successor, Donald Reid Cabral and finally, on April 24, 1965, a group of young army officers, led by Colonels Fernández Domínguez and Francisco Caamaño Deñó, began a revolt aimed at restoring the exiled Bosch to power. They succeeded in overthrowing the unpopular Reid Cabral, but the colonels quickly met with opposition from their right-wing superiors, headed by General Elias Wessin y Wessin. What had begun as a bloodless coup now threatened to develop into full-scale civil war as fighting broke out in the capital city of Santo Domingo between the colonels, supported by the Dominican left, and the generals, backed by the conservative upper class.

American officials in Santo Domingo sided immediately with the conservative generals. In the absence of Ambassador W. Tapley Bennett, who was on leave in the United States, Charge d'Affaires William B. Connett, Jr., sent a telegram to Washington stating, "All members of the country team feel Bosch's return and resumption of the government is against U.S. interests in view of extremists in the coup and Communist advocacy of Bosch return." Bennett hurried back to Santo Domingo and, soon after he arrived on April 27, one of the rebel leaders, fearful of defeat, asked him to arrange diplomatic negotiations with the generals to end the strife. Bennett refused, pleading lack of authority but undoubtedly influenced by the prospect of a conservative victory. The situation changed dramatically the next day, however, as the rebels gained strength from the pro-Bosch forces within the capital and the generals failed to press their advantage. Over a thousand Americans were trapped in the Embajador Hotel as the fighting raged nearby and, on April 28, Ambassador Bennett became concerned for their safety. His early cables that day had stressed the possibility of American intervention to prevent "a Castro-type solution" and to "protect American interests" but, by late afternoon, he was frightened.

President Johnson was in conference with Rusk, McNamara, Bundy, George Ball, and Bill Moyers when he received an urgent cable from Bennett: "American lives are in danger....If Washington wishes, they [American troops] can be landed for the purpose of protecting evacuation of American citizens. I recommend immediate landings." Though most of the White House discussion had centered on the danger of a Communist takeover in the Dominican Republic, Johnson made no mention of this possibility when he explained his decision to send in American marines in a brief television speech to the American people that evening. Instead, he laid exclusive emphasis on the need to protect the lives of American citizens. The marines, waiting for several days just off the Dominican coast on board the aircraft carrier *Boxer,* quickly established a ceasefire in Santo Domingo and then, in May, the Organization of American States agreed to deploy a hemispheric peace-keeping force to replace the American troops. By fall the last United States soldiers had left and, in the spring of 1966, Joaquin Balaguer, a moderate, was elected to head a new Dominican government.

In one sense, Johnson's policy had been successful. He acted promptly to save American lives and prevent the emergence of a Communist-dominated government, and he had been able to withdraw gracefully with OAS support. Yet the incident left deep scars on his Administration. Two days after his original justification, LBJ suddenly informed the nation that United States forces were seeking to prevent "people trained outside the Dominican Republic" from taking power. On May 2, he became more explicit, charging that "Communist leaders, many of them trained in Cuba," had infiltrated the rebel movement and that he had intervened to block the rise of another Castro. The American embassy in Santo Domingo then released the names of 54 Communists within the rebel ranks in a clumsy effort to document Johnson's new rationale. Many Americans found it difficult to accept the sudden shift from saving lives to halting Communist expansion, and liberals were quick to denounce the Adminstration for engaging in red scare tactics with its highly dubious list of Communists in the Dominican Republic. The more Johnson tried to explain his policy, the greater the outcry, as critics discovered that he had blatantly misquoted Bennett's April 28 cable, which spoke only of American lives being " in danger," to read "American blood will run in the streets" unless the United States intervened. In the Senate, William Fulbright finally broke with the President, denouncing him for misleading the American people. Many other Democrats reached the same conclusion: however effective Johnson might be on domestic issues, he could not be trusted to conduct foreign policy.

In the Dominican Republic, Johnson acted on his belief that "the last thing the American people wanted...was another Cuba on our doorstep." This same concern for domestic political repercussions shaped his Vietnam policy. He remembered the devastating impact of the loss of China and the Korean War on the Democratic party in the early 1950s, and he was determined not to repeat Truman's mistakes. Yet, in attempting to benefit from this past experience, Johnson alienated the people even more than Truman had, creating an intense and vocal opposition that ultimately drove him from office.

The Vietnam situation came to a new climax in early 1965. The political chaos in Saigon, combined with increasing military pressure by the Viet Cong, convinced Johnson's advisers that bombing the North was essential to boost the morale of the South Vietnamese. The Joint Chiefs had pressed for air attacks against the North since the spring of 1964; in November, LBJ had approved contingency plans for retaliatory air strikes, but he had withheld final approval, in part influenced by the opposition of his three chief civilian advisers, McGeorge Bundy, Robert McNamara, and Dean Rusk. By January 1965, Bundy and McNamara had changed their minds. In a long memo on January 27, Bundy reported that he and McNamara were "pretty well convinced that our current policy can lead only to disastrous defeat." They saw only two alternatives, either to "use our military power in the Far East and to force a change of Communist policy" or to "deploy all our resources along a track of negotiation." They favored the first alternative but, when Rusk disagreed, saying, "the consequences of both escalation and withdrawal are so bad that we simply must find a way of making our present policy work," Johnson sent Bundy to Saigon for a firsthand look at the situation before reaching a solution.

On February 7, Viet Cong terrorists attacked the American barracks at Pleiku, using mortars and satchel charges to kill eight sleeping soldiers and wound over a hundred more. Bundy went to Pleiku to inspect the damage and, sickened by the bloodshed, sent Johnson a recommendation that the United States retaliate with air attacks on North Vietnam. Johnson immediately called a meeting of the National Security Council and found his advisers unanimous in their support for bombing of the North. Johnson then gave the order to bomb four army barracks in North Vietnam and authorized the withdrawal of all American dependents from the South. "We have kept our gun over the mantel and our shells in the cupboard for a long time now," Johnson told his aides. "...They are killing our men while they sleep in the night. I can't ask our American soldiers out there to continue to fight with one hand tied behind their backs."

Bundy returned to Washington with a report that stiffened the President's determination to continue the bombing campaign. "The situation in Vietnam is deteriorating," Bundy began, "and without new U.S. action defeat appears inevitable — probably not in a matter of weeks or perhaps even months, but within the next year or so." He then went on to describe the stakes. "The international prestige of the United States, and a substantial part of our influence are directly at risk in Vietnam." The only solution, he concluded, was to wage a new kind of war — "sustained reprisal against North Vietnam." After a quick review by the National Security Council, Johnson concurred, and so what began as a limited retaliatory air strike to punish the Communists for the attack on Pleiku turned into a massive and sustained bombing of the North, dubbed Operation Rolling Thunder, that would continue for the next three years. Johnson had finally adopted the tough policy recommended by the Joint Chiefs and by his 1964 opponent, Barry Goldwater; unwilling to accept the possibility of defeat in Vietnam, he escalated the war in the name of national honor and prestige.

The air strikes against the North led inevitably to the buildup of American ground forces in South Vietnam. Once American planes were engaged in daily operations, LBJ had to provide the troops to protect the air bases in the South against Viet Cong mortar attacks. In April, there were 33,500 American soldiers in Vietnam. In the next two months, Johnson approved the piecemeal sending of several Army brigades and Marine battalions until by June the level had risen to 75,000. He also broadened their mission, permitting United States commanders to go beyond static defense to active patroling of the countryside and finally in June to a full combat role against the VC in War Zone D, northwest of Saigon.

The steady flow of troops began to change the nature of the war, transforming it from a local civil conflict into a struggle between the United States and North Vietnam, which responded to the American military buildup by sending its own cadres down the Ho Chi Minh trail. Once again LBJ sent one of his principal advisers to Saigon to examine the scene at first hand, this time choosing Robert McNamara. The Secretary of Defense reported back on July 21 with the gloomy assessment that "the situation in South Vietnam is worse than a year ago." The three choices facing the United States, McNamara concluded, were "(a) Cut our losses and withdraw.... (b) Continue at about the present level, with U.S. forces limited to say 75,000.... (c) Expand promptly and substantially the U.S. military pressure against the Viet Cong in the South and maintain the military pressure against the North Vietnamese...." McNamara recommended the last alternative, arguing that it offered "the best odds of the best outcome with the most acceptable cost to the United States." Specifically, he proposed increasing the force level in Vietnam from 75,000 to 200,000 by the end of 1965, with plans for an additional 100,000 men in 1966.

Nearly all the President's advisers concurred with McNamara's solution. McGeorge Bundy gave his approval; the military leaders supported it strongly; Maxwell Taylor, now the United States ambassador in Saigon, gave his enthusiastic backing. In Washington, only two men dissented. The first was George Ball, the Under Secretary of State, who had opposed bombing throughout 1964 and who thus played the role of devil's advocate within the Administration. Everyone listened politely to his reservations, flattering themselves with the feeling that they had thus considered the other side, and then quickly dismissed Ball's arguments. The other dissenter was Clark Clifford, a man whose judgment Johnson valued highly. "I don't believe we can win in South Vietnam," he told the President in a conference at Camp David on July 25. "If we send in 100,000 more men, the North Vietnamese will meet us. If North Vietnam runs out of men, the Chinese will send in volunteers....I can't see anything but catastrophe for my country."

The President reached his decision on July 27. He would authorize an additional 50,000 men for the war in Vietnam immediately and, for the future, he was prepared to "give our commanders in the field the men and supplies they say they need." Out of all the discussion, Dean Rusk's warning that an American failure to honor its commitments in Vietnam impressed him most. "If we ran out on Southeast Asia," Johnson recalled in his memoirs, "I could see trouble ahead in every part of the globe — not just in Asia but in the Middle East and in Europe, in Africa and in Latin America. I was convinced that our retreat from this challenge would open the path to World War III."

In reaching this momentous decision, LBJ remained a prisoner of the past, with the memory of Munich and China dictating his action. In a press conference on July 28, he announced the commitment of 50,000 more troops to Vietnam (though he made no mention of his plans to send over 100,000 more in the future). "We did not choose to be the guardians at the gate," he explained to the American people, "but there is no one else." "Nor would surrender in Vietnam bring peace," he continued, "because we learned from Hitler at Munich that success only feeds the appetite of aggression." He cited the earlier policies of Truman, Eisenhower, and Kennedy to resist Communist encroachment in Vietnam, and then he identified himself with the domino theory by asserting:

If we are driven from the field in Vietnam, then no nation can ever
again have the same confidence in American promise or in American protection. In each land the forces of independence would be considerably
weakened. And an Asia so threatened by Communist domination would
imperil the security of the United States itself. . . .

V

Johnson's decision to escalate the war in Vietnam split apart his beloved
consensus at home. The first sign of the rift came in the Senate, where only
Wayne Morse and Ernest Gruening had spoken out at the time of the Gulf of
Tonkin incident in 1964. But the bombing of the North and the dispatch of
combat troops brought growing Democratic defections. In the course of 1965,
Senators William Fulbright, Frank Church, Eugene McCarthy, and Vance Hartke
broke with Johnson on his Vietnam policy and began a steady attack on the
war. Mike Mansfield, the scholarly and gentle liberal who had succeeded LBJ
as majority leader, developed serious doubts that he tried to keep hidden. By
1966, fourteen Senators joined with Hartke, a former Johnson protégé, in signing a letter to the President urging him to halt the bombing. Fulbright and
Mansfield did not sign in deference to their roles of leadership within the Senate, but observers estimated that fully half the 66 Democratic Senators were in
sympathy with the Hartke letter.

A more ominous loss came with the alienation of American youth, the very
group that Johnson had tried to help with his education program. The rise of
the New Left predated the Vietnam War, but the conflict in Asia provided the
issue that permitted the new radicalism to spread across college campuses.
Many elements contributed to the sense of malaise that infected college students in the early 1960s — frustration with the size and impersonal nature of
the expanding universities, an urgent sense of grievance over such obvious social
ills as poverty and racism, which Middle America seemed so willing to tolerate
and, above all, the difficulties created by sheer numbers, as the post-World War
II baby boom overwhelmed the fragile structure of American colleges. Many
state universities more than doubled in size in the 1960s, going from relatively
viable communities of 15,000 to 20,000 students to swollen campuses of
40,000 and more, with all the attendant problems of huge classes, inadequate
facilities, and benign neglect by both faculty members and administrators.
Given this unprecedented growth, it was easy for students to become disen-
chanted with the traditional university structure and find themselves swept up
in a series of romantic and emotional causes.

The Students for a Democratic Society gave a focus to the campus unrest.
Founded in 1960 by radical students at the University of Michigan, it took
sharper form in 1962 with the adoption of the Port Huron statement that

officially proclaimed the existence of "the New Left" and declared pretentiously: "We are people of this generation, bred in at least modest comfort, housed in universities, looking uncomfortably to the world we inherit. Our work is guided by the sense that we may be the last generation in the experiment with living." Though never large in numbers, the SDS attracted great sympathy with its denunciation of social problems and its bogus cry for "participatory democracy," which amounted to little more than a romantic anarchism. One reason for its emptiness was the lack of an old left on which it could build and find expression. Since the defeat of Wallace's Progressive Party in 1948, there had been no radical political movement in America and the affluence of the 1950s had prevented the emergence of any genuine left-wing stirrings among American workers.

The radicals found their first cause in the universities themselves. On September 29, 1964, four student groups defied a university ban and set up tables by the main gate of the Berkeley campus of the University of California. Campus police arrested one of the protestors, leading to a wild scene in which a mob surrounded a police car and finally forced the university authorities to release the student. But, a few weeks later, attempts to discipline the students involved led to a far more violent demonstration headed by Mario Savio and his Free Speech Movement. In December, students took over Sproul Hall, the university's administration building, in a sit-in reminiscent of the strike technique of the 1930s. Savio indicted the entire university system, condemning it as "odious," and calling on his fellow students to "put our bodies against the gears, against the wheels...and make the machine stop until we're free." Savio served a brief jail sentence, and the University of California eventually weathered the crisis. But on campuses across the nation, students imitated the Berkeley example as they occupied administration buildings and forced harried deans and presidents to submit to their "nonnegotiable" demands.

Vietnam provided the most satisfying outlet for student unrest. As soon as LBJ escalated the conflict in 1965, students developed the novel institution of the "teach-in," a marathon discussion, often led by sympathetic faculty members, in which speakers denounced the war and demanded a drastic change in American foreign policy. Exhilarated by a cause that transcended their own limitations, radicals sought ways to relate the Vietnam War to local grievances by trying to force R.O.T.C. programs out of the curriculum, prevent Army and Navy recruiters from interviewing students in university buildings, and demand the removal of defense research from the campus. Above all, students found release in the parades and demonstrations in which they vented their anger at the President. "Hey, hey, LBJ, how many people did you kill today," ran the popular chant; even more cruel was the poster asking, "Where is Oswald now that we need him?" The man who had sought the title of "the education President" had become the chief target of the campus activists, the symbol of what the young radicals thought was wrong with American society.

At the same time, Johnson discovered that he had lost touch with the other group he had tried so hard to help — American blacks. The movement for Negro equality in American life underwent a major transformation in the mid-1960s. The drive against segregation, led by the NAACP, the Student Non-Violent Coordinating Committee (SNCC), and Martin Luther King, reached its fulfillment with the civil rights acts guaranteeing blacks the right to vote, to use public facilities, and to avail themselves of hotels, restaurants, and other privately owned businesses serving the general public. The movement now turned from the South to the North, where the problem was essentially economic, nor moral. Northern blacks had long enjoyed the abstract rights of equal access to the ballot and public services, but they found themselves cut off from the affluent life of mainstream white America by their poverty and lack of education. In northern and western cities, blacks worked at menial, low-paying jobs and were crowded into tenements and slums which, in the 1960s, became known as ghettoes, while the more prosperous whites fled to the suburbs. A feeling of alienation and discontent grew quickly as Negroes realized they were not sharing in the general prosperity; black unemployment rates were more than double those of whites, reaching a high of 37.6 percent in Chicago, and the wage levels for those with jobs were falling steadily behind the white average. The victory over segregation meant little to the northern ghetto dweller; he responded far more eagerly to the radical appeals of groups like the Black Muslims and leaders like Malcolm X who preached a fiery brand of black nationalism, calling on Negroes to assert their own identity and form a separate society alongside the prevailing white one.

The anger of the black masses dimmed the appeal of moderates like Martin Luther King and gave rise to a new group of radical spokesmen. The first to emerge was Stokely Carmichael, a native of Trinidad who had grown up in New York City and then as a young man had thrown himself into the freedom movement in the South, going to jail 27 times, once for 45 days in the Mississippi state penitentiary, for the cause. By 1966 Carmichael had grown disillusioned with King's nonviolent approach, and when he took command of SNCC in the spring, he came forth with the new slogan, "Black Power." Like many young blacks, Carmichael resented the way white liberals had dominated the civil rights movement, using their superior education and access to financial resources to take positions of leadership. Carmichael preached the doctrine of black separatism, telling his followers, "If we are to proceed toward true liberation, we must cut ourselves off from white people. We must form our own institutions, credit unions, co-ops, political parties, write our own histories." At times, he tried to keep his appeal for black separatism on a dignified level but, on the stump, he often resorted to demagoguery that terrified whites. "When you talk of black power," Carmichael shouted at one rally, "you talk of building a movement that will smash everything Western civilization has created." As the Black Power cry gained momentum, Carmichael himself proved too moderate, giving way eventually to H. Rap Brown, who told reporters after taking over the leadership of SNCC in 1967, "The white man won't get off our backs, so we're going to knock him off....If it comes to the point that black people must have guns, we will have means and ways to obtain those arms." By 1968 the new wave of black militancy had given birth to groups like the Black Panthers, led by Huey Newton, who openly advocated war between the races.

The feeling of black anger found its most tragic expression in a wave of violent riots that began in the Watts district of Los Angeles in the summer of 1965 and spread to cities across the country in the following two years. In Watts, the violence began on August 11 and lasted for a week. At its height, more than 10,000 blacks engaged in wanton acts of destruction, turning over cars, burning buildings, and looting stores while those who were armed ex-changed gunfire with the police and shot at the firemen trying to put out the flames. The cries of "Burn, baby, burn," and "Get Whitey" created fears of a race war but, aside from a few white motorists caught in the early stages and the police and firemen trying to restore order, the main victims were Negroes themselves. All but nine of the 34 people killed in Watts were black; the nearly 1000 buildings destroyed crippled life in the black ghetto for years to come. The next year, severe riots occurred in Chicago, Cleveland, and San Francisco, and lesser disturbances broke out in more than 20 other cities. But 1967 proved to be the worst summer, from the ten days of terror in Newark's Central Ward, where 200,000 blacks lived in squalor, to Detroit, the site of the most destructive riot of all. It finally took 14,000 paratroopers, National Guardsmen, and policemen, using tanks and machine guns, as well as the more conventional billy clubs and tear gas, to restore order in Detroit at the cost of 38 lives and property damage running to more than $500 million. The orgy of violence reached its climax in April 1968, following the assassination of Martin Luther King in Memphis, when rioting broke out in over 100 cities. In Washington, looters smashed windows within three blocks of the White House and arsonists set fire to much of the Negro district. "...terrified civil servants clogged the streets in a wild escape to their suburbs," British journalist Louis Heren recalled. "It was as if the city were being abandoned to an invading army. Clouds of smoke hung over the Potomac, evoking memories of the London blitz...."

A bewildered Lyndon Johnson sought a solution to the agony that threat-ened to tear the nation apart. The war on poverty had been designed to help blacks advance economically, but the small scale of the program (only $6.2 billion was spent from 1964 to 1967, less than 1 percent of the gross national product for those years) and the increasing financial demands of the Vietnam conflict had blunted this approach. The Kerner Commission, appointed by the President to find the sources of black unrest, reported, in February 1968, that the chief cause was white racism and recommended a sweeping program of reform, highlighted by an open housing bill. Johnson had met with defeat in 1966 and 1967 when he had pressed for a measure to end discrimination in housing, but the death of Martin Luther King finally shocked the Congress into passing the Civil Rights Act of 1968, which promised open housing by 1970. Time would prove that legislative fiat was not enough to end the patterns of residential segregation in America but, fortunately for the nation, the violence abated after King's death as blacks came to realize that they hurt only themselves in the long, hot summers of the 1960s. After he left office, the President himself realized that despite the many advances he had made in the cause of equal rights, "the American struggle for justice was just beginning."

VI

Vietnam came to dominate every aspect of American life in the late 1960s. The escalation that began in 1965 swelled the numbers of American troops from 75,000 to 125,000, then to more than 200,000 and finally, by the end of 1967, to 485,000. The casualties mounted as well, climbing steadily as American soldiers took on the brunt of the fighting, until by 1967 the deaths surpassed 20,000. The draft became a dreaded institution, reaching into the ranks of American youth each year to provide enough men to sustain the war; the deferments for college students meant that the disadvantaged in American society bore the greater burden of service. Discontent with the conflict also increased, as the teach-in's and parades on college campuses gave way to stormy Senate hearings, where such respectable figures as General James Gavin and George Kennan voiced their opposition, and to protests by affluent, middle-aged Americans, culminating in the march of 60,000 citizens on the Pentagon in November 1967.

Meanwhile, President Johnson tried to ignore the rising clamor and achieve victory in Southeast Asia. He hoped the bombing would force North Vietnam to stop its support for the Viet Cong, and periodically he would suspend the air attacks and send out peace feelers to the enemy. The most dramatic gesture began on December 24, 1965, when the President announced a bombing pause over the Christmas holidays that eventually lasted for 37 days. During that period, the President took personal charge of the peace effort, sending private envoys to talk with the world's major leaders: Hubert Humphrey spoke with Chairman Alexei Kosygin of the Soviet Union; UN Ambassador Arthur Goldberg conferred with the Pope, Charles de Gaulle, and British Prime Minister Harold Wilson; veteran diplomat Averell Harriman went behind the Iron Curtain to present Johnson's views to Communist officials in Warsaw and Belgrade and, through them, to the Chinese. All the diplomats carried the same message — if Hanoi would respond to the bombing pause by reducing its support for the Viet Cong, then gradually the war could be wound down and peace negotiations begun. On January 28, Ho Chi Minh responded on Radio Hanoi, broadcasting a statement condemning Johnson for "deceitful" and "hypocritical" maneuvers and insisting that the United States prove its good faith by withdrawing all troops from Vietnam and accepting the National Liberation Front, the political arm of the Viet Cong, as "the sole genuine representative of the people of South Vietnam." Three days later, Johnson authorized the resumption of bombing; his flamboyant peace campaign had failed.

Though there would be other peace feelers and several additional bombing pauses, Johnson relied more and more on military pressure to solve the Vietnam dilemma. Under General William Westmoreland, the United States built up a massive striking force consisting of 486,000 men in 278 battalions, supported by 28 tactical fighter squadrons and daily bombing sorties by giant B-52 bombers. Over 3000 helicopters moved the American troops rapidly in their effort to search out and destroy the Viet Cong. Massive fire power, in the form of free-fire zones, in which artillery barrages and bombing attacks were carried on indiscriminately, turned much of Vietnam into a cratered landscape that could no longer support life and drove 5 million people into makeshift refugee camps. And still the Viet Cong continued to control the countryside, moving from ambush to ambush with relative impunity. North Vietnam sent a steady stream of men down the Ho Chi Minh trail and, despite estimated losses of 165,000 during 1967, by the end of the year the enemy had 118,000 regular troops and 90,000 more guerrillas in South Vietnam. General Vo Nguyen Giap, the conqueror of Dien Bien Phu, admitted that the American escalation had deprived him of victory, but he was prepared to outlast the Americans in a deadly war of attrition, confident that the 200,000 North Vietnamese youth that turned 18 each year gave him the manpower reserve to match the American fire power.

The war had become a stalemate, a test of wills between Lyndon Johnson and Ho Chi Minh. LBJ could not understand how "a raggedy-ass little fourth-rate country" like North Vietnam could stand up to the power and technology of the United States. He became infuriated with the rising demand at home for negotiations with Hanoi, but gradually he moved toward a softer position. At first he had insisted that North Vietnam match any American move toward lessening the war. In a September 29, 1967 speech in San Antonio, however, he relented by announcing, "the United States is willing to stop all aerial and naval bombardment of North Vietnam when this will lead promptly to productive discussion." Not only did he not insist on a reciprocal move by Hanoi, but he stressed his desire for peace by declaring, "I am ready to send a trusted representative of America to any spot on this earth to talk in public or private with a spokesman of Hanoi." The North Vietnamese remained intransigent, apparently taking the San Antonio speech as a sign of weakening American resolve. Johnson was caught between the doves at home, who cried for peace at any price, and the hawks in Hanoi, who insisted on inflicting a humiliating defeat on the United States. Bitter with frustration, LBJ "hunkered down," as he put it, and went on with the increasingly unpopular war.

The economic consequences of Vietnam began to catch up with the Administration by 1968. When he stepped up the American role in 1965, Johnson tried to avoid putting the nation on a war footing, as the Joint Chiefs urged, for fear it would sabotage his Great Society program in Congress. The economy had finally reached the rate of rapid growth Kennedy had sought, and many of the President's advisers warned that the additional costs of the Vietnam War would produce a dangerous inflation. In fiscal 1966, the war cost the United States $8 billion ($5 billion more than the original estimate), and the projections for 1967 ran between $15 and $17 billion. Gardner Ackley, chairman of the Council of Economic Advisers, urged the President to ask Congress for a sharp increase in taxes in 1966 to pay the rising cost of the war and head off inflationary pressures. Johnson consulted both businessmen and Congressional leaders but, when he failed to inform them of the expected war expenses, they recommended against a tax increase. As a result, the deficit for 1967 jumped to $9.8 billion as the war cost the United States a whopping $21 billion. Not until late 1967 did Johnson ask Congress for a 10 percent income tax surcharge to help defray the costs of Vietnam, and this measure only passed when the President agreed to lop off $6 billion in domestic expenditures, thereby curtailing the Great Society and the war on poverty. And even then the tax boost came too late; in fiscal 1968, the war cost the United States $27 billion, resulting in an incredible deficit of $28 billion and a virulent inflation that wiped out many of the economic gains made earlier in the decade. "In effect, the Administration was going to war without really coming to terms with it," wrote David Halberstam; "they were paying for the war without announcing it or admitting it. Faking it."

The war had an equally serious impact on America's world position. From 1965 to 1968, the United States suffered a series of reverses as the preoccupation with Vietnam eroded American influence elsewhere. In Europe, Charles de Gaulle ended French military participation in NATO in 1966, forcing the transfer of the headquarters to Brussels, thereby weakening the Western alliance. Two years later, the Soviets moved with brutal disregard for world opinion and American retaliation in sending their army into Czechoslovakia to oust the liberal Dubcek government. In the Middle East, the United States played the role of passive spectator during the Six Day War as Israel won a stunning victory over its Arab neighbors. Johnson limited the United States activity to hot-line messages to the Soviet leaders to ensure Russian abstention and a brief summit meeting with Kosygin at Glassboro, New Jersey, which failed to produce any significant results. The Soviets exploited the Arab defeat to increase their influence with Egypt and Syria and with the oil-rich nations of the Persian Gulf. Even in Asia, the United States suffered humiliation when North Korea seized the *Pueblo,* one of the Navy's electronic intelligence-gathering ships, and imprisoned the crew. The only available striking force consisted of fighter planes in South Korea equipped with nuclear weapons; deeply involved in Vietnam, Johnson had no choice but to negotiate for the eventual release of the captured sailors. Despite some successes, notably the overthrow of Sukarno and the ending of Communist Chinese influence in Indonesia, Johnson's Vietnam policy had weakened America's position in the world by overcommitting the nation's resources and alienating world opinion through the indiscriminate use of weapons of mass destruction against a small country.

VI

By early 1968, Johnson had become virtually a prisoner in the White House. He could not move freely about the country; the Secret Service would not guarantee his safety from hostile demonstrators. The intellectuals had turned against him, criticizing him for the slaughter in Vietnam and with a few even hinting that he might have been involved in his predecessor's death. The Eastern Establishment began to voice its doubts, and former Kennedy aides like Arthur Schlesinger and McGeorge Bundy came out against the war. Robert Kennedy, now Senator from New York and a full-fledged political rival, criticized Vietnam but carefully refrained from challenging Johnson directly, apparently planning to wait until 1972 to run for the Presidency. Then, on November 30, 1967, Senator Eugene McCarthy of Minnesota announced his candidacy for the 1968 Democratic nomination. Johnson saw McCarthy as merely a stand-in for Bobby Kennedy, but the Minnesota Senator soon proved he was a serious candidate. He had come to detest not only Vietnam but the centralization of power in the Executive; McCarthy ran to give those who where troubled with the course of American politics in the 1960s a chance to vote their convictions. Dismissed by professional politicians as too romantic and idealistic, McCarthy appealed to the nation's young people precisely because of these traits. His ironic sense of humor ("If elected, I shall go to the Pentagon") and his courage in taking on an incumbent President won him a broad following among college students, who turned out in such numbers to help him that his campaign was quickly dubbed, "the children's crusade." Belatedly Johnson realized he faced a major political test as the accumulated grievances of American voters over inflation, black unrest, and Vietnam now found an attractive and articulate spokesman.

The Tet offensive dealt the beleaguered Administration a fatal blow. General Westmoreland had agreed to a three-day cease-fire during Tet, the Vietnamese new year celebration. Aware of the enemy's duplicity, he kept American forces on alert, but he concentrated his strength at the besieged fortress of Khesanh near the demilitarized zone in the north. The Viet Cong achieved total surprise by shifting their attack to the cities, launching simultaneous assaults on Saigon and 39 of the 44 provincial capitals. Eventually United States and South Vietnamese troops beat back the Viet Cong and inflicted heavy losses, estimated as high as 32,000. But, in pulling troops into the cities, Westmoreland lost control of much of the countryside. Far more important, however, was the psychological impact on the American people. Thanks to television, they were able to watch in their own homes the Viet Cong attack on the American embassy in Saigon, which directly contradicted the Administration's claim that the war was under control and soon would be won. Robert Kennedy spoke for millions of Americans when he claimed the Tet offensive proved that "a total military victory is not within sight or around the corner; that, in fact, it is probably beyond our grasp. Our enemy, savagely striking at will across all of South Vietnam, had finally shattered the mask of official illusion...no part or person of South Vietnam is safe from their attacks."

In New Hampshire, Eugene McCarthy took advantage of the Tet offensive to drive home his argument that Johnson was losing the war in Vietnam. Three days before the Democratic primary, the New York *Times* published reports that Westmoreland had asked for an additional 206,000 American soldiers. The army of college students canvassing the state for McCarthy made the most of this disturbing report. Pollsters still predicted an easy victory for Governor John King, who was Johnson's stand-in for the New Hampshire primary, but McCarthy astonished the nation on March 11 by polling 42 percent of the vote and coming within 230 votes of winning. Five days later, an embarrassed Bobby Kennedy ended his months of indecision and announced his candidacy. Suddenly Lyndon Johnson's control of the Presidency was in doubt.

All through February, LBJ struggled with the aftermath of the Tet offensive. Although he and Walt Rostow, who replaced McGeorge Bundy as National Security Adviser in 1966, claimed it was a major defeat for the Viet Cong, the fact remained that General Earle G. Wheeler, the Chairman of the Joint Chiefs, brought back a request from General Westmoreland for an additional 206,000 men — 108,000 right away, 42,000 by September, and a final installment of 55,000 by the end of 1968. Such an increase would lift the American troop level in South Vietnam to nearly 750,000 and require the mobilization of 250,000 reservists from all three services and increase the 1969 budget by $10 billion. Johnson decided to ask Clark Clifford, who had just replaced Robert McNamara as Secretary of Defense, to conduct a high-level study of these proposals. Clifford's task force advised that 20,000 men be sent right away, but then the new Secretary of Defense began to explore other alternatives. Though he had been a strong hawk, Clifford sensed the weariness of the American people with the war and he discovered that within the Defense Department there was growing disillusionment with the conflict.

Dissatisfaction with the war began to reach Johnson from other quarters. He called on Dean Acheson for advice and was surprised to hear that Cold Warrior express his lack of confidence in the military's judgment. In mid-March, Arthur Goldberg advised the President to stop the bombing of the North in an attempt to begin negotiations with Hanoi; a few days later, a group of distinguished senior advisers, including Acheson, Henry Cabot Lodge, General Matthew Ridgway and others who had played prominent roles in the conduct of the Cold War, advised Johnson to seek disengagement in Vietnam. Yet the President gave no sign of yielding. He blew up at Goldberg, telling him, "Let's get one thing clear! I'm telling you now I am not going to stop the bombing." In an address on March 16, he told his audience, "As your president, I want to say this to you today: we must honor our commitments in the world and in Vietnam. We shall, and we are going to win."

Despite this rhetoric, sometime during the last ten days in March, Johnson began to change his mind. He permitted Dean Rusk to develop a proposal to limit the bombing of North Vietnam to the area south of the 20th parallel, which would exempt nearly all the country, and to include a new peace proposal to Hanoi in a speech he planned to give the nation on March 31. Without informing his advisers, he then decided to announce that he would not be a candidate for reelection. In his memoirs, Johnson maintains that he had reached this last decision as early as 1965, and he waited only for the right moment to disclose it. He fails to make any mention of the upcoming Wisconsin primary, in which the polls indicated he would suffer a crushing defeat at the hands of McCarthy. Instead he claims that March 1968 "proved to be exactly the right month" to make the disclosure since "it coincided with the new effort I planned to seek the way to peace in Vietnam."

Whatever his motivation, Johnson's speech on March 31 proved historic. "Beginning immediately, and without waiting for any signal from Hanoi, we will confine our air and naval attacks in North Vietnam to the military targets south of the 20th parallel," the President declared. He invited Hanoi to respond by entering into peace negotiations and then startled the nation by announcing that with "our hopes and the world's hopes for peace in the balance...I shall not seek, and I will not accept, the nomination of my party for another term as your president."

VII

Lyndon Johnson's dramatic announcement did not end the Vietnam War; it was destined to last another four and a half bloody years. But it did terminate American escalation and, with it, the fruitless search for victory. And it meant the end of Johnson's political career. The man who achieved so much through his mastery of Congress and the legislative process had finally met with a failure in foreign policy that eclipsed his many accomplishments. He had passed more constructive legislation than Truman, Eisenhower, and Kennedy combined, yet he never received the adulation that he so ardently desired. His enormous egotism, his coarseness, and his lack of charisma prevented him from winning the kind of public relations victories that came so easily to Kennedy, or even the grudging respect that Harry Truman wrung from the American people. Yet the nation stood deeply in his debt for the progress he had made in the fields of civil rights, health insurance, aid to education, and the war on poverty.

Even on Vietnam, he was the recipient of unfair criticism and condemnation. He tried to follow a responsible policy, steering a middle course between the demands of the military, who wanted no limitations on the use of American power in Vietnam, and his civilian critics, who favored withdrawal but could never offer a workable formula. Johnson may have placed too high a premium on American pride and prestige, but all the public opinion polls of the mid-1960s indicate that the American people were as opposed to unconditional withdrawal as he was. The American public turned against him finally not because he escalated the war but because he failed to win it. The Tet offensive marked the climax; when, after three years of warfare, more than 20,000 deaths, and billions in expenditures, the United States could not prevent the Viet Cong from attacking the cities of South Vietnam, the American people had had enough. Johnson gambled on achieving victory without placing the nation on a war footing and lost. With his penchant for secrecy and dissimulation, he betrayed the confidence of the American people and, true to his code as a politican, he paid the price.

Johnson's ultimate failing was his inability to be honest, even with himself. Had he gone to the American people openly in 1965, explained the nature of the Vietnamese situation, and asked them to support a difficult and dangerous war by cutting back on their affluence, making sacrifices, and paying higher taxes, he might have won their support and been able to guide the nation through the difficult years that lay ahead. But instead he dissembled, telling himself and the people that they could have victory in Vietnam and the Great Society at home. Perhaps, as Louis Heren suggests, he had no other choice. "The natural gifts which made him the most successful Senate majority leader in history rendered him unfit to lead the nation in times of crisis," Heren concludes. "National leadership could not be exercised from a back room, with cajolery, fixing, and the rest of his tricks, and Johnson knew no other way."

7

Nixon and the Politics of Division

The tumultuous events of 1968 that led many to fear for the very future of the nation provided Richard Nixon with a unique opportunity. The assassinations of Martin Luther King and Robert Kennedy, the protest movements of Eugene McCarthy and George Wallace, the violence and bloodshed that overtook the Democratic convention in Chicago — all contributed to one of the most remarkable political comebacks in American history.

Richard Nixon had hit rock bottom in November 1962, when he lost the California governor's race to the lightly regarded Pat Brown and then revealed his bitterness by lashing out at the press in an impromptu news conference, claiming that the reporters had given him "the shaft" and promising them that "You won't have Nixon to kick around any more." Almost immediately, however, Nixon began to reconsider his course. He had run for governor primarily to duck a second contest with the popular John Kennedy in 1964; the California defeat proved humiliating, but he discovered it did not end his quest for the Presidency. He may have planned to leave politics, but there was no way that he could. "Once you've been in the arena," he later confessed, "you can't stay out." He shifted his base to the East Coast, used influential connections to become a partner in a big but stodgy New York law firm, and then undertook a careful self-analysis to prepare himself for the inevitable return to politics.

Fate proved kind to Nixon in the 1960s. The tragic death of John F. Kennedy made possible the Goldwater campaign, which enabled Nixon to emerge as the Republican Party's voice of moderation. Unlike the liberal Rockefeller, Nixon backed Goldwater in the election and thus won the grudging support of the right wing as he moved in to fill the vacuum of leadership with a carefully orchestrated "centrist" approach. In 1966 Nixon traveled 30,000 miles, appearing in 35 states on behalf of Republican candidates for the House and Senate and, when the GOP made significant gains in Congress, he received much of the credit. Nixon knew the dangers facing a front-runner, however, and he let the inept George Romney, governor of Michigan, play this role in 1967 and early 1968. When Romney destroyed himself by claiming that the Johnson Administration had "brainwashed" him on Vietnam, Nixon quietly forged into the lead for the GOP nomination, forcing Nelson Rockefeller to drop out of open contention and winning all eight primaries he entered. Last minute challenges from Rockefeller and California's conservative governor, Ronald Reagan, simply confirmed Nixon's command of the center and led to his first ballot triumph in Miami Beach in July 1968.

The fall campaign against Vice-President Hubert H. Humphrey proved a more difficult task and, once again, Nixon almost blew it. He had originally planned to make Vietnam a major issue but, when Johnson renounced his candidacy on March 30 and began peace negotiations in Paris, Nixon fell back on his slick New Hampshire primary formula, promising "policies which will end the war and win the peace as quickly as possible." When reporters pressed him for details, he declined with the explanation, "The pursuit of peace is too important for politics-as-usual." Instead he and his advisers stressed the "social issue" – the fear of violence engendered by the Vietnam protests, the rising crime rate, the black ghetto riots, and the violent scenes in Chicago at the Democratic convention. Nixon hoped to siphon off the disaffected lower-middle class attracted originally by George Wallace, who was running on a third-party ticket with General Curtis LeMay. He hammered away at Attorney General Ramsey Clark, a strong civil libertarian, and promised to restore the "first civil right of every American, the right to be free from domestic violence." Avoiding newspaper and magazine journalists, whom he still regarded as enemies, Nixon relied primarily on television; his aides developed a new technique, a series of taped interviews with pro-Nixon panels that allowed the candidate to express his views directly to the people without the embarrassing and critical questions that reporters liked to raise. "So Nixon," commented Joe McGinness, one of his media consultants, "could get through the campaign with a dozen or so carefully worded references that would cover all the problems of America in 1968."

Nixon enjoyed a comfortable early lead in the polls but, in mid-October, Humphrey's campaign gathered momentum as the Vice-President started to free himself from Johnson's static Vietnam policy. Humphrey closed with a rush, aided by LBJ's last minute announcement of an end to all bombing of North Vietnam, but Nixon hung on for a slim victory. The Republican candidate won easily in the electoral college, 302 to 191 for Humphrey and 46 for Wallace; the popular vote, however, showed Nixon barely nosing out Humphrey, 43.4 percent to 42.7 percent, with Wallace taking 13.5 percent (0.4 percent went to protest candidates). Conservatives could point to a handsome 56.9 percent vote by combining the Nixon and Wallace totals, but the Republicans found little solace. They had made only slight gains in the House and Senate, which were still controlled by the Democrats. Nixon thus became the first President elected in the twentieth century who failed to carry either House of Congress with him. Moreover, despite the addition of 5 million to the electorate since 1960, 2.4 million fewer people voted for him in 1968 than in his loss to Kennedy.

The narrowness of Nixon's margin goes far toward explaining his behavior in office. A secretive, insecure man by temperament, he had hoped to win a decisive victory that would enable him to restore a sense of order and calm, much as Eisenhower had done in the 1950s. Instead, he had slipped into the White House without a broad national mandate. For the next four years, his overriding goal would be to achieve the victory in 1972 he felt had been denied him in 1968. In the campaign, to the dismay of ideologically motivated followers, he had played down the issues to win election; in office, he would concentrate on manipulating both foreign and domestic problems to achieve his personal fulfillment. Richard Whalen, a conservative who had joined the Nixon crusade to help end the Vietnam war, dropped out after Miami in total disillusionment when he discovered that "not the war but the politics of the war issue absorbed Nixon." Nixon had told Whalen in 1967, "Flexibility is the first principle of politics." As President, he would demonstrate his devotion to that axiom.

I

In his victory speech on the morning after the election, Nixon recalled a sign a teen-age girl had held up in Ohio during the campaign imploring, "Bring Us Together Again." Telling his cheering supporters how much that message had touched him, the President-elect declared: "And that will be the great objective of this administration at the outset, to bring the American people together." Yet, as one of his speech writers quickly pointed out, "that wasn't the theme of the campaign"; indeed, throughout the fall Nixon had exploited the divisions within America — white against black, south against north, conservative against liberal, hawk against dove. In fact, the task of healing the nation's wounds and offering reconciliation clashed directly with the political need to transform the resentments and grievances of the 1960s into a solid Republican majority in 1972.

The Nixon cabinet gave little indication of the direction the new Administration would take. In attempting to fill the two most prestigious posts, State and Defense, the President met with rebuffs as William Scranton and Senator Henry Jackson declined to serve. Nixon finally appointed his old friend William Rogers, Attorney General in the Eisenhower Administration, as Secretary of State and chose Representative Melvin Laird of Wisconsin to head the Pentagon. Both men were skillful political operators, but neither possessed the intellectual capacity nor the personal drive to rival Nixon.

The other cabinet appointments were equally undistinguished. John Mitchell, Nixon's former law partner and campaign manager, brought an unshakable self-confidence (along with a delightfully outspoken wife) to the Justice Department, but no evident legal qualifications and little experience in national politics. Robert Finch, a long-time Nixon associate and former Lieutenant Governor of California with liberal credentials, headed the controversial Department of Health, Education and Welfare; David Kennedy, an obscure Chicago banker, took over at the Treasury; and Maurice Stans, Ike's Budget Director and ace Republican fund raiser, became Secretary of Commerce after financial leaders vetoed his bid to be Secretary of the Treasury. Three former governors, George Romney of Michigan in Housing and Urban Development, Walter Hickel of Alaska in Interior, and John Volpe of Massachusetts in Transportation, quickly irritated the President with their independent and at times flamboyant behavior. Two relatively unknown academics, Clifford M. Hardin as Secretary of Agriculture and George Shultz as Secretary of Labor, completed a group that inspired James Reston's comment, "The bland were leading the bland."

The mediocrity of the cabinet was no accident. The real power in the Nixon Administration lay in the White House and particularly in the tight inner circle of Presidential aides. Though this group included such diverse individuals as speech-writers Raymond Price, a liberal from the defunct New York *Herald Tribune,* and Patrick Buchanan, a conservative who had left the St. Louis *Globe Democrat* to work for Nixon in 1965, veteran political specialists such as Bryce Harlow, Eisenhower's liaison man with Congress who played the same role for Nixon, and Murray Chotiner, the architect of Nixon's early California campaign victories who was noted for his mastery of dirty tricks; the two dominant figures were the relatively unknown H. R. Haldeman and John Ehrlichman. Both came from the business community, Haldeman from the J. Walter Thompson advertising agency, Ehrlichman from a Seattle law practice where he specialized in real estate transactions; both were graduates of U.C.L.A; and both had served as Nixon advance men in the 1960 campaign, traveling ahead to drum up the crowds and perfect such tasks as "releasing the ballons precisely at the moment the candidate's arms shot skyward in a V." The two men had not joined Nixon's 1968 campaign until he had emerged as the front-runner in April, but they quickly took command, brushing aside the "writer and research types" as they applied their managerial skills to the election process. Known resentfully as "the Germans," they became Nixon's right-hand men in the White House, with Haldeman as Chief-of-Staff, controlling appointments and access to the President, and Ehrlichman emerging as chief domestic coordinator.

The rise of Haldeman and Ehrlichman reflected a crucial characteristic of Nixon's personality. Outwardly aggressive and self-confident, the President was actually a shy, insecure man who hated the hurly-burly of politics and the abrasive personal clashes inherent in the exercise of power. The long climb up from Whittier, socially, economically, and politically, had left him deeply scarred as he learned to control his emotions in the face of repeated snubs and defeats. Haldeman and Ehrlichman provided Nixon with the thing he prized above all else — isolation from the daily routine of governing and the time for personal reflection on the nation's problems. They erected what one aide termed "a Berlin Wall" around the President to keep out all intruders, whether anxious lobbyists, Republican Congressmen, or even members of the cabinet. "They see that he has to deal with only a few people, rather than having a great many people barge in and out," explained aide Leonard Garment. "Nixon can't handle that." They also served as hatchet men, saying no to those who wanted something from the President and dismissing employees who failed to meet Nixon's high standards but whom the President did not want to face. In short, they were indispensable to a man who, as British journalist Henry Brandon observed, "always liked power...but detested the public exposure of one's personality that the reach for power entailed."

Only a handful of men were able to penetrate the Berlin Wall. In the domestic area, two diametrically opposed individuals, economist Arthur Burns and sociologist Daniel Patrick Moynihan, vied for Nixon's ear. Burns, who had served as Chairman of the Council of Economic Advisers under Ike, seemed at first to have the advantage. Close personal ties going back to the Eisenhower days, fiscal orthodoxy rooted in a balanced budget, impeccable Republican emphasis on freeing business from government restraint — all gave Burns unusual leverage in his cabinet-rank position of Counsellor to the President. But Moynihan, a Kennedy-style liberal from Harvard whom Len Garment recruited ("He almost drank me under the table") as secretary of the newly created Urban Affairs Council, soon came to outmaneuver Burns in the White House. "Never underestimate the importance of proximity," the ebulient Moynihan told a friend, explaining that he had made certain his office was in the West Wing, only a few steps from Nixon's, while Burns worked in the Executive Office Building next door. Moynihan also made the most of his charm, writing freewheeling memos that sparkled and spinning out his ideas in sprightly conversation. Impressed by Moynihan's vibrant personality and the grace with which he endured attacks from his old liberal friends, Nixon accepted his argument against a wholesale dismantling of the Great Society. Instead, the President retained the Office of Economic Opportunity, though he reorganized it under

Republican Donald Rumsfeld, preserved the Job Corps while transfering it to the Department of Labor, and charged Moynihan with developing a new approach to the welfare problem that led ultimately to the single most constructive proposal of the Nixon Administration. By 1970, when Nixon appointed Burns to the chairmanship of the Federal Reserve Board, Moynihan had given a surprisingly liberal cast to the Administration's approach to domestic issues, one that gave some promise of fulfilling the pledge to bring the nation together again.

The emergence of another Harvard professor, Henry Kissinger, to a position of unrivaled influence in foreign policy proved even more dramatic. A Jewish refugee from Nazi Germany, Kissinger had relied on a first-rate mind, steely determination, and thinly disguised ambition to enter the inner circle of academia and win recognition as one of the nation's leading experts on international affairs. He became Nelson Rockefeller's foreign policy adviser in the late 1950s, and he served briefly as a State Department consultant under both Kennedy and Johnson. This service had led him to view Nixon with profound mistrust as late as mid-1968, and he was greatly surprised when Nixon invited him to a private meeting at the Hotel Pierre right after the election. The two men hit it off well from the start, finding that they shared a realistic outlook on world affairs and a personal bond as men who had struggled to get to the top and suffered from a deep sense of insecurity. After a second meeting, Kissinger was offered the position of National Security Adviser, and a week later he accepted. He quickly expanded the National Security Council, which had atrophied under Kennedy and Johnson, filling it with highly regarded specialists and doubling its budget. Nixon backed Kissinger's aggressive move to make the NSC the main coordinating body for American foreign policy; Secretary of State Rogers still enjoyed personal rapport with the President, but his task was essentially to keep the State Department bureaucracy from interfering with the White House conduct of diplomacy.

At the heart of the Nixon-Kissinger relationship lay a common world view. Both men realized that the Cold War had undergone a decisive change in the 1960s; the old polarity between the United States and Russia had broken down with the rise of new centers of power in China, France, Japan, and the Third World. The containment policy, begun with the Truman Doctrine in 1947, had led to global commitments far beyond the capacity of the United States. Kissinger's task was to chart a way for Nixon to beat a strategic retreat that would end the era of containment without sacrificing American world prestige. His solution, which Nixon fully accepted, was to practice classic balance-of-power politics, treating China and Russia as traditional great powers with interests and ambitions to defend and protect and not as ideological opponents. "They recognized a cold and logical world without fated allies or enemies — only interested parties," commented Richard Whalen. Both distrusted bureaucrats because of their resistance to change and both saw the need for a combination of secret diplomacy and bold public acts to carry out the revolution in foreign policy they were planning. There was no role for the American people – the Nixon-Kissinger diplomacy "went on above the heads of the American people as though it were a high-wire act involving the fate of the trapeze artists alone."

Kissinger, Moynihan, Burns – they all enjoyed access to the President, but none could rival Attorney General John Mitchell in influence. "He is my closest adviser, as you know, on all legal matters and on many other matters as well," Nixon told the press in 1969. The close bond between them stemmed from the merger of their law firms in 1966 and the role Mitchell played as campaign manager in 1968, bringing order and discipline when it was most needed. Nixon stood almost in awe of Mitchell, envying him his unshakable composure, his steely eyed self-assurance, and his domineering presence in any gathering – qualities that the President felt he himself lacked. Most of all, Nixon relied on Mitchell for political advice, advice that ran directly counter to the bring us together theme. Mitchell kept reminding the President of his constituency – Wallace supporters, law-and-order advocates, and businessmen who had contributed so heavily through Maurice Stans. Aware that Nixon had received only 43.4 percent of the popular vote, the Attorney General insisted on policies designed to forge a majority for Nixon in 1972. His advice rarely interfered with Kissinger's conduct of foreign policy, but the search for a Republican majority undercut Moynihan's liberalizing influence and contradicted Nixon's genuine desire for a "lowering" of voices and reconciliation with the disaffected in American society.

II

The first two years of the new Administration were marked by a series of bitter contests in Congress, in the courts, on the campuses, and even in the streets of the nation. Nixon struggled with the problems bequeathed to him by Johnson – the nuclear arms race, desegregation and civil rights, and the seemingly endless war in Vietnam.

The President gave the highest priority to the nuclear arms race. Ever since the Cuban missile crisis, the Soviets had engaged in a crash program to close the missile gap that Kennedy had opened up. They built over 1000 ICBMs, including the huge SS-9 with a 25 megaton warhead, they launched submarines with Polaris-type weapons on board and, in 1966, they began deploying antiballistic missiles (ABM) around Moscow. Johnson had tried to avoid a hasty response, hoping instead that as the Kremlin leaders approached a position of equality with the United States they would agree to strategic arms limitation talks (SALT). The massive nature of the Soviet arms buildup finally convinced

Johnson that he must respond and, in 1967, he ordered a reluctant Robert McNamara to announce plans for an American ABM system, dubbed Sentinel, designed to protect United States cities against a possible Chinese nuclear attack in the 1970s. Despite charges that Sentinel was only the opening wedge in a massive anti-Soviet ABM system, the Senate approved the new program in June 1968 by a vote of 46 to 27. Johnson planned to use the ABM authorization as a bargaining point in the SALT negotiations scheduled to start in the fall, but the Soviet invasion of Czechoslovakia in August 1968 forced an indefinite postponement of the talks and left the ABM issue hanging until after the election.

In his first press conference as President, Nixon signaled his willingness to forego the traditional American insistence on nuclear supremacy by speaking of "sufficiency." For the next six weeks, Laird and Kissinger undertook a major overhaul of LBJ's Sentinel program, which the President finally revealed to the nation on March 14. The new system, now called Safeguard, shifted the antiballistic missiles from American cities to the Great Plains where they would guard the nation's primary deterrent, the Minutemen missiles buried in concrete silos. Such a change, Nixon declared, was "vital for the security and defense of the United States." Members of the Administration, led by Defense Secretary Laird, acknowledged that the ABM could not protect urban populations, since the penetration of only one enemy missile could wipe out a city, but explained that Safeguard could meet the real danger, the possibility that Russia would use her huge SS-9 missiles to destroy the American Minutemen in a first strike. The new rationale made much better sense and, for the next five months, senators engaged in a highly sophisticated debate over ABM technology, ranging from neutron explosions in outer space to the vulnerability of high-speed computers and ground radar. To millions of Americans, however, the idea of protecting weapons instead of people seemed brutally callous and inhuman, raising as it did uncomfortable questions about the nuclear age that the nation had been dodging for two decades.

The Nixon Administration ignored the moral dilemmas inherent in Safeguard as it sought to achieve its first legislative victory. Privately, the President explained to wavering senators that he needed continued approval for the ABM to have a bargaining chip to match the Russian ABM when he resumed the SALT negotiations. This appeal helped preserve GOP votes, but many Democrats who had voted for Sentinel out of loyalty to Johnson now turned against Safeguard. Bryce Harlow, in charge of Congressional relations, concentrated on the southern bloc led by Georgia's Richard Russell, and he warned the President that the vote would be very close, forecasting a possible 50-50 tie. To Harlow's disgust, the "Germans" in the White House kept interfering in the lobbying effort, making heavy-handed threats to withhold patronage from GOP opponents of the ABM. At one point, Haldeman informed one of Harlow's assistants that he should "be up in the Senate telling Hugh Scott how to vote." Despite this interference, Harlow succeeded in mustering 50 votes to defeat a Democratic attempt to gut Safeguard and then sighed with relief as the Senate voted 51 to 49 in favor of continuing the ABM effort.

Nixon could take little solace in the legislative triumph, however. In his March 14 statement, he had predicted "a very spirited debate and a very close vote," but he might have shifted his ground had he known how long and costly the fight would be. The ABM debate tied up the Senate for five months, blocking all other legislation and leaving wounds that would not heal easily. Men like GOP Majority Leader Hugh Scott voted for the ABM out of party loyalty, but they deeply resented the arm-twisting by Haldeman and his assistants. Had the President explained publicly his need for an ABM authorization as a "blue chip" in the SALT negotiations, he might have rallied widespread support and have eased his critics' fears of intensifying the arms race. As it was, his lack of candor raised suspicions that he was still wedded to a policy of nuclear supremacy and made his Safeguard victory a very expensive one.

Civil rights proved an even tougher test of Nixon's political skill. In the fifteen years since the Brown decision in 1954, the South had interpreted "with all deliberate speed" in glacial terms to block desegregation in its schools. In 1964, Congress had decreed that no federal funds could be used for segregated schools, and two years later the Johnson Administration had laid down tough guidelines that threatened a withdrawal of federal support for recalcitrant southern districts. During the 1968 campaign, Nixon had ducked the school issue, giving vague approval for a "freedom of choice" plan favored by his southern supporters. Yet, when he took office, he discovered that the issue had suddenly reached a climax, with school districts across the South facing a September, 1969 cutoff of federal funds. Worried conservatives, led by South Carolina Senator J. Strom Thurmond, who had played a key role both in Nixon's nomination and election, bombarded the White House with demands for relief, while liberals within the Administration, notably HEW Secretary Robert Finch, wanted to move ahead with a rapid and orderly desegregation of southern schools and thus a fulfillment of the 1954 Supreme Court decision.

John Mitchell realized that the HEW plans would jeopardize his goal of building a solid Republican majority in 1972. If the Administration could shift the burden of desegregation to the courts, however, perhaps Nixon could maintain his appeal to the South. On July 3, the Administration issued an ambiguous statement permitting some delay in integration beyond the September deadline and then in August, in a shocking about-face, the federal government requested a three-month postponement in the court-ordered desegregation of 33 Mississippi school districts. The NAACP filed suit against the government which, in the past, had always been its partner in the quest for racial justice, and, on October 29, the Supreme Court in *Alexander* versus *Holmes* ruled unanimously in favor of immediate integration of the Mississippi schools. In an opinion written by Warren Burger, the man Nixon appointed as Chief Justice, the Court held that "the obligation of every school district is to terminate dual school systems at once and to operate now and hereafter only unitary schools."

The President informed the nation on December 8 that he would "carry out what the Supreme Court had laid down." "I believe in carrying out the law," he hastened to add, "even though I may have disagreed as I did in this instance with the decree...." The Mitchell formula of shifting the responsibility for desegregation, and hence the political wrath of the South, to the courts had been adopted. As a result, the process of integration moved rapidly. In the 1969–70 school year, 1,200,000 black children attended formerly all-white schools in the South, twice as many as in the previous year. The Supreme Court ruled in favor of busing as a means to achieve racial balance in education and the segregation issue began to affect northern as well as southern schools. Nixon spoke out sharply against busing but, at the same time, he requested additional funds from Congress to help school districts carry out their desegregation plans. Above all, he had managed the difficult political feat of permitting more rapid integration while convincing the South that he opposed the forced mixing of races in the schools.

Nixon pursued the southern strategy even more openly in his Supreme Court appointments. His first opportunity to alter the character of the Court came with Earl Warren's resignation as Chief Justice. Warren had offered to resign in 1969, but he stayed on when LBJ's choice of Justice Abe Fortas touched off a political fight in the Senate that forced Johnson to recall the nomination. Fulfilling a campaign pledge to appoint "strict constructionists" who would reverse the liberal trend of the Warren Court on civil liberties, Nixon chose Warren Burger, a conservative and respected federal judge, as Chief Justice, a nomination that met with quick Senate approval. In the summer of 1969, a sudden vacancy developed when disclosures of conflict-of-interest compelled Fortas to resign. Ignoring the tradition of a Jewish seat on the Court that dated back to Woodrow Wilson's appointment of Louis Brandeis, Nixon followed Mitchell's suggestion and nominated Clement F. Haynsworth, Jr., a federal judge from South Carolina. Haynsworth possessed strong legal credentials, a conservative judicial philosophy, and a consistently segregationist record as an appeals judge. With Haynsworth, the President could satisfy his southern supporters and thus carry forward the Mitchell strategy for 1972.

The appointment ran into trouble from the start. Democrats, angry over the Fortas affair, were spoiling for revenge; civil rights and labor leaders both found serious flaws in Haynsworth's past decisions. Conflict-of-interest, the issue that had undone Fortas, provided the rallying point for the discontented. Haynsworth had once ruled on a case where he had an indirect economic stake in the outcome. Though his judicial superiors had cleared him of formal charges, the Democrats, led by Indiana's Birch Bayh, succeeded in convincing many liberal and moderate Republicans that the same high standards should apply to all Court nominees. On November 21, 1969, the Senate voted 55 to 45 to reject Haynsworth; for the first time since 1930, a President had been rebuffed on a Supreme Court nomination.

Nixon, angrier than his aides had ever seen him, told Mitchell to find another southern conservative appointee and the Attorney General finally came up with G. Harrold Carswell, a federal appeals judge from Florida. When the President submitted Carswell's name to the Senate on January 19, observers expected rapid confirmation. The Democrats had achieved their revenge; a second rejection would appear petty and vindictive. Yet Carswell lacked Haynsworth's legal qualifications. Higher courts had regularly reversed his decisions, and seven judges of the eighteen on the Fifth Judical Circuit refused to sign a telegram to the President endorsing his nomination. Even his defenders admitted that his judical record was only "mediocre," and Senator Ernest Hollings of South Carolina, who eventually voted for confirmation, said Carswell "was not qualified to carry Judge Haynsworth's law books." Disclosures of past advocacy of racial segregation and growing opposition by the legal community ultimately doomed the nomination, though the final Senate vote was a surprisingly close 45 to 51.

The double Supreme Court defeat embittered Nixon. He tended to agree with Mitchell's comment, "if we'd put up one of the twelve Apostles it would have been the same," and he shared the Attorney General's belief that in losing on the appointments he had won the undying loyalty of the South. With Mitchell's help, he prepared an angry public statement accusing the Senate majority of "malicious character assassination" and of insulting "millions of Americans who live in the South." Bryce Harlow tried to dissuade Nixon from making this statement, but the President was adamant.

Many observers believed that Nixon simply used the Supreme Court appointments to advance the Mitchell strategy for 1972. Certainly the episode made the President a hero in the South, but the bitterness and emotion that characterized his outburst suggest that it came from the heart. Nixon did play politics with civil rights, as his stand on school desegregation showed. In the nomination of Haynsworth and Carswell, however, he revealed his deep desire to transform a major branch of the government and halt the liberal trend of the Warren Court. Blocked by the Senate, he finally settled on the more moderate and acceptable Harry Blackmun, a respected judicial conservative from Minnesota who easily won confirmation. Blackmun and Burger would move the Supreme Court away from the advanced position it had taken under Warren on social issues; they would not, as the desegregation and school busing cases proved, undo the historic 1954 decision.

Vietnam was the most troubling of all the issues confronting the new Administration. The military situation had been relatively stable since the 1968 Tet offensive, which had exhausted both the Viet Cong and the North Vietnamese; in Paris, the peace talks that finally began in November remained stalled. Though Nixon had spoken of a secret plan to end the war during the campaign, in fact he had no overall blueprint, and he therefore instructed Kissinger to conduct a thorough survey and present him with a list of alternatives by the time of the first meeting of the National Security Council in January 1969. Kissinger listed five options, ranging from an all-out military effort to win the war to a thinly disguised retreat from South Vietnam. The President quickly realized that his choice lay between a rapid pullout that risked political opposition at home and a slow, negotiated withdrawal. Laird and Rogers favored the first alternative, Kissinger the second, though he doubted the likelihood of a successful negotiation with North Vietnam.

Nixon chose the second alternative, a gradual retreat from South Vietnam, but he kept his decision secret from all but his closest advisers. The heart of the play lay in Vietnamization, the reliance on South Vietnamese troops to take over the fighting as American soldiers left the country. The United States would concentrate on a new pacification program designed to win over the peasants in the countryside, while at the same time reducing United States casualties. In March, Secretary of Defense Laird went to Saigon to sell the new plan to General Creighton Abrams, Westmoreland's successor. When Abrams protested, Nixon flew to Honolulu to persuade the General personally to withdraw 25,000 combat troops from Vietnam. The next day, after a meeting with South Vietnamese President Nguyen Van Thieu on Midway Island, Nixon made public the first reduction in American forces in Indo-China since LBJ began the escalation in 1965.

The President refused to disclose the full details of his Vietnamization program but, in August, he gave it a broader setting by announcing the Nixon Doctrine in the course of a press conference on Guam. He had gone to the Pacific to greet the returning American astronauts after the first moon landing on July 20, 1969. He explained to reporters that while the United States did not intend to become involved in future Vietnams, it did not plan to abandon Asia. Instead, he outlined a limited retreat by which the United States would ask the Asians to take over the burden of their own defense, with America providing moral support, economic assistance, and nuclear reassurance. Those present found the President's words ambiguous and, in later statements, Nixon stressed both his determination to help stem Communist advances in the Orient and his belief that "Asian hands must shape the Asian future." In fact, the Nixon Doctrine was simply a reaffirmation of the decision to withdraw slowly from Vietnam, but it also marked, as Henry Brandon noted, "an end to the containment policy against the Soviet Union and China."

The antiwar protesters at home found the plan too gradual. In the early fall, students across the nation decided to embark on a moratorium against the war with antiwar strikes they hoped would grow more massive each month the conflict continued. On October 15, more than a million Americans left their schools and jobs to participate in Vietnam Moratorium Day activities; the largest crowd gathered on Boston Common, where an estimated 100,000 people listened to speeches by Senators Edward Kennedy and George McGovern. When an even greater number prepared to attend a huge rally in front of the Washington Monument on November 15, President Nixon decided to break his silence on the war with a televised speech on November 3. In a hard-hitting address reflecting Mitchell's point of view, the President denounced antiwar protesters and appealed for the first time to "the great silent majority of my fellow Americans" for support. He claimed he planned eventually to withdraw all United States combat forces "on an orderly scheduled timetable," but he declined to make the schedule public. He also warned the enemy not to take advantage of the American withdrawal, saying, "I shall not hesitate to take strong and effective measures" to blunt any new Communist move.

Nixon's speech gave him the time he felt he needed. Although 250,000 people attended the Washington rally on November 15, public opinion polls showed a remarkable jump in the President's popularity. On December 15, he announced an additional troop withdrawal, making a total of 115,000 American soldiers brought home since he took office. These reductions, along with the lowering of draft calls and the decreasing size of the weekly casualty list, persuaded most Americans to back the President and robbed the antiwar movement of its vitality. But Nixon had only gained some breathing space; as Kissinger told a reporter in November 1969, "We will not be justified before the American people by the numbers we withdraw and the date we withdraw them, but by how it will come out a year from now."

The American military had long wanted to attack North Vietnamese bases just across the border in Cambodia, but both Johnson and Nixon had held back for fear of driving the neutral Prince Norodom Sihanouk into an alliance with Hanoi. But on March 18, 1970, anti-Communist General Lon Nol led a successful coup against Sihanouk and, when North Vietnam retaliated by moving large numbers of troops into Cambodia, the Pentagon proposed the use of South Vietnamese troops, backed by American air and logistical support, to destroy the Communist sanctuaries. The whole Vietnamization program in the Mekong delta seemed to be at stake; unless the United States helped South Vietnam wipe out the Cambodian bases, no more American troops could be safely withdrawan. After a series of NSC meetings in late April, Nixon retired to the solitude of Camp David. "You listen to everybody's arguments, but then comes the moment of truth," he told Henry Brandon later. "I remained secluded at Camp David for two days and weighed the odds with not much sleep." When he returned to Washington, he informed Kissinger that United

States combat troops would take part in the invasion, and then relaxed by watching the movie *Patton,* with its stress on bold military action, for the second time.

Despite strong opposition to the plan from Laird and Rogers, and more muted objections by Kissinger, Nixon insisted on going ahead. The Pentagon sent out the orders on Monday, April 27, and then Nixon once again isolated himself to write out the text of the speech to the nation on one of his famous yellow pads. On April 30, a somber, nervous President informed the American people of the operation already under way, using extravagant rhetoric to justify it. He explained the military objectives, but he concentrated on the larger implications. "We will not be humiliated. We will not be defeated," Nixon declared. "If when the chips are down the U.S. acts like a pitiful helpless giant, the forces of totalitarianism and anarchy will threaten free nations and free institutions throughout the world." And then, in a most revealing sentence, he put the issue as he saw it. "It is not our power but our will that is being tested tonight."

Nixon had been warned to expect a violent reaction to the Cambodian invasion, but he was not prepared for the massive dissent from the nation's youth. Students in 448 colleges and universities went on strike, forcing many campuses to close. Delegations of students descended on Washington, receiving sympathetic hearings from Laird and Rogers, who quietly leaked their objections to the press. Secretary of the Interior Walter Hickel sided with the young people in a letter to the President in which he pleaded with him not to "set out consciously to alienate those who could be our friends." Nixon appeared to be unmoved. On May 1 he told two aides, "You see these bums, you know, blowing up the campuses....Then out there [in Vietnam] we have kids who are just doing their duty. They stand tall and they are proud." On May 4, however, the entire nation was shocked when Ohio National Guardsmen opened fire on demonstrators at Kent State University, killing four students and wounding eleven more. The Vietnam bloodbath had finally extended into the heart of America.

The President, shaken by the violence, suddenly tried to reverse his course. He consulted with college presidents in a belated effort to understand the causes of campus unrest. He called the first presidential news conference in three months on May 8 and, in a contrite mood, spoke of the student desire "to stop the killing" and "to get out of Vietnam" to declare, "I agree with everything that they are trying to accomplish." Unable to sleep that night, the President slipped out of the White House at five in the morning to mingle with the students camped out around the Lincoln Memorial. Trying desperately to establish contact, he spoke of his desire for peace, relating experiences he had had in Warsaw and Prague. "We are not interested in what Prague or Warsaw look like," a young man shot back, "we are interested in what kind of life we build in the United States!" Despite this rebuff, Nixon found the dialogue exhilarating, and he followed it up by appointing William Scranton to head a special presidential commission to investigate the causes of the campus disorders.

A minor incident in New York on May 8 provided the first evidence that the student protest did not reflect the thinking of most Americans. A group of construction workers, enraged by an antiwar demonstration in front of City Hall, attacked the students and broke up the rally. Three days later, two thousand "hard-hats" marched through Wall Street chanting "All the way, U.S.A." and on May 20 construction unions organized a huge rally around City Hall to show their support for the President's Cambodian policy. Encouraged by the White House, patriotic leaders across the nation conducted an "Honor America Day" program in Washington on July 4 attended by more than 250,000 flag-waving members of the silent majority, who listened intently to a sermon by Billy Graham and relaxed to entertainment led by Bob Hope. When the Gallup poll revealed that most Americans blamed the students, not the National Guardsmen, for the Kent State massacre, Nixon shifted back to his original hard-line stand. "I want peace on the campus," he told reporters on July 20, "but my major obligation is to adopt policies that I consider will bring peace to the world."

The Cambodian operation ended on June 30 when the President announced that all American troops had left the country. Militarily, the invasion succeeded in its goal of destroying Communist sanctuaries, thus enabling Nixon to continue the gradual withdrawal of American soldiers from South Vietnam. Yet the price he paid was very high. The antiwar movement, weakened by the slow winding down of the conflict, had suddenly sprung to life again and, in the Senate, antiwar legislators succeeded in passing the Cooper-Church amendment that barred any further American fighting in Cambodia and signified Congressional impatience with the President's slow-paced Vietnamization program. Never again would Nixon be able to exercise his power as Commander-in-Chief so cavalierly. More important, the Cambodian affair polarized the nation. Although he had found surprising support from the silent majority, Nixon had sacrificed his goal of lowering the angry voices and achieving a new era of national reconciliation. He had now embarked on the politics of division, playing one segment of the electorate off against another and thus insuring continued turmoil and unrest.

III

On September 10, 1970, a smiling Spiro T. Agnew boarded a plane at Washington's National Airport to begin a two-month tour of the nation in behalf of Richard Nixon's quest for a Republican victory in the November Congressional elections. "...one of the principal issues is whether policies of the United States are going to be made by its elected officials or in the streets," the Vice-President told reporters. "I think that's the primary issue." Ted Agnew, virtually unknown at the time of his nomination in Miami Beach, had become a household word in 1969 with a series of slashing attacks on Nixon's enemies. He first won national attention on October 9 when he denounced "a spirit of national masochism...encouraged by an effete corps of impudent snobs who characterize themselves as intellectuals." He had written those words himself, but the President, impressed by Agnew's success in rallying conservative support, lent him speech-writer Pat Buchanan, who prepared the Vice-President's equally sharp attack on television news broadcasters as "a small and un-elected elite" who "bask in their own provincialism, their own parochialism." From that point on, Agnew became the Republican party's leading spokesman, appearing at fund-raising dinners across the country and delighting the faithful with his barbed attacks on liberals, intellectuals, students, and all other groups that did not qualify for membership in the silent majority.

The choice of Agnew to spearhead the 1970 campaign reflected Nixon's commitment to the hard line that emerged after the Cambodian affair. Agnew appealed to precisely those elements in the electorate that Nixon and Mitchell felt were essential for a victory in 1972. Two books confirmed this analysis. In the first, *The Emerging Republican Majority,* Kevin P. Phillips, a special assistant to Attorney General Mitchell, argued from demographic evidence that an entirely new voting pattern had developed in the United States in the late 1960s. "From space-center Florida across the booming Texas plains to the Los Angeles-San Diego suburban corridor, the nation's fastest-growing areas are strongly Republican and conservative," he wrote. All the Administration had to do was ignore the once-vital industrial states of the Northeast and Midwest and concentrate instead on winning the "Sunbelt" that stretched from Miami through Atlanta and Dallas to Los Angeles. Richard Scammon and Ben Wattenberg, two Democratic political analysts, tended to confirm Phillips' findings in *The Real Majority,* a book that claimed that most people who went to the polls were unyoung, unblack, and unpoor. The authors focused on "the Social Issue" — the prevailing dislike of many Americans for youth, crime, violence, permissiveness, drugs, and pornography. Candidates who understood this mood were most likely to win in 1970.

Nixon, encouraged by Mitchell and long-time political consultant Murray Chotiner, decided to wage the 1970 campaign on the social issue. He realized that the Republicans had little chance to control the House; at best they could make small inroads into the large Democratic majority. But the President did hope to capture the Senate, where a gain of seven seats would shift the balance to the GOP. Above all, he wanted not only a party victory but an ideological conquest, and so he would support conservative Democrats like Henry Jackson in Washington and Harry Byrd, Jr. in Virginia and oppose liberal Republicans such as Charles Goodell in New York. He relied on Agnew to carry the message, waging an all-out verbal assault on "the radical liberals in the United States Senate," (sometimes just the "Radiclibs"), the men who wanted to sell out Vietnam to the Communists and allow crime to run rampant in the streets of America.

The Nixon strategy backfired. The Democrats had read the same books and, in 1970, their candidates came out strongly for law and order and against permissiveness. Hubert Humphrey, running for the Senate in Minnesota, reversed himself by opposing gun controls; Adlai Stevenson, III, campaigned in Illinois with an American flag in his coat lapel. More important, as Scammon and Wattenberg had warned, the economic issue rivaled the social issue as a growing recession gripped the nation in the summer and fall of 1970.

The Administration's failure to solve the deteriorating economic situation it had inherited from Johnson proved politically disastrous. When Nixon took office, the inflation created by the Vietnam war was eating away at the prosperity of the 1960s. The deficit for 1968 amounted to a record $25 billion. Many economists favored drastic measures to halt the spiral, ranging from wage-and-price controls through strict federal guidelines to Kennedy-style jawboning. Nixon rejected these alternatives, preferring to rely on a passive governmental role while the private sector adjusted itself. In 1969, the President announced his "game plan" — a sharp cut in federal spending to end the budget deficit and a rapid curtailment in the money supply by the Federal Reserve Board to force high interest rates and consequent business cutbacks on expansion. These fiscal and monetary policies would hopefully curb inflation without creating a recession and increased unemployment.

The Nixon game plan failed to work. The inflationary spiral continued unabated, since the government failed to force any restraints on prices. Business activity, hurt by rising interest rates, slowed more quickly than expected, leading to a sharp drop in federal revenue and a budget deficit in 1969 of $2.8 billion (instead of the predicted $5.6 billion surplus). The unemployment rate, which had dropped to 3.5 percent in the late 1960s, climbed to over 5 percent in mid-1970, with over 4 million men and women out of work. In June, economists officially declared a state of recession, the fifth since World War II, as production dropped below 1968 levels. Walter Heller summed up the failure in a memorable phrase when he labeled the unholy combination of inflation and recession "Nixonomics."

By October, the President, realizing that the economic decline was jeopardizing his dream of winning Senate control, decided to enter the contest personally. He left Washington on October 17 on the first stage of a trip that would carry him to 23 states over the next two weeks. Everywhere he went, he gave essentially the same speech, hitting hard at the social issue ("I can tell

you that the violent few that you see on your TV screens are not a majority
of the American youth today and they will not be leaders of America tomorrow.") and ignoring the economic decline. On several occasions, angry demonstrators played into his hands by throwing rocks and shouting obscenities;
on October 29 Nixon deliberately goaded a hostile crowd in San Jose by flash-
ing a V-for-victory salute and then ducking into his bullet-proof limousine as
television cameras recorded the barage of eggs and rocks thrown by angry youths.
On election eve, the Republicans played a badly recorded black-and-white video-
tape of Nixon's hard-nosed Phoenix speech, in which he piously announced,
"no band of violent thugs is going to keep me from going out and speaking
with the American people." The Democrats, in contrast, presented a calm,
reasoned appeal by Senator Edmund Muskie, the 1968 vice-presidential candidate, who called on the voters to reject the GOP's "politics of fear."

The next day, the voters gave Richard Nixon a sharp setback. The Democrats
picked up nine additional House seats, eleven governorships, and held the Republicans to a net gain of two Senate seats. The President could take some satis-
faction in the defeat of Goodell in New York (beaten by the independent conservative James Buckley), Albert Gore in Tennessee, and Joseph Tydings in
Maryland, but his party fared poorly in the South, losing bids to take over
Senate seats in Texas and Florida and dropping gubernatorial elections in South
Carolina, Arkansas, and Florida as black voters led a surprising Democratic
resurgence. The election proved that gut economic issues still affected Americans more deeply than uneasy fears of social change and thus served as a warning to the President for 1972.

IV

Nixon put the best possible face on the election outcome, calling it "a victory" that gave him "a working majority" in the Senate. While critics scoffed,
the President proceeded to complete a major reorganization of his cabinet. Earlier in 1970, he had replaced HEW Secretary Robert Finch, an ineffective ad-
ministrator, with Elliot Richardson, a superb manager who had proved his ability
as Under Secretary of State, and had appointed Secretary of Labor George
Schultz head of the new and powerful Office of Management and Budget (Under
Secretary George Hodgson became the new Secretary of Labor). With the
election over, the President wanted to remove Interior Secretary Walter Hickel,
who had incurred his wrath during the Cambodian affair and, when Hickel refused to step down, Nixon fired him publicly. GOP National Chairman Rogers
Morton took Hickel's place, but not before H.R. Haldeman personally removed
all six assistant secretaries at Interior. The most significant shift, however,
came in the Treasury Department, where the quiet, competent, but politically
inept David Kennedy was permitted to return to his Chicago bank. In a bold

move, Nixon persuaded former Texas Governor John Connally to become Secretary of the Treasury, despite Connally's inexperience in finance and his strong Democratic affiliation. The forceful Texan possessed, as journalists Rowland Evans and Robert D. Novak commented, "the imperious air of authority, self-possession and masterfulness that Nixon lacked and, therefore, so admired in others." Nixon took a calculated risk in appointing such a strong personality to a cabinet post; he hoped to boost his standing with conservative Democrats without alienating loyal Republicans.

The President sought to convey the sense of a new, more dynamic administration in his State-of-the-Union message to Congress on January 22. He offered "six great goals" designed to bring about "a New American Revolution." Several of the measures, notably proposals for health insurance, environmental protection, and a full employment budget simply restated traditional Democratic concepts that were relatively noncontroversial. A fourth suggestion, for a massive governmental reorganization to consolidate all the Departments except State, Treasury, Defense, and Justice into four new superagencies, marked a genuine departure. The last two goals, federal revenue sharing with the states and Moynihan's Family Assistance Plan (FAP) for welfare reform, were parts of Nixon's original legislative program that Congress had failed to enact. If the measures were relatively mundane, the rhetoric was cosmic. Congress, the President declared, had the opportunity to carry out "a peaceful revolution in which power was turned back to the people — in which government at all levels was refreshed and renewed, and made truly progressive. This can be a revolution as profound, as far-reaching, as exciting as that first revolution 200 years ago...."

The New American Revolution soon proved abortive. The Democratic Congress made only modest advances in environmental control; health insurance for those under 65 led to controversy but no action; the consolidation never materialized. The President was able to implement his full employment budget, which meant a planned federal deficit of $20 billion on the theory that if unemployment were at its normal 4 percent, instead of an actual 6 percent rate, there would be sufficient revenue to balance the budget. Not all skeptics were convinced by Nixon's description of the new concept as "a self-fulfilling prophecy: By operating as if we were at full employment, we will help to bring about that full employment." Actually, the planned deficit marked Nixon's disguised conversion to Walter Heller's new economics — the President was ignoring the problem of inflation in relying on heavy government spending to overcome the continuing recession.

The Family Assistance Plan and revenue sharing generated the most discussion in Congress. Moynihan had sold the President on FAP in 1969. The original proposal had called for replacing the existing cumbersome system with a flat payment of $1600 to each family on welfare, and was thus a variation of the Democratic concept of a guaranteed annual wage. Nixon had approved it largely because he liked the idea of substituting "cold cash" for bureaucratic services and because George Schultz added the working poor to those getting benefits and insisted on a work requirement for all recipients except the physically disabled and mothers with preschool children. Conservatives opposed FAP as a handout, however, and even liberals objected to the work rule and the very low level of payments. Despite an upward revision to $2400 a year, the Administration could find no consensus in Congress and finally let FAP die. Revenue sharing provoked an equally sharp reaction in Congress, leading one GOP stalwart to comment, "Maybe I'm old-fashioned, but I believe most sincerely that with the pleasure of spending public funds there should also be the odium of collecting them," but the Administration persisted and finally secured Congressional approval in 1972. This compromise measure provided for the distribution of $30.1 billion in federal funds over a five-year period under a complex formula that allocated one third to state governments and the remainder to city, town, and county authorities. Much of the effectiveness of revenue sharing was offset, however, by the ceiling of $2.5 billion that Congress placed on federal spending for social services, forcing local officials to use most of the new money on welfare programs previously funded by Washington.

The failure to carry out the New American Revolution was only one of several setbacks that Nixon encountered in 1971. On April 20, a unanimous Supreme Court ruled in favor of busing as an indispensable method of removing "the last vestiges" of racial discrimination from southern schools. The President expressed his strong disagreement on August 3 when he denounced a federally drawn plan that called for extensive busing in Austin, Texas. "I have consistently opposed the busing of our nation's schoolchildren to achieve a racial balance," Nixon declared, "and I am opposed to the busing of children simply for the sake of busing." The President then directed an unhappy Elliot Richardson to draw up an amendment to forbid the use of federal education funds for busing and allowed Press Secretary Ronald Ziegler to warn government employees that they risked their jobs if they worked to implement the Court's insistence on busing to achieve desegregation. Despite this unprecedented attempt to interfere with judicial procedure, when schools opened in September, nearly half-a-million southern children attended newly integrated classrooms. The long battle against de jure segregation in the South was nearly over; in the future the struggle would shift to de facto separation of the races in northern schools.

The President had a new opportunity to transform the Supreme Court in the fall of 1971 when Justices Hugo Black and John Harlan retired due to ill health. Ziegler announced that Nixon would move "as swiftly as possible" to fill the vacancies and the President himself hinted that he was considering the appointment of a qualified woman and possibly an individual who was not a practicing lawyer. After the American Bar Association gave him a rude jolt by branding six potential Nixon nominees as "unqualified" (a finding that the Washington *Post* cited as evidence of the President's "relentless pursuit of mediocrity"), Nixon named Lewis F. Powell, a Richmond, Virginia lawyer, and William H. Rehnquist, an assistant attorney general, to the Court. Powell, a distinguished attorney and former president of the ABA, quickly won approval in the Senate, with only one dissenting vote, and thus became the southern conservative Nixon had so long sought, while Rehnquist, an able legal scholar who was more extreme in his judicial philosophy, survived a closer scrutiny to win confirmation by a vote of 68 to 26.

The desegregation fight and the Bar Association action proved embarrassing to Nixon, but the growing anguish over the continuing war in Vietnam created far more dangerous political opposition. A second American-sponsored incursion into a neutral country in Indo-China, this time Laos, touched off a prolonged controversy. Acting on the advice of the Pentagon and especially of Defense Secretary Melvin Laird, the President approved a plan to invade the panhandle of Laos in order to halt the flow of supplies coming down the Ho Chi Minh trail. Learning from the Cambodian experience, Nixon insisted that no American ground troops take part in the operation, and he refrained from identifying himself personally with the invasion that began on February 8, 1971. The South Vietnamese Army (ARVN), supported by American air strikes and helicopter supply missions, moved 16 miles into Laos before the North Vietnamese unleashed a furious counterattack. The inexperienced ARVN troops began a retreat that turned into a rout for some units; unfortunately for Nixon, American television reporters filmed scenes of South Vietnamese soldiers fleeing for their lives, hanging on to the landing skids of U.S. helicopters and giving the impression of mass panic. For many Americans, already fed up with the prolonged Vietnam struggle, Laos became the final indignity.

In the midst of the Laotian fiasco, an Army court-martial found Lieutenant William Calley guilty of the premeditated murder of more than 20 villagers in Mylai, South Vietnam. Though Calley was spared the death penalty, the American people reacted angrily at the sentence of life imprisonment, feeling that Calley was being made a scapegoat for higher-ranking officers who had ordered the attack on Mylai and the resulting massacre. With White House mail running 100 to 1 in favor of clemency, the President quickly ordered Calley released from the stockade at Fort Benning pending an appeal and announced that he would review the case personally before sentence was carried out.

The Calley verdict and the Laos affair brought about a sudden resurgence in the antiwar movement, which had been relatively quiet since the Cambodia spring. Ignoring a Presidential speech in early April promising the withdrawal of an additional 100,000 American troops in 1971, demonstrators poured into Washington wearing buttons with the simple slogan, "Enough." For four days, over 1000 Vietnam Veterans Against the War, many on crutches or in wheelchairs, conducted rallies climaxed by an emotional scene in which more than 700 men threw their medals and ribbons, ranging from Purple Hearts to Silver Stars, over a wire fence before the Capitol. Their spokesman, John Kerry, voiced the veterans' "determination to undertake one last mission, to reach out and destroy the last vestige of this barbaric war...." Senator George McGovern called the demonstration "the most effective protest to date"; a frightened Richard Nixon asked aide John Dean, who had mingled with the veterans, for a first-hand account. Nixon's concern was so great, Dean later told the Watergate Committee, that "we prepared hourly status reports and sent them to the President."

The demonstrations reached their peak in early May. Rallies of up to 200,000 took place around the nation, but the main focus was on Washington, where a militant group known as the people's coalition for peace and justice planned to shut down the government. The Mayday Tribe, as these radicals became known, set out to disrupt the rush hour traffic into the capital on the morning of May 3. Ordering that the city be kept "open for business," Nixon countered with a massive force of 5000 policemen and 4000 federal troops, with 7500 more soldiers in reserve. During the next two days, Attorney General Mitchell supervised the arrest and detention of over 12,000 individuals, paying scant attention to their civil liberties as they were herded into makeshift jails at places such as a practice football field and the Washington Coliseum. Many were released without being formally charged and, by mid-May, the city had returned to normal. The President had survived the militants' challenge but, in the process, he had lost much popular support by using equally extreme and undemocratic means.

For Richard Nixon, the sensational publication of the Pentagon Papers in newspapers across the country in mid-June 1971 came as the final indignity. Secretary of Defense Robert McNamara had ordered the preparation of this massive study of Vietnam policy from 1945 to 1968, and Daniel Ellsberg, one of his former aides, had leaked it to the New York *Times,* the Washington *Post,* and other papers. Though the Pentagon Papers contained no documents on the Nixon Administration, nor any from the White House files at any time, the President felt that the release of hitherto secret information breached the basic principle of governmental confidentiality. Accordingly, the Justice Department filed suit to enjoin the newspapers from publishing the Pentagon Papers; the New York *Times* and the Washington *Post* lost an appeal from a court ruling that they could not print any material that the government claimed was vital to the national security. The two papers appealed to the Supreme Court, claiming that the restraining order was "a classic case of censorship" and thus a clear violation of the First Amendment guarantee of a free press. The Court ruled six to three in favor of the newspapers, though only three Justices accepted the First Amendment grounds (the other three in the majority ruled simply that the government had failed to prove that publication involved immediate and irreparable damage to the nation). The three dissenting judges, including Nixon appointees Burger and Blackmun, favored a continued restraint on publication.

The President had suffered a stinging defeat, one made even more painful by the ringing opinion of the dying Hugo Black (the last one he would ever write), "I believe that every moment's continuance of the injunctions against these newspapers amounts to a flagrant, indefensible, and continuing violation of the First Amendment." Ever since the Congressional elections, the tide of events had moved against him. He had failed to secure the "ideological majority" he hungered for in Congress; he had overreacted to the Vietnam protest movement; he had run afoul of the Supreme Court on busing and now on his belief in government secrecy. Worst of all to this most political of Presidents, he found his standing in the Gallup poll declining throughout the spring. From a high of 56 percent in January, the percentage of those approving of his conduct had dropped to 50 percent in March and then to an all-time personal low of 49 percent in April. He had to reverse this dangerous trend or his dream of winning a sweeping reelection and ruling with a broad popular mandate might never be fulfilled.

V

The President responded in the summer of 1971 with a series of actions designed to restore his sagging popularity. Some measures were highly publicized, others were kept deeply secret; some dealt with domestic problems, others with foreign affairs. All involved dramatic reversals from previous Administration policy and led to a sharp upswing in the polls. Yet, despite this short-run success, the "Great Nixon Turnaround," to use Lloyd Gardner's apt phrase, led ultimately to disaster.

Nixon made his first move secretly. A week after the Pentagon Papers began appearing in the New York *Times*, he authorized John Ehrlichman to create a special White House unit to "stop security leaks and to investigate other sensitive security matters." The President had long expressed concern over such leaks. In 1969, he had permitted the FBI to tap the private telephones of Henry Kissinger's National Security Council staff, and a year later he had approved a plan submitted by aide Tom Charles Huston to set up an "Interagency Group on Domestic Intelligence and Internal Security" composed of agents of the FBI, the CIA, and other intelligence units acting under White House direction. Only strenuous objections from FBI Chief J. Edgar Hoover, who opposed plans for extensive electronic surveillance, for the interception and opening of mail, and for the lifting of restrictions on "surreptitious entry" against domestic radicals and foreign diplomats, forced the President to cancel the operation after five days of existence. In mid-June 1971, however, the recent Mayday violence and the Pentagon Papers affair led to what John Dean termed "a quantum jump" in White House concern and formation of "the plumbers."

The new investigating group, led by Egil Krogh and David Young, began operations in July with the hiring of E. Howard Hunt, a 20-year veteran of the CIA, and G. Gordon Liddy, a former FBI agent who loved guns and playing tough. Daniel Ellsberg became their first target; the plumbers hoped to find damaging evidence linking Ellsberg with domestic radicals, and hopefully, with foreign governments. When FBI attempts to gain information from Ellsberg's California psychiatrist, Dr. Lewis J. Fielding, failed, Hunt and Liddy borrowed CIA regalia, including a camera concealed in a tobacco pouch, and recruited three Cuban exiles who had served with Hunt in the Bay of Pigs invasion to break in and steal Ellsberg's file from Dr. Fielding's office in Beverly Hills. On September 4, the three Cubans rifled the office while Hunt kept watch on Dr. Fielding at his home and Liddy cruised nearby streets looking out for the police and maintaining contact with a walkie-talkie. The burglary, authorized indirectly by Ehrlichman, went off smoothly, but the Cubans failed to find Ellsberg's file, which Dr. Fielding kept in a safer place.

The President may not have known about these clandestine and clearly illegal activities, but he must have been aware of the "enemies list," a project carried out by White House aide Charles Colson, who specialized in political projects, and his assistant, John Dean. In August 1971, Dean prepared a memorandum describing ways "we can maximize the fact of our incumbency in dealing with persons known to be active in their opposition to our Administration." "Stated a bit more bluntly," Dean continued, "how we can use the available Federal machinery to screw our political enemies." There followed suggestions for income tax audits, for denial of federal contract awards, and for Justice Department litigation aimed at a group of prominent individuals including such diverse figures as the 12 black Republicans in Congress, the presidents of Harvard, Yale, and M.I.T., and Jet football star Joe Namath, mistakenly identified as a New York Giant. The enemies list, along with the Ellsberg psychiatrist breakin, reveals the siege mentality that permeated the White House in the summer of 1971. New York *Times* reporter R.W. Apple, Jr., summed it up perfectly when he observed later, "Paranoia toward outsiders, absolute faith in insiders — result, disaster."

The President's second step proved far more constructive. By early August, he finally realized that his original economic game plan had failed — the reliance on gradualism had led to a recession that still plagued the country while inflation grew worse. Secretary of the Treasury John Connally began to advocate a bolder policy and, though George Shultz pleaded for a free market, Federal Reserve Chairman Arthur Burns sounded a renewed call for government action.

After a long meeting with all his economic advisers, the President announced a startling new program designed to curb inflation, speed the sluggish recovery from the recession, and solve the nagging international problems of a continuing gold drain and an unfavorable balance of trade, the first in more than 40 years. The chief domestic measure was a 90-day freeze on all wages and prices that went against Nixon's heated public opposition to all forms of government economic controls. In addition, the President asked Congress to repeal existing excise taxes on cars, speed up a planned increase in personal income tax exemptions to beef up consumer spending power, and to delay for a year action on both his welfare-reform and revenue-sharing proposals. On the international scene, Nixon took the equally surprising step of suspending the traditional United States practice of converting dollars to gold. "Opening the gold window," as the new departure was called, in effect left the dollar free to float on international monetary exchanges and automatically devalued it, making American goods cheaper, and thus more competitive in foreign markets. The President also placed a temporary 10 percent surtax on imported goods in an effort to redress the adverse balance of trade.

The sudden monetary and tariff moves came as a rude shock to America's trading partners, especially Japan and the Western European nations. They faced losses in the American domestic market, since their goods would now be higher priced, as well as uncertainties in international monetary rates. After considerable foreign pressure had been exerted, Secretary Connally agreed to a series of meetings in which he proved to be a hard bargainer, winning a reputation as "the bully boy on the manicured playing fields of international finance." The talks culminated in an agreement in December, signed at the Smithsonian Institution in Washington, by which the European nations and Japan agreed to revalue their currencies while the United States resumed buying gold at a new rate of $38 an ounce, an increase in $3 over the old level. In the Smithsonian agreement, Connally had effectively devalued the American dollar by more than 12 percent, insuring a sharp movement in the balance of payments and return of a large portion of the 50 billion in dollars that America's trading partners held abroad.

The domestic economic program worked almost as well. In October, Nixon ended the 90-day freeze, replacing it with a group of new government agencies: a fifteen-member Pay Board that would attempt to hold wage increases below a 5.5 percent annual level, a seven-member Price Commission whose task was to keep inflation at a 2.5 percent annual figure, and a Cost of Living Council chaired by John Connally for overall supervision and the development of new policies. Phase II, as the new setup became known, brought inflation under temporary control for the first time since 1968, giving the nation a new sense of economic confidence. By the first quarter of 1972, the economy had moved out of the recession as industrial production surged 5.3 percent ahead of the previous year. Though there was still an alarming gap between production and full industrial capacity, the country's corporations reported record profits — an average increase of 11.7 percent over 1971, with the automobile industry, benefitting from devaluation and the surcharge, leading the way. For the first time since he took office in 1969, Nixon had taken steps that improved the economic outlook.

The President's foreign policy reversals proved even more sensational. On July 15, 1971, Nixon informed the nation by television that he would visit Peking within the next year to confer with Communist Chinese leaders in order "to seek the normalization of relations between the two countries." This startling announcement was the fruit of more than two years of probing carried on through established channels, the American and Chinese embassies in Warsaw, and through helpful third parties like Pakistan. The Chinese responded cautiously at first, but with increasing interest as they realized that Nixon, despite his past record of antagonism toward Communist China, genuinely desired improved relations. For Mao Tse-tung and Chou En-lai, the timing was perfect. China was just emerging from the self-imposed isolation of the tumultuous cultural revolution of the late 1960s and was seeking counterweights to the Soviet Union, with nearly a million men mobilized along the Siberian border, and to an economically revived Japan.

The first hint of China's receptivity came in April 1971, when Peking invited an American ping-pong team, in Japan for a world tournament, to visit the People's Republic. American newsmen were permitted to accompany the table tennis players, the first United States group to visit the mainland since the mid-1950s, and Chou En-lai was on hand at the Great Hall of the People in Peking to greet his country's guests personally, telling them, "You have opened a new page in the relations of the Chinese and America people. I am confident," he continued, "that this beginning again of our friendship will certainly meet with the majority support of our two peoples." In America, two decades of "yellow peril" rhetoric vanished overnight as a new China craze swept the nation. Nixon joined in by announcing the relaxation of a 20-year-old embargo on trade with China, and then he sent Henry Kissinger on a secret mission to Peking to gain Chinese agreement before making the July 15 disclosure of his forthcoming trip to China. The only hostile comment came from foreign capitals: in Moscow, *Pravda* warned against "any designs to use the contacts between Peking and Washington for pressure against the Soviet Union"; in Tokyo, Japanese officials expressed shock and anger at Nixon's failure to inform them in advance of the sudden American about-face with Japan's Asian rival; and in Taipei, the Nationalist Chinese, feeling betrayed by the opening to Peking, warned darkly about "increasing the danger of subversion and attack upon democratic nations."

The close American ties to Chiang's government on Formosa created the most sensitive and difficult issue for Nixon and Kissinger. For more than 20 years, the United States had led the fight to block Red China's admission to the United Nations; on August 2, Secretary of State Rogers announced that the United States would now support the seating of mainland China, but at the same time would fight against the expulsion of the Nationalists. When Peking refused to join the UN as long as Chiang's regime was represented, the other nations overrode American objections and voted 59 to 55 to expel Taiwan, touching off a wild demonstration of hand-clapping and jeering at the expense of the United States, and then admitted the Peking government by an overwhelming margin, 76 to 35. President Nixon, taken aback by the emotional scene in the UN, denounced the "undisguised glee" at the expulsion of Formosa as "shocking," and permitted Press Secretary Ronald Ziegler to warn that it could "impair support for the UN in the country and in the Congress."

The President did not permit a fit of pique to alter his new China policy, however. In February 1972 he made the trip to China, accompanied by a planeload of American journalists and with full television coverage beamed back to the United States by satellite. After a cool and formal greeting at the airport outside Peking, he met briefly with Mao and then held a series of talks with Chou En-lai. The two men exchanged views candidly but reached little agreement, particularly on the fundamental issue of Taiwan. In their final communique they glossed over the deadlock with the ambiguous statement "that all Chinese on either side of the Taiwan Strait maintain there is but one China and that Taiwan is a part of China." The President did affirm "the ultimate objective of the withdrawal of all U.S. forces and military installations from Taiwan," but no timetable was set, nor did the two leaders take any further steps toward establishing formal diplomatic relations between China and the United States.

The real significance of Nixon's visit was symbolic. By going to Peking, the President allowed the American people's long love affair with China, dormant since the Communist rise to power, to bloom once again. Liberal Democrats suddenly found themselves lavishing praise on Richard Nixon: Senator Edward Kennedy called the communique "one of the most progressive documents" in American history, while Frank Church gushed, "Nixon's great accomplishment is that he has changed the public image of China." A few skeptics pointed to the enormous political advantage the President had gained in making this well-publicized journey at the outset of an election year, but they made little dint in the chorus of praise. Disregarding the partisan angle, most Americans rejoiced at the President's bold stroke in fulfilling his inaugural promise to end the long years of Cold War confrontation and open up a new era of negotiation with the Communists.

VI

"Americans are engaged in a great enterprise," Nixon proclaimed in August

1971, "...to build a generation of peace, something that Americans have not enjoyed in this century." The key, he realized, lay in Moscow, not Peking, and thus his quest for "a generation of peace" led to the boldest of his foreign policy reversals, the detente with Russia.

The President had plotted his effort to end the Cold War with the greatest care. When he came into office in 1969, he and Kissinger worked out a comprehensive strategy based on the idea of "linkage." Instead of a series of ad hoc bargains with the Russians, they would insist on a general settlement linking together such troublesome issues as the Vietnam war, Middle East tension, Berlin and, above all, the nuclear arms race. In time, the President departed from this plan in Vietnam, as he realized that the Kremlin had relatively little leverage on Hanoi. But for the most part he held to his conviction that detente could only come from a broad relaxation of tension with the Soviet Union. Kissinger became the prime mover in this operation, developing a friendly and productive relationship with Anatoly Dobrynin, the Russian ambassador in Washington who had direct contact with Brezhnev and Kosygin in Moscow. The two men began meeting even before Nixon was inaugurated, and their close contact became the main channel for the slow and halting evolution of detente.

In the first two years of the Nixon Administration, Kissinger made little progress. Though each side wanted to improve relations, the past distrust was hard to overcome. In the Middle East, an ominous Soviet buildup of jet planes and surface-to-air missiles in Egypt alarmed the United States and, in the fall of 1970, Nixon put American troops in Germany on alert and reinforced the Sixth Fleet in the Mediterranean during a crisis between Jordan and Syria in order to deter Russian interference. A few weeks later, newspaper accounts of the construction of a Soviet submarine base near Cienfuegos in Cuba led Kissinger to remind Dobrynin of the 1962 Kennedy-Khrushchev understanding that banned strategic weapons from the island. The Russians quickly halted work as Dobrynin privately assured Kissinger that his country would stand by the 1962 agreement. The tough American stand in the Middle East and Cuba may have helped persuade the Soviets of Nixon's refusal to make piecemeal concessions, but the only real progress toward detente came over Berlin, with the beginning of four-power talks.

Both sides realized the crucial importance of the Strategic Arms Limitations Talks. SALT began in Helsinki in the fall of 1969 after Nixon received the ABM authorization from Congress, and for the next three years the talks continued on a rotating basis between the Finnish capital and Vienna. At the outset, the strategic balance seemed relatively even. The Soviets had established a lead in ICBMs with a heavy building program still under way (1200 to 1054 for the United States), while America had far more Polaris submarine-launched missiles (656 to 200) and more than twice as many long-range bombers (450 to 200). The exclusive American possession of MIRV (multiple independently targeted reentry vehicle, that is, a missile with from three to ten separate war-heads that could be sent to widely spaced targets in the Soviet Union) more than offset the 64 ABMs the Russians had placed around Moscow. With MIRV, the United States had the technical capacity to more than triple its nuclear striking power and thus overcome both the Russian ABM and ICBM advantage.

The SALT talks quickly reached a deadlock. The Russians wanted to limit the agreement to an ABM treaty in order to prevent a rapid American buildup of this defensive weapon; the United States insisted on a numerical limitation of ICBMs, especially the huge SS-9, which had the capacity to destroy American missiles in their concrete silos. While the technical experts meeting in Vienna and Helsinki, led by American Gerard Smith and Russian Vladimir Semyonov, failed to make progress, Nixon permitted Henry Kissinger to open up "back channel" negotiations with Dobrynin in Washington that were kept secret even from Smith and Semyonov. After four months of give and take, Kissinger and Dobrynin worked out an agreement in principle that Nixon and Brezhnev announced to the world on May 20, 1971. The United States and Russia agreed to place limits on the number of ABMs each side could deploy and to freeze ICBMs at their existing level, with a further Russian pledge to hold down the number of the dreaded SS-9s.

This breakthrough still left the SALT negotiators with the difficult and time-consuming task of working out the details, such as the numerical limits on ABMs and whether to include submarine-launched missiles in the freeze. In October, when Nixon announced that he would travel to Russia in May for a meeting with Brezhnev and Kosygin, reporters speculated that the President undoubtedly planned to sign the long-sought nuclear arms limitation treaty at the Moscow summit.

A sudden renewal of the fighting in South Vietnam in March 1972 cast a long shadow over this promising outlook. Hanoi launched a major offensive, complete with Soviet-supplied tanks, at three points in South Vietnam, gaining the most ground in Quangtri province just below the 17th parallel. After initial reverses, the South Vietnamese forces fought back with surprising strength. Angered by the assault, which he interpreted as a deliberate attempt to take advantage of continued American troops withdrawals, Nixon responded by a massive use of air power. For the first time since 1969, American planes attacked targets deep within North Vietnam, hitting the outskirts of both Hanoi and Haiphong, the major port city. Nearly 200 huge B-52s, each carrying 24 tons of bombs, struck from high altitudes while Air Force fighters from bases in Thailand and Navy Phantom jets from six carriers in the Gulf of Tonkin used new "smart" bombs, equipped with television and laser beams, to destroy bridges with an amazing degree of success. When this aerial counteroffensive failed to stop the North Vietnamese attacks on the South, Nixon ordered the Navy to mine the approaches to Haiphong harbor. Naval officers had advocated such a step since 1966, but President Johnson had vetoed it for fear of sinking Russian and Chinese vessels and thus risking a widening of the war. Both Laird and Kissinger objected to the mining, but the President sided with Treasury Secretary John Connally, who now became the most outspoken Administration hawk.

Liberal critics predicted a Russian cancellation of the forthcoming summit meeting, but the President refused to call off either the bombing or the mining and, to general astonishment, the Moscow meeting took place as scheduled in mid-May. For a week, Nixon met with the Russian leaders, spending 42 hours in face-to-face discussion with Brezhnev as the two men hammered out the final details of arms limitation. Unlike the Peking trip, the Moscow summit led to a series of agreements capped by the signing of two documents that comprised SALT I. The first was a treaty limiting the two nations to 200 ABMs in two separate systems, one to defend the national capital and one to protect offensive missiles. Experts thought it unlikely that either country would build that many ABMs; the treaty's importance lay in the assurance that neither could construct a large system. The second document was an executive agreement by which Nixon and Brezhnev promised not to build any additional land-based ICBMs after July 1, thereby permitting Russia to maintain its numerical lead but not to increase it, and regulated the number of submarine-launched missiles, giving the Russians the opportunity to build about 300 more than the United States. The offensive missile agreement was to last five years, and though on the surface it seemed to favor the Soviet Union, it place no limitation on MIRV, which remained the great American qualitative advantage.

The real significance of SALT I was its recognition of Russian parity in nuclear striking power. Nixon was willing to forego insistence on American numerical superiority in order to secure limits on both the Russian defensive and offensive missiles. Though many hailed the documents as the beginning of effective arms control, most experts realized that it simply transferred the competition from the assembly lines to the laboratories. Both sides would use the five-year freeze to perfect new and more destructive weapons. The Soviets immediately launched a major effort to master MIRV technology while Secretary of Defense Laird insisted, as the price for Pentagon cooperation in obtaining Congressional approval of the agreements, on securing funds to develop the B-1 bomber and the Trident submarine. Instead of an immediate reduction in defense spending, SALT I led to a new round of strategic arms expenditures as the United States sought to build the weapons of the future.

Yet meager as the impact of SALT I was on the nuclear arms race, it did mark a major turning point in the Cold War. By traveling to Russia and signing these agreements, Nixon had gone far toward achieving "the generation of peace" that he had promised. The Moscow summit made detente a reality, and the President was ready to harvest the fruit of his foreign policy coup when he faced the voters in the fall. As he proudly told the Congress on his return:

> An unparalleled opportunity has been placed in America's hands....We can seize this moment or lose it; we can make good this opportunity to build a new structure of peace in the world, or let it slip away. Together, therefore, let us seize the moment so that our children and the world's children live free of the fears and free of the hatreds that have been the lot of mankind through the centuries.

VII

Despite Nixon's strong rebound, a half dozen prominent Democrats vied for the chance to run against him in 1972. Senator Edmund Muskie of Maine, the moderate who had been the Democratic vice-presidential candidate in 1968, was the frontrunner, while Hubert Humphrey, once regarded as an outspoken liberal, contested for the party's middle ground with strong labor backing. On the right, Senator Henry Jackson of Washington appealed to Democratic hawks with an undisguised Cold War stance and Governor George Wallace of Alabama, returning to the fold after his 1968 third-party candidacy, sought the votes of those disaffected by the federal government's racial, economic, and social policies. John Lindsay, the former Republican mayor of New York City, hoped to cash in on his vaunted charisma by wooing the newly franchised 18-to-21 year olds; Senator George McGovern was the other leading contender on the left, with a small but growing following among college students, women's rights advocates, and the intellectuals.

The spring primaries quickly destroyed the Muskie candidacy, as his failure to win a majority in his neighboring state of New Hampshire followed by miserable showings in Florida and Wisconsin all but drove him out of the contest. McGovern displayed surprising strength, scoring well in New Hampshire and sweeping to victory in Wisconsin with a well-organized and efficiently run campaign. George Wallace proved equally popular, winning in Florida and threatening to become a major contender until Arthur Bremer's assassination attempt in mid-May left him paralyzed from the waist down and forced him to withdraw. The Democratic showdown came in California when Hubert Humphrey waged an all-out effort to portray McGovern as a radical, challenging the South Dakota Senator's dovish defense proposals and ridiculing his poorly conceived welfare plan. McGovern's lead in the polls, once as high as 15 points, vanished in the last week and he barely escaped with a narrow victory over Humphrey. The 271 California delegates assured him of the Democratic nomination, but Humphrey's savage assault destroyed the momentum McGovern had been building since New Hampshire and left him open to future Republican attacks.

The Miami Beach convention provided a turbulent and often exciting spectacle for the nation. The McGovern forces beat back last minutes challenges by the Democratic Old Guard, but the reform rules that insured participation by women, blacks, and young people led to some wild scenes as the convention debated resolutions on such controversial topics as abortion and homosexuality, delaying the proceedings and forcing McGovern to make his acceptance speech at three in the morning to a meager nationwide television audience. Intent on winning the nomination, McGovern had failed to consider the choice of a running mate in advance, and at the last minute he selected the relatively unknown Thomas Eagleton, Senator from Missouri, whose only qualifications appeared to be a prolabor voting record, border state appeal, and the fact that he was a Catholic. When newspapers reported a week later that Eagleton had been hospitalized for psychiatric care on three separate occasions in the 1960s, McGovern at first stood behind him, saying he was "1000 per cent for Tom Eagleton." But, as opposition mounted, McGovern shifted his ground, until he finally forced Eagleton to quit the ticket. The Democratic National Committee quickly selected Sargent Shriver as his replacement, but the episode proved disastrous. An underdog from the outset, McGovern's only chance to win lay in his appeal as a sincere and candid man. The Eagleton affair made him appear devious and expedient, thus disappointing his idealistic supporters and putting him on the defensive throughout the campaign. McGovern worked hard to demonstrate that he was not the radical Humphrey had portrayed, but he succeeded only in convincing many voters that he was an indecisive and inept man who could not be trusted with presidential responsibility.

Nixon, meanwhile, savored the Democratic disarray from the safe confines of the White House, which he rarely left during the fall campaign. He carefully stage-managed the Republican convention, which followed a prepared script that broke down the entire proceedings into minutes and seconds, with specified allotments for each speaker, each outburst of applause and even each demonstration, complete to the number of balloons to be released. To the delight of conservatives, Spiro T. Agnew remained on the ticket, though many party regulars grumbled over the creation of the Committee to Reelect the President, which directed Nixon's campaign with lavish funding and kept it entirely separate from the Republican National Committee. The President limited his participation to a few televised appearances and let Agnew and members of his cabinet carry on the campaign as his surrogates. He held no press conferences throughout the fall as he sought to avoid making any controversial statements that could endanger his reelection.

The only threat came from the overzealous activities of his aides. On June 17, Howard Hunt and Gordon Liddy, the former "plumbers" now employed by the Committee to Reelect the President, engineered a breakin at the Democratic National Committee's headquarters in the Watergate complex. Police caught the actual burglars, including ex-CIA agent James McCord and Cuban exile Bernard L. Barker, and the Democrats, seeking to exploit this incident, immediately termed it "a blatant act of political espionage" and filed a $1 million damage suit against the Committee to Reelect the President. The White House publicly denied any complicity (Press Secretary Ron Ziegler dismissed it as "third-rate burglary") but, behind the scenes, presidential aides John Dean, Haldeman and Erhlichman began a huge cover-up operation that included payment of the burglars' legal fees, larger sums to induce their continued silence, and even promises of executive clemency. Despite continued Democratic outcry, and some heroic investigative reporting by the Washington *Post* team of Robert Woodward and Carl Bernstein, the American people displayed little interest.

The President more than made up for any losses from Watergate by spectacular developments in the Paris peace talks on Vietnam. For nearly four years, Henry Kissinger had been meeting secretly with North Vietnamese diplomat Le Duc Tho; in the course of their 15th meeting, on October 8, they broke the long deadlock when each side made a crucial concession. North Vietnam dropped its demand for a coalition government, accepting instead a military cease-fire without a specific political settlement, while in return the United States agreed to permit the more than 100,000 North Vietnamese troops in South Vietnam to stay after the fighting stopped. Kissinger initialed the draft agreement, but then ran into unexpected trouble when South Vietnamese President Thieu refused to approve the terms. On October 26, North Vietnam, apparently fearful that Nixon would revoke the agreement after the election, broadcast a summary of the accord. Smarting from this disclosure, Kissinger told a Washington news conference that "peace is at hand," thereby ensuring Nixon's reelection. Rejoicing at the premature news of the war's end, the American people did not become troubled at the continued refusal of Thieu to accept the agreement.

On November 7, Nixon captured 60.7 percent of the popular vote in a landslide victory almost as great as Johnson's triumph over Goldwater in 1964; George McGovern carried only the District of Columbia and Massachusetts. In several ways, however, Nixon's victory was deceptive. The low turnout, only 55 percent of the electorate, confirmed observers' reports that many Americans voted for the lesser of two evils, displaying a noticeable lack of enthusiasm as they cast their ballots for the President. Nixon succeeded in picking up the Wallace vote, but he failed to establish the Republican majority he had been seeking since 1968; the Democrats maintained their control of Congress, picking up two additional Senate seats and losing just twelve House places. The inept campaign waged by McGovern padded the margin of victory and thus disguised the shallowness of Nixon's appeal to the American people.

The President ignored these considerations as he savored his long-sought victory. For the first time in his career, he had won big in a national election. Now he could look ahead to four more years in the White House, years of serenity in which he would be secure from the nagging fear of rejection by the voters.

The only cloud that remained was the stubborn refusal of the Vietnamese, both in Saigon and Hanoi, to accept the peace terms Kissinger had worked out. When North Vietnam continued to haggle over details, the President lost his patience and resumed massive bombing of the North, unleashing B-52 attacks that outdid all previous assaults and led to cries of outrage in the United States. Even the staunchly Republican Los Angeles *Times* denounced Nixon for "directing against this small Asian country a rain of death and terror that to the whole world makes the United States of America appear a barbarian gone mad." But the very ferocity of the attack apparently convinced Hanoi of Nixon's determination, and on January 23 the two nations announced that they would sign the much-delayed cease-fire agreement on January 27. The final terms showed little change from those released by Hanoi in October: total withdrawal of American troops within 60 days without a matching North Vietnamese pull-out, the release of all American prisoners of war, an International Control Commission to police the cease-fire, and only vague provision for a future political settlement between Hanoi and Saigon. The truce did not achieve "the peace with honor" that Nixon had promised; it was, in fact, a cease-fire in place, very similar to one proposed by Democrat Cyrus Vance in 1968. But at least it ended direct American military involvement in Vietnam and allowed the Vietnamese to settle their own fate free of foreign interference.

The triumphal reelection and the end of the Vietnam war marked the zenith of Nixon's political career. For four years, he had made political success the ultimate test of both his domestic and his foreign policies and, despite such setbacks as the Haynsworth and Carswell rejections, the Mayday riots and the Pentagon Papers affair, he had won the overwhelming support of the American people. The war in Vietnam had played an integral role in his political maneuvering and it seemed fitting, and perhaps inevitable, that he ended it only after he was safely reelected. For above all else, Richard Nixon was a purely political man. His abrupt reversals on economic and foreign policy in 1971 reveal his exclusive preoccupation with the election process. "Flexibility," he had told Richard Whalen in 1969, "is the first principle of politics"; his first four years in the White House suggest that it was the only principle he possessed.

Epilogue: The Unmaking of a President

On January 20, 1973, Richard Nixon began his second term in a confident and triumphal mood. Reelected by an overwhelming majority, he could look forward to the ending of the Vietnam War in a few days and tell the American people that they "stood on the threshhold of a new era of peace in the world." At home, he planned to use his electoral mandate to prune away the reforms adopted in the 1960s and put tight reins on federal spending. By the end of the month he had announced plans to eliminate 112 Great Society programs, including the Office of Economic Opportunity and Model Cities, and had shocked Congressional leaders by affirming his right of impoundment, refusing to spend some $8.7 billion in funds appropriated by Congress in 1972. A great constitutional struggle appeared to be shaping up, a struggle in which the President had all the advantages. Yet, within 18 months, Nixon had met with a stunning series of reversals that finally forced him to resign the Presidency.

Nixon's decline stemmed from a combination of developments that occurred early in his second term. A new wave of inflation that began with food prices and then spread to every sector of the economy went far toward eroding the President's postelection popularity. Consumers first began to notice the sudden rise in grocery prices in early 1973; in February alone, the cost of meat, poultry and fish jumped an astonishing 5 percent. Wholesale food prices increased at a spectacular 53.2 percent between December and February as farmers and ranchers benefitted from a worldwide crop failure, the stimulus of a massive wheat sale to the Soviet Union, and the growing demand of more

and more affluent American consumers. The Administration was caught totally unprepared. On January 11, Nixon had announced Phase III in the economic stabilization program, ending wage and price controls on all except the food,
health care, and construction industries and thereby touching off a hectic round
of price increases by manufacturers who sought to make up for the nearly two
years of enforced price restraint. By March, the cost of living had increased
to an annual rate of 9.6 percent, the highest since the Korean War.

Belatedly, the President sought to offer relief. On March 29, he placed
price ceilings on beef, pork, and lamb in an effort to placate angry housewives
who were organizing meat boycotts. He held back from bolder steps, telling
a news conference on May 2 that he had resisted "the temptation" to "go for
the superficially simple solution — to freeze prices," but on June 13, in yet
another turnaround, he ended Phase III and froze all prices for 60 days while
his aides prepared a new system of economic control to battle inflation. Phase
IV, announced on July 18, reimposed government supervision of prices but
permitted businesses to pass on additional costs to consumers. The new system
worked no better than its predecessors. Food prices continued to rise at a
phenomenal 20 percent rate, and the overall cost of living advanced by more
than 8 percent through 1973. In April 1974, the President finally abandoned
Phase IV, ending the experiment in economic controls that had begun in August 1971 to such great applause and yet that had led only to the worst inflation in the nation's history. By mid-1974, inflation had become the people's
most pressing domestic concern and the Administration's vacillating policies
had cast doubt on Nixon's ability to govern effectively.

The disclosure of scandal and corruption, beginning with the Watergate revelations in the spring and summer of 1973, provided an even greater threat to
Nixon's hopes for a triumphal second term. The first break came on March
23, 1973, when Judge John Sirica, who had tried the seven men accused of the
actual burglary of the Democratic National Headquarters in the Watergate complex, read a letter from convicted defendant James McCord charging that witnesses had committed perjury at the trial and that he and the other defendants
had been under "political pressure...to plead guilty and remain silent." By
April 17, Nixon was admitting that "major developments" had led him to make
a new inquiry into the Watergate case and press secretary Ronald Ziegler, who
had repeatedly condemned the Washington *Post* for its earlier disclosures, announced that all previous White House disclaimers were now "inoperative."
The President then went before a national television audience on April 30 to
announce the resignations of Attorney General Richard Kleindienst, White House
counsel John Dean, and his two closest advisers, H. R. Haldeman and John
Ehrlichman, He accepted full responsibility for the Watergate affair, though he
denied any personal involvement and even tried to exonerate Haldeman and
Ehrlichman by calling them "two of the finest public servants it has been my

privilege to know." He appointed Elliot Richardson, former Secretary of HEW and Defense, as Attorney General and allowed him to designate Harvard Law Professor Archibald Cox as special prosecutor in charge of the Watergate probe.

Congress, however, prevented the President from containing the scandal. A special Senate investigating committee headed by North Carolina's Sam Ervin, a passionate advocate of restoring congressional prerogatives against presidential encroachment, began televised hearings in May that soon led to a series of startling revelations. The nation watched in fascination as witnesses testified to acts of perjury, revealed White House plans to carry on covert intelligence operations, most notably the famous "plumbers" unit, spoke matter of factly of cash payments to Watergate defendants, gave details of dirty tricks played on Democratic presidential hopefuls ranging from forged letters to newspaper editors to distributing spurious and embarrassing campaign leaflets, and disclosed the compilation of an "enemies list" designed to enable federal agencies, notably the Internal Revenue Service, to harass political opponents. John Dean proved to be the most damning witness, telling the committee that he had warned Nixon on March 21 that "there was a cancer growing on the presidency" as he disclosed the nature of the coverup in progress since the burglary in June. Despite the warning, according to Dean, the President failed to take the decisive steps needed to clean up the Watergate mess. Other witnesses, particularly Maurice Stans and John Mitchell, denied all wrongdoing, but the disclosure by Alexander Butterfield that the President, unknown to nearly everyone in the White House, regularly taped all conversations and phone calls in the Oval Office, put the President in the gravest jeopardy yet. The truth of Dean's charges, it seemed, could now be tested by the tapes.

When both the Watergate committee and the special prosecutor issued subpoenas to acquire the tapes, Nixon invoked executive privilege in refusing to comply. On July 23, the President informed Senator Ervin that the tapes would remain under his "sole personal control." He added that he had listened to several of the key conversations and claimed that they were "entirely consistent with what I know to be the truth," but admitted that they did "contain comments that persons with different perspectives and motivations would inevitably interpret in different ways." Cox insisted that he needed the tapes to prosecute the Watergate case and, after both Judge Sirica and a federal appeals court ordered the President to release the tapes, Nixon demanded that the Attorney General dismiss Cox. First Elliot Richardson and then Deputy Attorney General William Ruckelshaus resigned rather than comply; Solicitor General Robert Bork, hastily appointed Acting Attorney General, finally fired Cox. The "Saturday night massacre," as reporters dubbed the affair, led to a deluge of telegrams critical of the President's action and to demands for his impeachment. Stung by the outcry, Nixon agreed belatedly on October 23 to surrender the tapes in question to Judge Sirica. A week later, Bork appointed a new special prosecutor (Nixon earlier had announced his intention of abolishing the office), Leon Jaworski, a conservative Democrat from Texas, who received a presidential promise that he would not be dismissed without the consent of a "substantial majority" of a bipartisan group of eight congressional leaders.

The removal of Cox marked the beginning of an even steeper decline in the President's position. Like a series of hammer blows, he reeled in the next few months under the impact of the resignation of Vice-President Spiro Agnew, who pleaded no contest to a charge of income tax evasion stemming from the receipt of bribes while serving as governor of Maryland, a startling revelation of a dubious tax deduction for Nixon's vice-presidential papers that reduced his income tax for 1970, 1971, and 1972 to a total of $5969, less than the sum paid by the typical wage earner making $15,000 a year, and an inexplicable gap of 18½ minutes in a tape of a key presidential conversation with Haldeman on June 20, 1972, three days after the original Watergate breakin. Repeated efforts to regain the public's confidence, including a series of meetings with members of Congress and a blunt assertion to a group of newspaper editors, "I am not a crook," failed to halt the President's decline. He dropped below 30 percent in the Gallup poll in the fall of 1973 and stayed there month after month. The new Vice-President, Gerald Ford of Michigan, former House minority leader, tried to rally the GOP, but more and more Republicans began deserting after GOP candidates lost four of five by-elections in the spring of 1974 in districts that were traditionally Republican, including Ford's own. Even staunch conservatives, once thought to be Nixon's ultimate source of support, began to waver, with independent Senator James Buckley of New York calling for his resignation and rumors spreading that Barry Goldwater had privately urged the same course.

Nixon made his most desperate counterattack on April 29, 1974, when he went on national television to announce that he had ordered the release of portions of 42 taped conversations sought by the House Judiciary Committee for its impeachment deliberations. Citing carefully selected passages from the more than 1200 pages of transcripts, the President claimed he was innocent of all charges of wrongdoing and was striving simply "to do what was right." "I hope, and I trust," Nixon concluded, "that, when you have seen the evidence in its entirety, you will see the truth of that statement." The public received the edited transcripts the next day, and those who read them were appalled at the many omissions, the frequent "expletive deleted" notations, and the total lack of moral sensitivity on the part of the President and his associates. The transcripts revealed Nixon as an indecisive, perplexed man struggling for political survival with no apparent regard for the national welfare. The released material failed to resolve the outstanding Watergate issues, but it did suggest that the President was willing to tolerate if not approve the payment of hush money to convicted defendant E. Howard Hunt and to obstruct justice by advising aides to "stonewall" when testifying before the grand jury. Above all, the White House transcripts undermined Nixon's support among Congressional moderates and thereby increased the chances for impeachment in the House of Representatives.

Even foreign policy no longer seemed likely to redeem the Nixon Presidency. People quickly forgot about the SALT agreements and detente in the turmoil over Watergate. Brezhnev continued the mood of growing accommodation between the United States and Russia by coming to Washington in June 1973, but the only result was a vague nonaggression pledge to avoid military confrontations likely to lead to "the outbreak of nuclear war." Henry Kissinger, elevated to the post of Secretary of State, continued to receive most of the credit for the international accomplishments, often to Nixon's displeasure.

The peaceful mood vanished suddenly in early October 1973, when Egypt and Syria launched coordinated attacks on Israel on Yom Kippur. The Arab states gained the initial advantage, with Egyptian troops securing a foothold on the east bank of the Suez Canal and Syrian forces driving into the Golan heights but, by mid-October, the Israelis had advanced to within 20 miles of the Syrian capital of Damascus, well within artillery range, and had launched a brilliant counterattack that trapped an entire Egyptian army in the Sinai. More ominous, both Russia and the United States had abandoned all pretense of neutrality in sending vast quantities of arms to the Middle East, with Soviet weapons pouring into Egypt and Syria while the United States conducted a "massive airlift" of tanks, airplanes, and antiaircraft missiles to Israel. Kissinger engaged in personal diplomacy, flying to Moscow to arrange a cease-fire with Russian cooperation but, on October 25, the danger of nuclear war developed when the President ordered a worldwide alert of American military forces in response to reports of Russian plans to airlift 40,000 troops into Egypt. The two superpowers backed away from a possible confrontation, and the cease-fire took effect in the Middle East in late October.

In the months that followed, Kissinger once again proved his superlative skill as a diplomatic negotiator, first arranging for a pullback of Egyptian and Israeli troops along the Suez and then arranging a similar military realignment on the Syrian front. But the brief war created a far more serious domestic problem for the Administration when the oil-producing Arab states invoked an embargo on the United States on October 17. For the next five months, America was cut off from crude oil it had previously relied on to make up the difference between the 10 million barrels produced domestically and the nearly 17 million barrels Americans consumed each day. Long lines began to appear at filling stations, car sales dropped sharply, and pleas for conservation of energy began to drown out the traditional call for Americans to consume more and more goods. The Arab oil embargo brought home the relationship between foreign and domestic policy with a vengeance. Congress quickly put the nation on year round daylight savings time and ordered the highway speed limit reduced to 55 miles per hour, while the President created a new Federal Energy Office, asked gas stations to close on Sunday to discourage weekend trips, and appealed to Americans to lower their thermostats in the cold winter months. Most Americans cooperated with the government to reduce demand, but the energy crisis only intensified Nixon's unpopularity, as people simply added the grievances created by the fuel shortage to the existing discontent over inflation and Watergate. Dire predictions of massive brownouts and heavy unemployment failed to materialize, however, when the Arab states lifted the boycott in late March; by summer, Americans were consuming more oil than ever before.

In other foreign policy areas, the President met with a conspicuous lack of success. The Congress, reacting to the way Nixon and his Democratic predecessors had waged war in Indo-China, particularly in Laos and Cambodia, passed a War Powers Act that required the President to report to Congress within 48 hours of committing American troops to a foreign conflict and to withdraw them within 90 days if Congress refused to concur, or immediately if both Houses so requested in a concurrent resolution. Nixon vetoed the bill, terming it "unconstitutional and dangerous," but both the House and Senate overrode the veto for the first time in Nixon's second term. Congress also resisted further steps toward detente with the Soviet Union as a bloc of Democratic senators, led by Henry Jackson of Washington, refused to grant Russia favorable tariff and credit treatment until the Kremlin eased its restrictions on Jewish emigration. Despite the resulting legislative deadlock that prevented further Soviet-American trade deals, Nixon preserved the image of detente by traveling to Moscow in June 1974. Brezhnev and Nixon signed an agreement further restricting the deployment of ABMs by each side, but they failed to make progress on the far more vital issue of MIRVs, the multiple and independently targeted warheads aboard offensive missiles. The American lead in MIRV technology had made the Soviet advantages in number of rockets and size of warheads bearable in the original SALT agreement, but evidence that the Russians had finally achieved MIRV capability created the possibility of Soviet nuclear supremacy by the end of the 1970s. Both Nixon and Kissinger had wanted desperately to achieve a breakthrough in the stalemated SALT II talks; their failure was the clearest sign yet that the President's domestic reverses had seriously weakened his ability to conduct foreign policy.

I

The President's sudden fall from grace gave rise to widespread speculation over the causes of his difficulties. Many veteran Nixon-watchers saw in Watergate the logical culmination of his political career. Haunted by insecurity and fear of failure, Nixon had first gained political power by cruel and malicious attacks on his opponents in California. As Vice-President, he had chafed under the benign neglect and faintly patronizing treatment by Dwight Eisenhower, resenting it so deeply that his failure to bring the popular General into his 1960 campaign until the last minute helped doom his candidacy. The loss to John Kennedy and the California defeat in 1962 left deep scars and, even after his amazing political recovery led to the narrow victory in 1968, Nixon hungered for the security of a landslide triumph. Everything was subordinated to the quest for power, and those who resisted, from the scraggly antiwar protesters who streamed into Washington after the Cambodia invasion in 1970 to the newspaper editors and television broadcasters who made so much of Daniel Ellsberg's leak of the Pentagon Papers, were marked for retribution. It was Nixon's almost paranoid desire for total victory in 1972 that led to the excesses on the part of his aides that proved his ultimate undoing. Fearful of opposition and dissent, Nixon sought to achieve a Presidency in which he would be absolutely secure, free from criticism from the press, restraint by the Congress and disagreement within the Executive branch.

Others saw the fault in the system, not the man. Senators like William Fulbright and Sam Ervin viewed Nixon's actions as the ultimate corruption of presidential power that had been developing since 1945. Truman had begun the process, threatening both unions and business with unprecedented federal action and sending troops into the Korean conflict without the consent of Congress. Eisenhower had shown greater respect for Congressional prerogatives, but even this cautious President had engaged in such questionable tactics as the CIA operation in Guatemala in 1954 and the U-2 fiasco. The trend toward excessive presidential power had taken a sharp upswing under John F. Kennedy who, stymied by Congressional opposition on domestic measures, took bold initiatives in foreign policy, challenging Khrushchev over Berlin, committing American prestige in South Vietnam, and risking nuclear war in the Cuban missile crisis without consulting Congress in advance. Johnson had continued the consolidation of power in the White House, escalating the war in Vietnam and forcing a reluctant Congress to support the conflict. By the time Nixon became President, the tradition of presidential supremacy was so well established that he found it easy to conduct foreign policy without consulting Congress — such major steps as the Cambodian invasion and the mining of Haiphong came in defiance of the House and Senate. Nixon's major innovation, according to Arthur Schlesinger, Jr., in his influential book, *The Imperial Presidency,* was to extend presidential power over domestic as well as foreign affairs and thereby to free himself from the checks imposed by the Constitution. Impoundment, efforts at establishing a supercabinet, and the covert activities revealed during the Watergate hearings all reflected Nixon's determination to rule without interference.

The argument over whether it was Nixon's personal drive or the inevitable drift toward a runaway Presidency that led to Watergate seems artificial. The arrival in the White House of an insecure man who sought insulation from criticism and opposition at a time when power was flowing away from Congress toward the Presidency proved fatal. Just when the nation needed another Eisenhower with his inherent sense of restraint, it got Nixon with his bent for mastery. As George Reedy has so wisely observed, the greatest danger in the White House is isolation — the President can easily lose touch with reality. Anxious aides seek to reassure him that all is going well, the reverent, almost deferential attitude people display toward him mutes any criticism, and the trappings of royalty in the White House lead to a false sense of well-being. Reedy observed this phenomenon while serving President Johnson, who tried to stay in touch by meeting frequently with congressmen and senators and by watching three television sets mounted on his office wall. Nixon relied on aides like Haldeman and Ehrlichman to protect him from outside intruders; he had LBJ's television sets removed from the Oval Office and instead relied on a summary of the media prepared by hard-line speechwriter Pat Buchanan. This self-imposed isolation reinforced the separation from everyday life inherent in the White House and meant that Nixon became more and more removed from Congress, the press, and the main currents of public opinion.

Nixon's fate sustains the view that the President's relationship with the people is the single most vital aspect of the American political system. Elected by the entire population, a President can stand out as the people's representative, rising above the more parochial outlook of congressmen and senators. He can take the broad view, assessing issues for their impact on the entire nation, rather than simply how they effect one industry, one state, or one class in society. But, to govern effectively, a President must be sensitive to the changing nature of the public mood and nourish a continuing confidence in the wisdom and maturity of his judgment. After his massive reelection in 1972, Nixon felt he could rule on the basis of that mandate for the next four years and thus proceeded to ignore his continuing need for popular support. When the Watergate revelations began to undermine public confidence in his Presidency, he found it more and more difficult to reestablish the all-important ties with the American people. The attempts at winning back public favor — "operation candor," the infrequent news conferences, and the final, desperate release of the White House transcripts — all boomeranged, leaving the President more isolated than ever before. The more that Richard Nixon struggled to persuade the American people that he deserved their support, the more he convinced them that he had betrayed their trust.

II

The end came quickly for Richard Nixon. Ironically, the Supreme Court, the body that he had tried so hard to reform, delivered the decisive blow. On July 24, the Court ruled that he must turn over tapes he had withheld from special prosecutor Leon Jaworski, thereby denying Nixon's claim of executive privilege and, unknown to all but the President himself, insuring that Nixon's complicity in the cover-up would become public knowledge. Several months earlier Nixon had listened in private to the tapes in question, which included a conversation with Haldeman on June 23, 1972, just six days after the Watergate breakin. In that fateful conversation, the President had approved Haldeman's suggestion that he tell the FBI to "stay the hell out" of the Watergate investigation. When James St. Clair, Nixon's attorney, and Alexander Haig, the White House chief-of-staff, heard the tape, they realized that any further resistance would be futile. Bitter at being betrayed by their leader, they forced the President to publish a transcript of the tapes as they prepared for an orderly transfer of power to Vice-President Gerald R. Ford, the man Nixon had appointed to replace Agnew.

Meanwhile the House Judiciary Committee climaxed six months of deliberations by voting to impeach the President on two broad charges—obstruction of justice in the Watergate affair and the abuse of Presidential power. Although a group of loyal Republicans, led by Representative Charles Wiggins of California, provided a spirited defense, seven G.O.P. members joined with all the Democrats on the committee to place impeachment beyond partisanship. The nation watched the televised proceedings as commentators, assuming similar action by the full House, speculated on the likelihood of a guilty verdict in the Senate trial, now scheduled for the fall. The disclosure of the incriminating tape transcript spared the nation that final agony. Overnight, Nixon's defenders deserted him. Charles Wiggins, who had been given the transcript in advance by Haig and St. Clair, now called on the President to resign; all ten Republicans on the House Judiciary Committee who had voted against impeachment publicly changed their vote, making the indictment unanimous.

Despite the growing pressure, the President still hesitated, torn between the alternatives of a long, agonizing Senate trial and the humiliation inherent in resignation. On August 7, he summoned the top G.O.P. Congressional leaders to the White House for consultation. They quickly destroyed any illusions Nixon may have had about the outcome of a Senate vote. Senate Majority Leader Hugh Scott informed the President that he could not count on more than 12 to 15 votes; Barry Goldwater was even more blunt, telling Nixon, "I can only vouch for four or five who would stay with you right to the end." Later that day, the President reluctantly decided to resign. The next evening, August 8, six years to the day since his triumphal acceptance speech to the Republican convention at Miami Beach, he informed the American people of his decision in a calm and restrained television address. He admitted no wrongdoing, only mistakes in judgment, as he recited his successes in office and explained his departure on the narrow ground of lost support in Congress. On August 9, after an embarrassingly emotional farewell to his White House staff, Nixon formally left office, flying to California on Air Force One for the last time while Gerald Ford took the oath of office as the thirty-eighth President.

The outlook was bleak. Despite the sense of national relief over Nixon's resignation and the willingness of most Americans to give their new leader a chance, Ford faced a difficult set of problems, ranging from the aftermath of Watergate to an ever-increasing inflation. But the greatest challenge of all lay in the condition of the Presidency. In the past, the office had brought out the best in apparently mediocre men, transforming an obscure Senator like Harry Truman into a decisive national leader. Richard Nixon, however, had reversed the process, lowering the office to his level by engaging in political chicanery of the worst kind. Nixon's abuse of the Presidency, as revealed in the Watergate scandals, had reached a climax with his assertion of executive privilege to cover up evidence of his own guilt. Ford faced the awesome task of restoring public confidence and giving the American people a new faith in the Presidency. In the long run, his place in history would turn on his ability to remove the terrible stain that Nixon had left on the White House.

Suggestions for Additional Reading

The literature on political and diplomatic developments since 1945 is very extensive, though uneven. Scholarly study of the Truman period is already far advanced; journalistic accounts predominate for the Kennedy, Johnson, and Nixon administrations. The Eisenhower years received relatively slight attention from contemporaries and academic historians have yet to explore many of the fascinating aspects of this period.

The citations that follow are not exhaustive; I have selected the books that I found most helpful in writing this account of the post-World War II years.

THE TRUMAN YEARS

The most satisfactory general history of the Truman Administration is Cabell Phillips, *The Truman Presidency: The History of a Triumphant Succession* (1966). Phillips is generally sympathetic to the President and though there are some notable omissions, particularly on domestic policy, he provides the fullest narrative coverage of the Administration in print. Harry S. Truman, *Memoirs* (2 Vols., 1955, 1956) reveals the former President to be as partisan and self-confident as a writer as he was in office. William Hillman, *Mr. President* (1952) and Margaret Truman, *Harry S. Truman* (1973) give excessively flattering portraits along with many useful letters and documents not otherwise available to historians. The essays edited by Barton J. Bernstein, *Politics and Policies of the Truman Administration* (1970) provide a much more critical evaluation, as does the biography by Bert Cochran, *Harry Truman and the Crisis Presidency* (1973).

On domestic issues, Richard Neustadt gives the best overall analysis of the Fair Deal in "Congress and the Fair Deal: A Legislative Balance Sheet," *Public Policy*, V (1954), 351-81. Arthur F. McClure, *The Truman Administration and the Problems of Postwar Labor, 1945-1948* (1969) deals broadly with labor policy during Truman's first term; R. Alton Lee focuses more sharply on the major legislative act in *Truman and Taft-Hartley* (1966). Three scholarly monographs, William C. Berman, *The Politics of Civil Rights in the Truman Administration* (1970), Allen J. Matusow, *Farm Policies and Politics in the Truman Administration* (1967), and Susan M. Hartmann, *Truman and the 80th Congress* (1971), each deal fully with important aspects of Truman's domestic program. In *The Truman Scandals* (1956), muckraking journalist Jules Abels describes in somewhat exaggerated style the corruption in government that came to light during Truman's second term.

Samuel Lubell gives a perceptive analysis of the underlying political realities in *The Future of American Politics* (1952). Clifton Brock, *Americans for Democratic Action* (1962) describes the split in liberal ranks. On the election of 1948, Irwin Ross stresses Truman's personal efforts in *The Loneliest Campaign* (1968), while Richard Kirkendall emphasizes the role of all elements in the Democratic Party in "Election of 1948", an essay in the fourth volume of Arthur M. Schlesinger, Jr. and Fred L. Israel, eds., *History of American Presidential Elections, 1789-1968* (1971). For Henry A. Wallace's challenge to the Truman Administration, see Edward L. and Frederick H. Schapsmeier, *Prophet in Politics: Henry A. Wallace and the War Years, 1940-1965* (1971), a routine biography; Norman D. Markowitz, *The Rise and Fall of the People's Century: Henry A. Wallace and American Liberalism, 1941-1948* (1972), an analytical study of his ideas and actions; Karl M. Schmidt, *Henry A. Wallace: Quixotic Crusade* (1960), a sympathetic treatment of his presidential bid; and Curtis D. MacDougall, *Gideon's Army* (3 Vols., 1965), an impassioned defense of the 1948 Progressive campaign. Three biographies, Joseph B. Gorman, *Kefauver* (1971), James T. Patterson, *Mr. Republican: A Biography of Robert A. Taft* (1972), and Joseph Lash, *Eleanor: The Years Alone* (1972), illuminate important political trends.

The most judicious treatment of the red scare of the late 1940s is Earl Latham, *The Communist Conspiracy in Washington* (1966). Walter Goodman traces the role of the most important Congressional investigating body in *The Committee: The Extraordinary Career of the House Committee on Un-American Activities* (1968); Alistair Cooke describes its most famous case, the charges against Alger Hiss, in *A Generation on Trial* (1950). Alan D. Harper, *The Politics of Loyalty: The White House and the Communist Issue, 1946-1952* (1969) is a sympathetic account of Truman's loyalty program. For a critical perspective, see Richard M. Freeland, *The Truman Doctrine and the Origins of McCarthyism* (1972) and Athan Theoharis, *Seeds of Repression* (1971). These revisionist writers argue that Truman himself created the emotional climate that spawned the red scare. The two best books on McCarthyism are Richard H. Rovere, *Senator Joe McCarthy* (1959), which stresses the Senator's lack of a coherent program, and Robert Griffith, *The Politics of Fear: Joseph R. McCarthy and the Senate* (1970), which concentrates on his domination of Congress.

A marked upsurge in the Truman literature took place while this book was being written. By far the most significant recent contribution is Alonzo L. Hamby, *Beyond the New Deal* (1973), a penetrating analysis of Truman and the liberal reform movement. Richard F. Haynes treats Truman's performance as commander-in-chief critically in *The Awesome Power* (1973); Donald R. McCoy and Richard T. Ruetten deal sympathetically with Truman's advocacy of civil rights in *Quest and Response* (1973); Robert Divine analyzes the influence of events overseas on the election of 1948 in *Foreign Policy and U.S. Presidential Elections, 1940-1948* (1974); and Robert Griffith and Athan Theoharis have edited an anthology of critical essays on the relationship between the Cold War and McCarthyism in *The Specter* (1974). Merle Miller, *Plain*

Speaking (1973) is a biography of Truman based on a series of frank interviews taped in 1962 that give a salty but superficial view of the President.

Gar Alperovitz touched off a heated debate among historians on the origins of the Cold War in *Atomic Diplomacy* (1965), in which he develops the revisionist argument that American possession of the atomic bomb led the Truman Administration to take a hard line toward Russia, particularly in Eastern Europe. Marvin Herz takes a more neutral position in *Beginnings of the Cold War* (1966), with major emphasis on the Polish issue. The revisionist case appears in more extreme form in Gabriel Kolko, *The Roots of American Foreign Policy* (1969), David Horowitz, *The Free World Colossus* (1965), and Denna F. Fleming, *The Cold War and its Origins* (2 Vols., 1961), a pioneering New Left study. John L. Gaddis has transcended the revisionist debate by analyzing the domestic pressures that led to the containment policy in *The United States and the Origins of the Cold War* (1972).

Accounts by contemporaries provide a useful insight into the deterioration of relations between the United States and Russia after World War II. Two Secretaries of State, James Byrnes and Dean Acheson, tell their respective version of events in *Speaking Frankly* (1947) and *Present at the Creation* (1969). Walter Millis, ed., *The Forrestal Diaries* (1951) provides a wealth of material on the views of the first Secretary of Defense, while Arthur Vandenberg, Jr., ed., *The Private Papers of Senator Vandenberg* (1952) gives a Republican perspective on bipartisan foreign policy. Lucius Clay, the general in charge of German occupation, traces American policy there through the Berlin blockade in *Decision in Germany* (1950). By far the most readable memoirs are those by George Kennan, *Memoirs, 1925-1950* (1967), in which the veteran diplomat traces his career in the foreign service and his contributions to the containment policy.

There are several favorable accounts of the development of the Truman Doctrine and the Marshall Plan. Joseph Jones, a former State Department officer, gives an inside account that conveys the sense of crisis felt by many in the government at the time in *The Fifteen Weeks* (1955). Robert H. Ferrell, *George C. Marshall* (1966) and Gaddis Smith, *Dean Acheson* (1972) trace the achievements of two of Truman's Secretaries of State from a sympathetic point of view. Herbert Feis describes the onset of the Cold War from the Administration's standpoint in *From Trust to Terror* (1970).

Joyce and Gabriel Kolko have written the most sweeping revisionist indictment of the Truman Administration's policies in *The Limits of Power: The World and U.S. Foreign Policy, 1945-1954* (1972). Committed to a rigid economic analysis, the Kolkos argue that the United States used the confrontation with Russia to dominate the world's resources and markets. Lloyd Gardner offers a less dogmatic and more persuasive critique of American policymakers in *Architects of Illusion* (1970). The views of those who opposed containment at the time, ranging from Henry A. Wallace on the left to Robert A. Taft on the right, are given in the essays edited by Thomas G. Paterson, *Cold War Critics* (1971). For an important contemporary criticism of the Truman Doctrine, see Walter Lippmann, *The Cold War* (1947).

A number of books detail various aspects of American policy in Asia during the Truman years. Herbert Feis describes the events during and immediately after World War II in the aptly-titled volume, *The China Tangle* (1953). Tang Tsou takes the story on down through the defeat of the Nationalists in *America's Failure in China, 1941-1950* (1963), criticizing the United States for refusing to give China priority. The subsequent refusal to recognize and deal with Mao's Communist regime is traced in Foster R. Dulles, *American Foreign Policy Toward Communist China, 1949-1969* (1972). David Rees has written the most comprehensive account of the Korean conflict, *Korea: The Limited War* (1964). Glenn D. Paige analyzes Truman's action in entering the war in *The Korean Decision, June 24-30, 1950* (1967), while Matthew B. Ridgway, the man who replaced MacArthur, gives a critical account of the struggle from the vantage point of the later Vietnam experience in *The Korean War* (1967). The best account of Chinese intervention is Allen S. Whiting, *China Crosses the Yalu: The Decision to Enter the Korean War* (1960); John Spanier deals fully with the issues raised by MacArthur's recall in *The Truman-MacArthur Controversy and the Korean War* (1959). For the truce negotiations, see C. Turner Joy, *How Communists Negotiate* (1956) and William H. Vatcher, *Panmunjon* (1958). Ronald J. Caridi deals with the Republican party's reaction to the conflict in *The Korean War and American Politics* (1968). Revisionists have not yet turned their attention to the Korean conflict, but I. F. Stone offers some interesting critical speculation in *The Hidden History of the Korean War* (1952).

There is no fully satisfactory survey of the nuclear arms race since 1945; Chalmers Roberts gives a brief overview in *The Nuclear Years: The Arms Race and Arms Control, 1945-70* (1970). Walter Millis examines many significant aspects of defense policies in the late 1940s and early 1950s in *Arms and the State* (1958). Two books, Joseph I. Lieberman, *The Scorpion and the Tarantula* (1970) and Thomas W. Wilson, Jr., *The Great Weapons Heresy* (1970), offer readable but superficial accounts of the Baruch Plan and the decision to build the H-bomb. There is a great deal of material on both issues in David E. Lilienthal's journal, *The Atomic Energy Years, 1945-1950* (1964). Bernard G. Bechhoefer, *Postwar Negotiations for Arms Control* (1961) is the best analysis of the unsuccessful efforts to achieve nuclear disarmament. The second volume in the offical history of the Atomic Energy Commission, Richard Hewlett and Frances Duncan, *Atomic Shield, 1947-52* (1969), is disappointing on weapons development. Rigid security rules prevented the authors from dealing in detail with such fundamental issues as the size of the atomic bomb stock-pile and the nature of the hydrogen bomb breakthrough.

Two books deal broadly with important themes in the Cold War years. H. Bradford Westerfield analyzes the neglected relationship between politics and diplomacy in *Foreign Policy and Party Politics: Pearl Harbor to Korea* (1955). In *The Roots of War* (1972), Richard J. Barnet describes the fundamental change World War II wrought in transforming the United States into a nation that accepted war as a normal state of affairs.

THE EISENHOWER YEARS

Herbert S. Parmet has written the fullest general account of the Eisenhower administration in *Eisenhower and the American Crusades* (1972). Although his treatment is somewhat uneven, Parmet presents a convincing and well-documented case for Eisenhower's skill as a political leader. Robert J. Donovan gives a highly partisan account of Eisenhower's first term in office in *Eisenhower: The Inside Story* (1956), a book written for the 1956 campaign. The two-volume selection of letters, speeches, and memoranda edited by Robert L. Branyan and Lawrence H. Larsen, *The Eisenhower Administration: A Documentary History* (1971), offers a sample of the material available in the Eisenhower presidential library in Abilene, Kansas. Two influential contributions to the rehabilitation of Eisenhower's political reputation are Murray Kempton, "The Underestimation of Dwight D. Eisenhower," *Esquire*, LXVIII (September 1967), 108-09 and Arthur Larson, *Eisenhower: The President Nobody Knew* (1968). See also Peter Lyon, *Eisenhower: Portrait of the Hero* (1974).

The memoir literature still provides the most penetrating insights into the politics and diplomacy of the 1950s. Eisenhower contributed two long and quite revealing volumes, *Mandate for Change, 1953-1956* (1963) and *Waging Peace* (1965). Emmet John Hughes has written by far the most graceful and perceptive memoir of the Eisenhower years, *The Ordeal of Power* (1963). Sherman Adams, *Firsthand Report* (1961) is equally valuable because of the author's key role in the Administration. Other useful accounts by participants include Robert Cutler, *No Time for Rest* (1965), Charles E. Bohlen, *Witness to History, 1929-1969* (1973) Ezra Taft Benson, *Crossfire* (1962), and Richard M. Nixon, *Six Crises* (1962), which has chapters on the secret fund episode in 1952, the vice-presidential nomination in 1956, and the election of 1960. Nixon's own account should be supplemented with Garry Wills, *Nixon Agonistes* (1970), which offers a shrewd evaluation of the strained relationship between Eisenhower and Nixon.

Five books on John Foster Dulles provide an overall view of American

222

foreign policy in the 1950s: a laudatory biography by John R. Beal, *John Foster Dulles* (1957), a cooler British analysis by Richard Goold-Adams, *John Foster Dulles: A Reappraisal* (1962), an uncritical account by Louis L. Gerson, *John Foster Dulles* (1968), a recent defense of the Secretary's foreign policy concepts by Michael A. Guhin, *John Foster Dulles: A Statesman and His Times* (1972), and a highly critical reassessment by Townsend Hoopes, *The Devil and John Foster Dulles* (1973). G. Bernard Noble analyzes the contributions of Dulles's successor in *Christian A. Herter* (1970).

The general survey by Foster Dulles, *American Foreign Policy Toward Communist China,* cited for the Truman years, contains chapters on the two Formosa Straits crises. Ellen J. Hammer, *The Struggle for Indo-China, 1940-1955* (1966) is the best book on the Indo-China problem through the Geneva Conference, but see also the revealing article by Chalmers M. Roberts, "The Day We Didn't Go to War," *Reporter,* XI (September 11, 1954), 31-35.

In regard to other foreign policy crises of the 1950s, Hugh Thomas gives a well-rounded account of the 1956 Middle East blow-up in *Suez* (1967). Herman Finer is highly critical of the Secretary of State in *Dulles Over Suez* (1964), but his book contains much useful information on American policy. Jack M. Schick gives an interpretive summary of a major source of Cold War tension in *The Berlin Crisis, 1958-1962* (1971). On Cuba, two former American ambassadors, Earl E. T. Smith and Philip W. Bonsal, provide contrasting views in *The Fourth Floor: An Account of the Castro Communist Revolution* (1962) and *Cuba, Castro and the United States* (1971), respectively. Theodore Draper analyzes the nature of the Cuban turmoil in *Castro's Revolution: Myths and Realities* (1962). For Latin America in general since 1945, see Gordon Connell-Smith, *The Inter-American System* (1966). An article by James C. Dick, "The Strategic Arms Race, 1957-1961," *Journal of Politics,* XXXIV (November 1972), 1062-110, gives a useful corrective to the contemporary view of the missile crisis; there is also a penetrating and generally favorable analysis of Eisenhower's strategic policy in George H. Quester, *Nuclear Diplomacy: The First Twenty-Five Years* (1970).

In the domestic area, the books cited earlier on McCarthy, particularly those by Robert Griffith and Richard Rovere, are pertinent to developments in the 1950s. Michael Straight has a good account of the Army-McCarthy hearings and their impact in *Trial by Television* (1954); Michael P. Rogin analyzes the reaction of intellectuals to the Wisconsin demagogue in *The Intellectuals and McCarthy* (1967). Harold G. Vatter, *The U.S. Economy in the 1950's* (1963) and Edwin L. Dale, Jr., *Conservatives in Power* (1960) trace the economic developments in this decade and the battle over the budget in detail. David A. Frier reveals the surprisingly large number of cases of improper political behavior that occurred during the Eisenhower years, culminating in Sherman Adam's downfall, in *Conflict of Interest in the Eisenhower Administration* (1969).

In *Portrait of a Decade: The Second American Revolution* (1964), Anthony Lewis uses long excerpts from the New York *Times* to document the civil rights revolution that began with the Supreme Court desegregation decision in 1954. Louis E. Lomax examines this development from a black perspective in *The Negro Revolt* (1962), while David L. Lewis traces the emergence of the movement's most prominent leader in *King: A Critical Biography* (1970). The failure of Eisenhower to provide moral leadership in the civil rights area comes through clearly in E. Frederic Morrow, *Black Man in the White House* (1963). For the South's diehard reaction, see Numan V. Bartley, *The Rise of Massive Resistance* (1969).

Two commentators, Samuel Lubell and Louis Harris, survey the prevailing political mood of the 1950s in *Revolt of the Moderates* (1956) and *Is There a Republican Majority?* (1954). In *Lyndon B. Johnson: The Exercise of Power* (1966), Rowland Evans and Robert Novak provide a detailed analysis of LBJ's success as Senate majority leader during the Eisenhower years. Adlai Stevenson has attracted many sympathetic biographers; the two most useful studies of his political role are Stuart G. Brown, *Conscience in Politics: Adlai E. Stevenson in the 1950's* (1960) and Kenneth S. Davis, *The Politics of Honor: A Biography of Adlai E. Stevenson* (1967). For the background of the two candidates in 1960, see James MacGregor Burns, *John Kennedy: A Political Profile* (1960), a superior campaign biography, and Earl Mazo, *Richard Nixon: A Political and Personal Portrait,* which is much more partisan in tone. The standard account of the 1960 election remains Theodore H. White, *The Making of the President 1960* (1961), the first and still the best in White's quadrennial series.

THE KENNEDY YEARS

The extensive literature on John F. Kennedy's presidency reflects a growing divergence in judgment. The early books, written by close associates, unreservedly praise Kennedy and bemoan his untimely death. The two fullest accounts are Theodore C. Sorenson, *Kennedy* (1965), the more revealing, and Arthur M. Schlesinger, Jr., *A Thousand Days* (1965), the more satisfying work of history. Hugh Sidey, a *Life* journalist who covered Kennedy, writes in an admiring vein in *John F. Kennedy, President* (1964), as does Pierre Salinger in *With Kennedy* (1966). More recent accounts offer a far more critical view of Kennedy's presidency. Henry Fairlie stresses the arrogance and dangerous overconfidence of the New Frontiersmen in *The Kennedy Promise* (1973); Nancy Gager Clinch probes, not altogether convincingly, the underlying psychological weaknesses of the male members of the Kennedy family in *The Kennedy Neurosis* (1973). In *Coming Apart* (1971), William L. O'Neill takes a critical look at the entire decade of the 1960s and is particularly skeptical of Kennedy's leadership.

John F. Kennedy and the New Frontier, (1966) edited by Aida DiPace Donald, provides the most balanced view of the Kennedy Administration with essays written by both friendly and hostile commentators. Helen Fuller gives a shrewd contemporary appraisal of Kennedy's first twelve months in office in *Year of Trial* (1962).

Writers on the Kennedy presidency have generally neglected domestic developments, but there is a good account of the President's inability to deal effectively with Congress in Tom Wicker, *JFK and LBJ* (1968). For the New Frontier's approach to economic problems, see Hobart Rowen, *The Free Enterprisers* (1964), a lively, journalistic account, Seymour Harris, *Economics of the Kennedy Years* (1964), a friendly appraisal by a liberal economist, and Jim F. Heath, *John F. Kennedy and the Business Community* (1969), a judicious monograph. Victor S. Navasky provides a highly critical account of Robert Kennedy's performance as Attorney General, particularly in the civil rights area, in *Kennedy Justice* (1971). Anthony Lewis gives a detailed picture of the Oxford and Birmingham crises in the previously cited *Portrait of a Decade* (1964). There are many conflicting accounts of Kennedy's assassination; the standard treatment is William Manchester, *Death of a President* (1967), but see also Edward Jay Epstein, *Inquest* (1966) for a dissenting view.

The many foreign policy crises of the Kennedy years have attracted the attention of a large number of authors. Roger Hilsman, an influential State Department official under Kennedy, gives a revealing insider's view in *To Move a Nation* (1967), while journalists Edward Weintal and Charles Bartlett write from a sympathetic point of view in *Facing the Brink* (1967). Richard J. Walton, *Cold War and Counterrevolution* (1972) and Louise FitzSimons, *The Kennedy Doctrine* (1972) are far more critical, portraying JFK as a rigid Cold Warrior. The showdown over Berlin is traced in Jack M. Schick, *The Berlin Crisis, 1958-1962* (1971), which emphasizes American moves, and in Robert M. Slusser, *The Berlin Crisis of 1961* (1973), which focuses on Soviet policy.

The best account of the Cuban missile crisis is Elie Abel, *The Missile Crisis* (1966). Robert A. Divine, ed., *The Cuban Missile Crisis* (1971) presents a wide variety of viewpoints. Robert F. Kennedy's posthumous memoir, *Thirteen Days* (1969), gives a personal view, while Graham T. Allison analyzes the crisis as a case study in bureaucratic decision-making in *Essence of Decision: Explaining the Cuban Missile Crisis* (1971). Of the many books on Vietnam, David Halberstam, *The Best and the Brightest* (1972) gives the fullest account of the decisions made during Kennedy's presidency. The New York *Times* edition of *The Pentagon Papers* (1971), edited by Neil Sheehan, contains many revealing documents on JFK's policies in Vietnam.

THE JOHNSON YEARS

The literature on Lyndon Johnson's Presidency has been slow to emerge. The best brief account, critical yet not unsympathetic, is Louis Heren, *No Hail, No Farewell* (1970). Rowland Evans and Robert Novak give a perceptive portrait of Johnson's political style and achievements in their previously cited book; Eric F. Goldman, *The Tragedy of Lyndon Johnson* (1969), contains the fullest treatment of the Great Society program. LBJ gives his own account in *The Vantage Point* (1971), which despite its defensive tone offers a great deal of useful material. Other books on Johnson include Hugh Sidey's sympathetic *A Very Personal Presidency* (1968) and two critical biographies, Alfred Steinberg, *Sam Johnson's Boy* (1968) and Robert Sherrill, *Accidental President* (1967). Few of Johnson's associates have written their memoirs, but two excellent ones are George E. Reedy, *The Twilight of the Presidency* (1970) and Harry McPherson, *A Political Education* (1972). For a contemporary view of the men around Johnson, see Charles Roberts, *LBJ's Inner Circle* (1965).

Lyndon Johnson's domestic achievements have attracted virtually no scholarly attention, aside from Goldman's inside account, and John C. Donovan's analysis of the Economic Opportunity Act of 1964, *The Politics of Poverty* (2nd ed. 1973). For the election of 1964, see Theodore White, *The Making of the President, 1964* (1965), Robert D. Novak, *The Agony of the G.O.P. 1964* (1965), and Joseph C. Goulden, *Truth is the First Casualty* (1969), which explores the way Johnson exploited the Gulf of Tonkin affair.

The best general account of black activism in the 1960s is Benjamin Muse, *The American Negro Revolution* (1968). For the urban riots, see Robert Conot, *Rivers of Blood, Years of Darkness* (1967) for Watts and John Hersey, *The Algiers Motel Incident* (1968) for Detroit. David Lewis's biography of Martin Luther King cited previously is indispensable for an understanding of the civil rights movement in the 1960s while Stokely Carmichael and Charles V. Hamilton document the new militancy in *Black Power* (1965). Three absorbing personal memoirs, James Baldwin, *The Fire Next Time* (1963), Malcolm Little,

The Autobiography of Malcolm X (1964), and Eldridge Cleaver, *Soul on Ice* (1968) reveal the agony and desperation of American blacks in the 1960s.

In *Coming Apart* (1971), William L. O'Neill supplies useful vignettes of many aspects of American life in the 1960s and is particularly informative on the student unrest and rise of the New Left. For the SDS, see Jack Newfield, *A Prophetic Minority* (1966) and Kirkpatrick Sale, *SDS* (1973). The best contemporary account of the new radicals is Christopher Lasch, *The Agony of the American Left* (1969); Irwin Unger offers a more detached analysis in *The Movement* (1974).

There is a much more extensive literature on the foreign policy crises of the 1960s. Philip Geyelin gives a critical view of LBJ's approach to diplomacy in *Lyndon B. Johnson and the World* (1966) while Walt W. Rostow offers a vigorous defense in *The Diffusion of Power* (1972). The most influential contemporary critique of LBJ's foreign policy was William Fulbright, *The Arrogance of Power* (1967). For a penetrating analysis of the national security crisis managers, see Richard J. Barnet, *Intervention and Revolution* (1968).

The fullest account of the Dominican intervention is John Bartlow Martin, *Overtaken by Events* (1966), written by Johnson's chief negotiator. More critical assessments include Theodore Draper, *The Dominican Revolt* (1968), Tad Szulc, *Dominican Diary* (1967), Jerome Salter, *Intervention and Negotiation* (1970) and Abraham Lowenthal, *The Dominican Intervention* (1972).

Two books previously cited on Vietnam, Halberstam's *The Best and the Brightest* and the New York *Times* edition of *The Pentagon Papers,* are as useful for the Johnson as for the Kennedy years. Frances FitzGerald, *Fire in the Lake* (1972) provides the best description of how the war affected the Vietnamese. Chester Cooper gives a balanced and informed account of the conflict in *The Lost Crusade* (1970). The failure of Johnson's peace efforts is described in detail in David Kraslow and Stuart H. Loory, *The Secret Search for Peace in Vietnam* (1968). For the growing opposition to the war in America, see Dan Wakefield, *Supernation at Peace and War* (1968), Norman Mailer, *Armies of the Night* (1968) and Don Oberdorfer, *Tet!* (1971). Townsend Hoopes supplies an insider's view of Johnson's decision to reduce the bombing and withdraw from politics in *The Limits of Intervention* (1969), but on this issue see also Johnson's *Vantage Point* and Harry McPherson's *Political Education.*

THE NIXON YEARS

The Nixon literature is already surprisingly large. Garry Wills provides a fascinating and controversial portrait in depth in *Nixon Agonistes* (1970), while Bruce Mazlish offers a briefer and more tentative psychohistorical probe, *In Search of Nixon* (1972). A friendly but fair assessment of Nixon's career appears in Earl Mazo and Stephen Hess, *Nixon: A Political Portrait* (1968). More extreme views are Ralph de Toledano, *One Man Alone: Richard Nixon* (1969), highly laudatory in tone, and Frank Mankiewicz, *Perfectly Clear: Nixon from Whittier to Watergate* (1973), a hostile account by McGovern's 1972 campaign manager. Jules Witcover describes RN's amazing political recovery in the 1960s in *The Resurrection of Richard Nixon* (1970).

A trio of English journalists, Lewis Chester, Godfrey Hodgson, and Bruce Page, give a blow-by-blow account of the turbulent 1968 election in *An American Melodrama* (1969). Theodore White provides a more intimate but less comprehensive view in *The Making of the President, 1968* (1969). For critical, inside perspectives on the Nixon campaign, see Joe McGinnis, *The Selling of the President* (1969) and Richard J. Whalen, *Catch the Falling Flag* (1972), an especially revealing book by a disillusioned conservative.

By far the best account of the first Nixon Administration is Rowland Evans, Jr., and Robert D. Novak, *Nixon in the White House* (1971), which goes down to early 1971. John Osborne, the keenest observer of the Nixon years, has collected his contemporary columns in four useful volumes, *The Nixon Watch* (1970), *The Second Year of the Nixon Watch* (1971), *The Third Year of the Nixon Watch* (1972) and *The Fourth Year of the Nixon Watch* (1973). Other books on domestic topics include Leonard Silk, *Nixonomics* (1972), a lively account of changing Administration economic policy, Walter J. Hickel, *Who Owns America?* (1971), a personal memoir by the Secretary of the Interior who fell from grace, and Allen Drury, *Courage and Hesitation* (1972), a conservative's lament.

A spate of books have appeared on the changing political scene of the

1970s. Richard M. Scammon and Ben J. Wattenberg discount the importance of youth and poverty in *The Real Majority* (1970); Kevin P. Phillips develops the case for the GOP's southern strategy in *The Emerging Republican Majority* (1969). The opposite point of view, stressing the need to appeal to new elements in the electorate, is presented by Jack Newfield and Jeff Greenfield in *A Populist Manifesto* (1971) and by Frederick G. Dutton in *Changing Sources of Power* (1971). More balanced accounts are David S. Broder, *The Party's Over* (1971) and Samuel Lubell's two volumes *The Hidden Crisis in American Politics* (1970) and *The Future While it Happened* (1973).

Theodore White has had considerable competition in chronicling the 1972 presidential election. In addition to his *The Making of the President, 1972* (1973), which is marred by a strong pro-Nixon bias and a failure to take account of the Watergate revelations, see especially Hunter Thompson, *Fear and Loathing: On the Campaign Trail '72* (1973), an unorthodox but rewarding account, and Timothy Crouse, *The Boys on the Bus* (1973), which focuses on the press coverage of the campaign. The underside of the 1972 election can be glimpsed in Anthony Sampson, *The Sovereign State of I.T.T.* (1973) and the New York Times edition of *The Watergate Hearings: Break-in and Cover-up* (1973), an extremely helpful digest of the Ervin committee exposures.

By far the best account of Nixon's foreign policy is Henry Brandon, *The Retreat of American Power* (1973). Brandon, a British journalist, gives a detailed and lucid analysis, ranging from the Nixon Doctrine to the search for detente. James Chace provides a sympathetic view in *A World Elsewhere* (1973), while Lloyd C. Gardner has collected a very useful group of contemporary articles in *The Great Nixon Turnaround* (1973). Two books concentrate on the background and experience of Henry Kissinger: David Landau, *Kissinger: The Uses of Power* (1972), a critical study, and Stephen R. Graubard, *Kissinger: Portrait of a Mind* (1973), a stout defense. Most of the books on the Vietnam war stop short of the Nixon years, but Seymour Hersh gives a horrifying account of the massacre that led to Calley's conviction in *My Lai* (1971) and Stanley J. Ungar describes the Administration's unsuccessful efforts to block publication of the Pentagon Papers in *The Papers and the Papers* (1972). For a penetrating account of SALT I based on extensive interviews with those close to the negotiations, see John Newhouse, *Cold Dawn* (1973). Robert E. Osgood and a half-dozen other John Hopkins University political scientists offer an overall analysis of Nixon's foreign policy in *Retreat from Empire?* (1973).

In the aftermath of Watergate, two scholars have provided penetrating analyses of the presidential office. In *The Imperial Presidency* (1973), Arthur Schlesinger, Jr., describes the way the usurpation of the war-making power unbalanced the Constitution; Emmet John Hughes gives a more detached view of the evolution of the office in *The Living Presidency* (1973). George Reedy,

The Twilight of the Presidency, though based on experience in LBJ's White House, is relevant to Nixon's experience. For a legal analysis of the impeachment process, see Raoul Berger, *Impeachment: The Constitutional Problems* (1973).

Carl Bernstein and Robert Woodward tell how they exposed the Watergate cover-up in *All the President's Men* (1974), while the Nixon version of the famous tapes appears in *The White House Transcripts* (1974). For a penetrating analysis of how Nixon's White House functioned, see Dan Rather and Gary Paul Gates, *The Palace Guard* (1974). Jeb Stuart Magruder offers an eye-witness account of the Watergate affair in *An American Life* (1974).

Index